UNIVERSAL
BASIC
INCOME

UNIVERSAL BASIC INCOME

PENNIES FROM HEAVEN

PAUL O'BRIEN

The History Press

First published 2017

The History Press
The Mill, Brimscombe Port
Stroud, Gloucestershire, GL5 2QG
www.thehistorypress.co.uk

© Paul O'Brien, 2017

British Library Cataloguing in Publication Data.
A catalogue record for this book is available from the British Library.

ISBN 978 1 84588 367 6

Typesetting and origination by The History Press
Printed in Great Britain

CONTENTS

ACKNOWLEDGEMENTS

Gratitude for assistance with developing the text is due in particular to John Baker, Deirdre Coveney, Deirdre de Burca, Michael Fitzgerald, Liam Flynn, John Goodwillie, Joan Healy, Roy Johnston, Claus Kazmaier, Neville Keery, Martina Langan, Ruth Kerr, Garreth McDaid, Seanan Mac Corra, Aoife Sheehan, and Sean Ward. My thanks go to all the members of Basic Income Ireland, and to those who attended meetings from time to time. I should also acknowledge the original Group on Alternative/Green Economics (GAGE) who were foregrounding similar ideas in the Irish Green Party from the 1980s onwards, and helped to shape my perspective. Thanks also to the staff at History Press Ireland: to Ronan Colgan for his deep interest in and support of the project, and to Beth Amphlett for her painstaking work in preparing the text for publication.

INTRODUCTION

This book is about a radical idea: the idea that each of us deserves enough money on which to live – and that it should be paid independently of our personal means, and independently of whether we work, or even want to work.

There are two main arguments in favour of a basic income for everyone: a moral reason and a social/political reason, as it is difficult to see how our society will survive, at least in its present form, without such a thing happening.

Universal basic income is, as its name suggests, a payment made unconditionally to everyone. For convenience I will refer to it as UBI.

The book is aimed at the intelligent general reader. It is not primarily intended as an academic book, though it makes use of a fair amount of academic material, and may be of interest to scholars of the subject as well. There's a considerable body of scholarly literature by now on UBI, going back several decades. Much of the literature is extremely erudite, and some of it is hard to follow without a background in one (or more) academic lines of study.

I hope the interested reader will be able to follow the argument without having done a lot of previous reading in areas that are touched on here (such as politics, philosophy, sociology, economics and cultural theory). Some of the references, though, may open up lines of further enquiry for those interested in pursuing them, whether from the point of view of general interest, or at a more scholarly level.

My hope is that the reader will not constantly have to go back and puzzle out the meaning of a paragraph, or need to have continual recourse to a dictionary or encyclopaedia. At the same time, I hope that, in the cause of making things accessible, I haven't distorted some very complex arguments.

If the reader wishes to follow up a particular line of enquiry, the end-notes may be of help. The discussion in them is, in parts, more detailed than the account in the main text. However, the reader who wishes to obtain a general overview of the subject will not need to continually refer to the discussions in the endnotes.

The bibliography may be of use to anyone who wants to delve more deeply into the topic. It includes most of the 'hard-copy' material, in terms of books and journal articles, mentioned in the endnotes, with online versions where available. It also includes some of the online material mentioned in the endnotes, where this seemed to be of particular relevance.

The book focuses on some political, economic, philosophical and ideological arguments around UBI, rather than on the mathematical details involved in regard to its implementation (whether actual, experimental or planned for the future) in various parts of the world. However, it includes information in the endnotes regarding further access to sources on this, for those who wish to follow them up.

There is also a (fairly brief) account at the end of the book of some detailed proposals regarding the implementation of UBI in the context of Ireland, since that is where I live and where I have had most experience of these debates, going back to the 1980s.

Academic writing has been of crucial importance in this area, in terms of getting the discussion established and taken seriously by people in the intellectual sphere. The concept of UBI, and political proposals to implement it, are now reaching the mainstream,[1] and discussion of these subjects is becoming an everyday matter in the media.

Some decades ago, the notion of an unearned income for everyone, without means testing or work requirement, was viewed as an outrageous proposition. (It was, perhaps, comparable to debates about close encounters with UFOs, in terms of acceptability as a topic for discussion in the mainstream media.) However, our economic system has reached such a perilous state that proposals which seemed shocking some decades ago are now much more acceptable, even by the establishment media.

It is to the credit of a relatively small group of persevering academics that this discussion has now gone beyond academic circles and is reaching the mainstream of political debate. For a long time the academics involved were, to some extent, 'out in the cold' on this, and they deserve much gratitude for sticking with the idea and working out the issues that it involves.

At this stage, however, it's vital, for all kinds of social, political and economic reasons, that the discussion should enter a more general arena – particularly regarding the underlying values involved. Much of the resistance to UBI is based not on mathematics but on ideology, as I will try to show. (The term 'ideology' has about a dozen different meanings, but I'm using it here in the sense of thinking that does not have much obvious claim to logicality, or coherence.)

At the same time, there are some rational objections to UBI and, for the sake of honest debate, I try to note them and respond, as appropriate, in the discussion that follows.

I don't need to labour the political upheavals caused by globalisation, technological development, and the move away from fossil fuels, for traditional patterns of employment. These have had seismic consequences in the US and the UK, and threaten to do so as well on the European mainland, where the rise of far-Right parties offering an authoritarian nationalist alternative is of particular concern. (Anti-globalisation, which 15 or 20 years ago was emphasised mainly by the Left, now seems to be largely taken over by the Right as a rallying cry.)

Ireland may not be immune from such issues either, though we seem to have emerged from our recent economic dislocation relatively unscathed, at least in terms of the economic figures. (Of course, this is not counting the many lives that have been lost or ruined in the process.)

To some extent, writers in the academic world are curtailed by a number of factors. One of them is specialisation: the focus on a particular subject, or aspect of a subject, means that the writer is producing work for a fairly narrow audience. As a result, academic writing becomes a kind of shorthand, which is understood by the writer's peers, but may not be easily accessible to the general public.

Nevertheless, there is an (arguable) case that the philosopher or theorist should try their best to make their work as understandable as possible, in order to help break down the barrier between theory on the one hand and the everyday concerns of ordinary people on the other.

There are good examples of clear (or clear-ish) writing in philosophy, such as the work of the nineteenth-century thinkers Arthur Schopenhauer and John Stuart Mill (whether or not one agrees with their ideas). There are also bad examples of clarity in philosophical writing – for example Immanuel Kant and Georg Hegel – two thinkers who are, however, regarded as being in the first rank of philosophical thought.

Another point to note is that the phenomenon of over-specialisation means that people tend to lose sight of the broader picture, which in fact may encompass many different disciplines or lines of enquiry, but which no one person has the expertise to cover and link together.

Our society is characterised by an overriding concern for analysis rather than synthesis, for breaking things up into ever-smaller bits rather than looking for general patterns that may cut across different areas of enquiry.[2]

As the cynical saying goes, as a student at university you spend your time learning more and more about less and less, until eventually you end up knowing everything about nothing.[3] Over-specialisation is not just an academic problem but a political problem as well – if thinkers lose touch with the public, there is a danger that the public may lose touch with rational thought itself.

Personally, I agree with George Orwell[4] that a writer should aim for simplicity and clarity as much as possible. There is, of course, another school of thought that believes that aiming for clear writing surrenders to the prevailing, simplistic mindset of society – a mindset that is presumed to be false. I believe, though, that that viewpoint is misconceived.

For one thing, the question arises as to what basis we have for saying that anything is true or false. There is no consensus in the academic world on this issue. Academics tend to be divided between 'realists', who believe there is a knowable world independent of thought, perception and language and 'relativists', who believe that the situation is much more challenging than that. There are problems with both positions, and most writing with any claim to sophistication has to negotiate an uneasy pathway through them.

For example, even the most dedicated relativists (or postmodernists) presumably believe that there are fundamental laws of physics, independent of thought, perception or language. If they did not, they might hesitate to step outdoors, since, at any time, some random change in the laws of gravity could spin them off into outer space.

On the other hand, the analysis of language (going back at least as far as Friedrich Nietzsche) has called into question the relationship between language and reality. In parallel, developments in physics raise issues about the relationship between the observer and observed reality.

The issue of 'truthiness' has recently come to the fore in regard to discussion of political and media matters – defined as referring to something that feels true, whether or not it actually is. The question of the supposed disappearance of truth from public discourse has recently been the focus of much debate.

However, the issue of truth itself has been the focus of discussion in philosophical circles for many decades – it would be wrong to believe that there is any academic consensus on what truth is (if, indeed, there is such a thing).

That brings us back to the question of whether the beliefs of ordinary people are true or false. As noted above, when you push the discussion to an extreme, it's by no means clear that there is any substantial basis for saying that any belief at all (whether held by the multitude or by the élite) is lacking in truth, since there is no consensus in the academic world on what truth is, or on how it can be established.

The recent criticism of the supposed lack of concern with objective facts and truth, particularly in media discourse, as if it were something new, is somewhat strange – in fact, this criticism has been levelled at the postmodern or relativist trend in academia for decades.

Bearing these difficulties in mind, from one point of view one could argue that ordinary people are just as likely to be aware of important issues to which the intellectual élite is blind, than the reverse.

In fact, the ordinary person with no claim to being an intellectual may get things drastically wrong in terms of the political solutions that he/she may endorse, but everyday citizens are sometimes more keenly – and accurately – aware of the nature of their economic and social problems than are the 'experts' who claim to understand them, but who may themselves have no direct experience of the struggles that everyday people have to undergo. In other words, the bad press that 'populism' has may have been undeserved, at least in some respects.

A parallel issue is that, if you never make an effort to communicate radical ideas to the public at large, they will never take them seriously. In 2016, we saw the devastating political fallout (for example Brexit and the US presidential election result) that arose from the exclusion of ordinary people from political debate.

This brings us back, though in somewhat of a roundabout way, to UBI.

While some of the discussion on this topic in the academic world is complex, and much of it is necessarily so, it seems important that an effort should be made to make the ideas accessible to people for whom they may be of crucial importance in everyday life. Such people may not necessarily have an academic background, but may nevertheless be acutely aware of the problems that face citizens in their everyday lives (perhaps more so in some ways than are the – supposed – experts on the way society functions).

My own interest in UBI goes back some decades, to a time when I was spokesperson on economic affairs for the Green Party in Ireland. I subsequently convened an economic policy group in the Green Party, where UBI was high on the agenda. Politically, I'd describe myself as a Left-libertarian Green, though my confidence in the ability of parliamentary politics to be the source of any substantial progress has taken quite a hit in recent times.

As with many people, my disenchantment happened around the time of the financial crisis in Ireland, when the Greens were part of a coalition government that was confronted with impending economic collapse, and faced the challenge of dealing with it. The results were mixed at best.

On the one hand, things could have been a lot worse. In Ireland, we have come through the bad times into a boom economy once more (indeed, we may be well into another bubble, for example in the housing market).

On the other hand, many ordinary people and families have suffered much as a result of 'austerity', not to mention the massive increase in Ireland's national debt. It seems to be in the nature of the capitalist system that, like a bipolar individual, it lurches from exuberance to depression and back again, without being able to experience stability or security. (The exceptions are the people at the top of the economic pile, who have mostly done very well in recent decades. It is in their economic interests to maintain the system, at least until it becomes so unstable that it comes crashing down.)

In the interest of full disclosure, I should say that I still pay my subscription to the Green Party, though without any particular enthusiasm for the possibilities that parliamentary politics offers for radical change.

At this point the main priority, in a global sense, seems to be to try to avoid a disastrous regression to the authoritarian politics of the 1930s – to avoid dystopia rather than to bring about utopia (though aiming for the latter may actually be the best way to avoid the former). But for that to happen, it's essential to alleviate the situation of economic and social alienation that faces large swathes of the population even of developed countries. UBI would be one of the tools in that toolbox, though by no means the only one.

The issues arising from austerity and the loss of economic sovereignty that faced the Irish people subsequent to the economic crash, and the devastation that it caused for many individuals and families, call into question the economic values that pervade the Irish mindset. These include economic individualism (in the negative sense of everyone for him/herself), or the ideology of neoliberalism;[5] the work ethic (in the negative sense of the overvaluation of paid employment, as distinct from other kinds of activities that may be of equal or greater worth); and the unquestioning adherence to the ideology of economic growth (infinite growth on a finite planet is surely a contradiction in terms).

There are also, it should be mentioned, some economic issues in Ireland that are not normally discussed to any great extent in the media (such as the historical ownership of land) as well as political issues (such as what it means to be a citizen of a republic, as distinct from a half-resentful, half-admiring former subject of a former colonial power).

The issues involved in being a citizen of a republic and a democracy are surely things that should be prioritised in any school curriculum. The fact that they are not means that the powers that be may not be interested in opening up the radical questions that discussion of such issues may raise.

A related matter is that of the European Union, and Ireland's place in it. Whatever about its economic effects, culturally speaking the EU was, arguably, a godsend in terms of emancipating Irish people from the either/or, Irish/British duality that previously set their mental boundaries.

With Brexit, and the possible break-up of the EU looming in the future, there is a danger – if Ireland draws back into the orbit of the UK as a result – that we may once more descend to our former mindset. That is, a cap-in-hand, post-colonial mentality with its associated feelings of 'malignant shame'[6] arising from centuries of defeat and oppression – a simultaneous (unconscious) admiration for, and resentment of, the former colonial oppressor.

This is, arguably, a particular danger if we look to the UK as our future economic mainstay rather than the EU (if, indeed, either still exists as political entities in the future). At a time of crisis, we can grasp the opportunity to progress, or else fall into a tailspin of cultural, and perhaps economic, regression. Staying still is not an option.

There is still a tendency for Irish people to copy their British neighbours (consciously or unconsciously) and it's possible that this may happen in the future in regard to Irish attitudes to the EU – particularly if the EU's view of Ireland's current corporation-tax arrangements should harden.

Ireland is a small country with an open economy that is vulnerable to economic shocks. If it should face economic dislocation in the future (for example from currency collapse or industrial relocation as a result of pressures on our corporation-tax structure) UBI would be one of the things that might help to soften the blow for ordinary people.

My interest in UBI arose from an interest in Leftist critiques of capitalism,[7] though I've never been happy with the alternatives that are usually put forward. In terms of a political programme, I've always thought that the notion of instituting a society of freedom and justice through increasing the role of the state was problematic, for reasons that I will outline later.

In terms of political economy, and putting the objection very crudely, the conventional Marxist idea of base and superstructure seems deeply questionable. It's the idea that you can explain everything, or most things, or most things that are important in a society, with reference to the economy. That, it seems to me, is a bit like the notion that you could satisfactorily explain a statue by a close examination of the plinth – or that you could satisfactorily understand a house in all, or most, important details through a study of its foundations.

The underlying problem with Karl Marx's analysis is a fairly straightforward one: an over-exaggeration of the explanatory power of the economy. This boils down to the tendency to believe that because the economic level is essential to society, it therefore ultimately explains it in all ways that are important.

In the same way, for example, Sigmund Freud may have overemphasised sex in an explanatory sense, and Friedrich Nietzsche may have overemphasised power. (The nineteenth-century tendency to explain things in overly simplistic ways is called 'reductionism' by critics.)

Clearly, many of the things we often do, such as engaging in a search for beauty and truth, or being willing to sacrifice our lives in the service of a higher ideal (such as freedom, for example) are not economically determined, yet our societies could not function in any recognisable way without them.

On the negative side, people's willingness to sacrifice themselves for a lower ideal – such as religious tyranny – is not economically determined either, at least in an ultimate sense. (Though it may be made worse by economic and political issues, for example the desire for oil, or neoconservative meddling on the part of the West.)

Furthermore, even if historical materialism were key to explaining the way things are, or have been, there is no reason why that should always be the case: we could envisage a society, for example, where higher ideals predominated, and where economic motivations and interests were relegated to the sidelines. (Conversely, we could envisage a nightmare dystopia where the atrocities of religious extremism were the norm, as is, unfortunately, the case in many parts of the world at the moment.)[8]

Consequently, while economics may explain much of what goes on in the world, it does not account for everything. The issue with historical materialism is that it's never clearly defined by Marx or his followers: consequently, the riposte to any criticism is usually along the lines 'well actually, it means something different'.

We cannot, of course, deny that historical materialism (the methodology of Marxism as applied to the study of history and society) may often have a useful function, even though it may be defective as an overall theory of the way things always, or necessarily, work.

For example, many of the high-flown ideals that people have may, on examination, be exposed as being rooted in their own economic interests, or in those of the class to which they belong (or to which they would like to belong) rather than being self-evidently true or justifiable. Examining the economic level may often explain much of what goes on in society – but not always, and not everything.

When it comes to the claim of Marxism to be a fundamentally explanatory system, I've never come across any watertight reason why Marx's analysis should be preferred to any other (apart from the fact of its success in the world of ideas).

In a yet more general sense, there is the issue of whether any social analysis – or indeed any theory in whatever context – has a legitimate claim to truth (as distinct from a claim to have triumphed over other explanatory systems – which is, actually, not to be completely ignored in terms of a claim to explanatory power).

At the same time, it should be said that anyone who has read Marx, in particular his major work *Capital,* his early writings on alienated labour, and his observations on the politics of his time, will realise that his intellectual contribution is of unparalleled value in terms of the explanation it offers of the nature of society, not only his own society but those that preceded it – and perhaps our own as well. Marx's work is unequalled in the ways that it highlights the injustice and dehumanisation that pervade the system of capitalism.

This is the case even though it seldom offers us any worked-out reasons why we should actually oppose capitalism. (After all, if you are doing well out of the system, you might decide that it's in your interest to support it.)[9]

Anyway, and to put it in a nutshell, I would argue that a Marx-based approach is often – though not always – useful in understanding society. Consequently, while I've never been a Marxist, I'd consider myself something of a '*marxisant*' (to use the French term): that is, someone who sometimes uses ideas rooted in Marx, while not necessarily endorsing other elements of his thought.

In that way, one can utilise Marx as a useful source of ideas and methods, just as one might use Adam Smith, Kant, Hegel, Nietzsche, Freud, or any other major thinker, without necessarily subscribing to their overall analysis as an ultimately explanatory one.

And that brings us to the point that the issues raised by the Right are not always to be dismissed. Sometimes, Left and Right may have important things in common. In a US context for example, there appears to be some common ground between conservatives and progressives on issues such as opposition to military adventurism, support for the decriminalisation of recreational drugs, and opposition to government support for banking and finance.

On the other hand, Left and Right may differ radically on other issues such as gun control, the role of science in education, and reproductive rights – not to mention the key area of disagreement: the role of the market vis-à-vis the state.

In addition to the agreement noted above between Left and Right on certain issues we should, arguably, look for some kind of 'crossover' support on the issue of UBI as well – though there may be major disagreements on the form that it should take in practice, the amounts that it should involve, or the knock-on effect on state spending in other areas. (The concept of UBI already has such 'crossover' Left-Right support, as will be seen later, though the majority of support appears to be Left-wing in nature.)

While the Left/Right distinction is somewhat inadequate, may be outmoded and sometimes needs to be transcended, if pushed to it I would have to say that I'm on the Left for all practical purposes. However, I disagree with the unquestioning endorsement of economic growth, the state, and the traditional work ethic in terms of maximising 'jobs' that are often to be found in Leftist circles.[10]

At the same time, though, I find it refreshing to read the works of conservative thinkers such as Edmund Burke (the best-known Irish philosopher, whose statue may be found outside Trinity College in Dublin), and Friedrich Hayek.[11] Even if one disagrees with their overall, conservative perspective, their ideas may highlight issues that are ignored by Leftists (sometimes for bad reasons). We can often learn more from our critics than from our friends.

There are, it goes without saying, obvious and deep-rooted problems with capitalism itself, which do not need much elaboration at this stage. They include, but are not limited to, structural unemployment,[12] massive inequality in the distribution of wealth, the atrophy of human potential, and mindless consumerism, combined with the inability of large sections of the population to afford the consumer goods that capitalism produces.

In the environmental sphere, capitalism has given us resource depletion, deforestation, the loss of biodiversity, and the terrifying prospect of runaway global warming and climate change. These issues are much clearer than they were back in the late 1980s and early '90s, when (with the fall of the Soviet Union) it seemed to some that capitalism had triumphed, and that all that remained was to tie up the loose ends.

At the same time, of course, it would be wrong to imagine that capitalism is completely bad (even Marx never claimed that – in some ways he was enthusiastic about capitalism).

Capitalism has, for example, helped to give us freedom from superstition and outmoded social constraints, not to mention its facilitation of democracy – at least when it suits capitalist goals – and technological development (though the role of the state should not be underestimated in that).

From a Right-wing perspective, one could imagine a form of capitalism that might work, or at least one that might work better than capitalism does at present. Such a system might consist of the minimal state (confined to defence, security, the guarantee of contracts, and the redistribution of wealth through a negative income tax). However, a workable capitalist system would need more than that if it were adequately to address the problems of the modern world.

For example, companies that grew beyond a certain size would need to be broken up into smaller ones so they did not achieve inordinate political and social influence (you would need a powerful state mechanism to accomplish that goal).

Furthermore, given our environmental crisis, such a society would also need robust environmental governance, and there's a question as to what would become of people with mental and physical challenges, in the absence of state support (private charity might not be enough to supply their needs).

Nevertheless, if so inclined, one could make an arguable case for such a form of capitalism. What is much more difficult to justify – from any political perspective – is the form of capitalism that predominates at present.

Capitalism has morphed, particularly in the US in recent times, into a form of corporatism: a monstrous system that combines the worst Orwellian nightmares of socialist bureaucracy with the depredations of bloated corporations; engenders massive inequality; deprives large sections of the population of adequate health care; engages in foreign adventurism to slake the appetites of the military-industrial complex, engendering chaos, misery and social upheaval as a result; imprisons for profit large sections of the population as punishment for things (like drug possession) that ought not to be crimes in the first place; oppresses minorities; turns everyday policing into ultra-militarist martial law; engages in forms of surveillance of which Hitler and Stalin could only dream (see Oliver Stone's recent film *Snowden* on this); persecutes whistleblowers; facilitates corporate and media control of the whole society; fosters crime, social fragmentation and atomisation, and generally applies the principle of 'socialism for the rich, capitalism for everyone else.'

While people at the lower end of the scale are faced with unemployment (or underemployment), poverty, insecurity and a declining quality of life, even those more comfortably off are not immune to the perilous prospects offered by contemporary capitalism/corporatism.

Uncertainty about the status of currencies and the possibility of future currency collapse; low, non-existent (or even negative) interest rates; the prospect of bank 'bail-ins', whereby depositors' money could be confiscated in the event of an economic crisis; a stock market that has recently boomed, but may be in a bubble; a property market that simultaneously prices out renters and makes it more difficult to buy one's home; the takeover of mortgages by 'vulture funds' – all of these increase insecurity not just for the working class but for the middle class as well.

The Trump phenomenon in the US is an attempted response to some of this. On the one hand, Trump's foreign policy appears, on the face of it, somewhat more restrained than that of Hillary Clinton, his main opponent in the presidential race, and of his predecessor Barak Obama, at least in regard to US–Russian relations, or military adventurism abroad. It remains to be seen whether his response (in terms of 'protectionism' and investment in jobs and infrastructure) to the issue of economic globalisation will work in practice. Interestingly, though, it attempts to address a problem (globalisation) that was widely high-lighted by the Left right up to 9/11, when attention was suddenly directed elsewhere.

However, Trump's policies in other areas – including, crucially, energy, immigration and the environment – seem to involve a major step back-wards. It is entirely possible that the economic problems of the United States are due much more to wasting money on militarism, rather than to globalisation and outsourcing.[13]

As seldom before, there is a need at this point for freedom lovers across the political spectrum to come together. Support for UBI is one area where this could occur, subject to some caveats I will mention later. There may be more in common between libertarians on both Left and Right than is commonly imagined, in terms of a common rejection of the corporate state. (Otherwise, we will continue to see the legitimate concerns of ordinary people appropriated by the far Right.)

The answers traditionally offered by Left and Right to our current social and economic problems have been quite different. On the one hand, the offer is some form of socialism (or social democracy) with its well-known problems of bureaucracy and intrusiveness. On the other hand, the offer is the minimal state, with its problems of inequity, lack of care for those less able than others, and the development of a pow-erful capitalist class, which erodes the values of freedom and justice for society as a whole.

More recently, as noted above, a Right-wing form of protectionist anti-globalism has emerged with the Trump phenomenon, though it is too early to see how this will work out in practice. (Initial indications look less than promising, to say the least.)

In terms of UBI, while the discussion of this has, in recent times, been largely on the Left, the idea may also appeal to some people of a conservative bent who wish to cut back on the overreaching state, as it seeks to monitor and control every detail of our lives. (Indeed, the prominent neoliberal economist Milton Friedman supported a nega-tive income tax, whereby the government, through the integration of taxes and transfers, pays you rather than you paying the government (if you fall below a certain threshold), which might be seen as a variant of UBI.)

The difference is that Leftists wish to increase social solidarity through state redistribution and other forms of provision, while Rightists want to cut back on the extent of the state, in the interests of individual (and business) freedom. The implications of a basic-income society would be quite different in each case, depending on the political emphasis with which it was pursued.

There is, of course, also the anarchist alternative. Anarchism has influenced people on both Left and Right: the former in terms of anarcho-communism; the latter in terms of support for the 'minimal state', and the libertarian project of freeing up business enterprises from what are seen as the interfering tentacles of the state. A coherent case may be made (as it has been, for example by people like the US politician Ron Paul) for the minimal state (whether or not you like the prospect is another matter).

However, the anarchist notion of doing away with the state altogether seems deeply problematic. Abolishing the state would, surely, give free rein to all kinds of antisocial elements. Even if, as anarchists argue, the antisocial tendencies are ultimately the product of state repression (which is by no means obvious) it would surely take several generations to eradicate them. In the meantime, chaos would ensue.

While some anarchists might endorse UBI in the short term (since it offers to cut down on bureaucracy and increase human freedom) it could hardly survive in an anarchist society itself. The obvious reason is that, even if such a society retained money in some form or other (from gold and silver at one end of the scale to digital currency at the other) it would need some kind of centralised structure to administer a system of UBI. (Whether or not one would necessarily call such a structure an element of the state is to some extent, I suppose, a matter of terminology.) Nevertheless, one could imagine some anarchists supporting UBI as an interim measure at least, towards their goal of a society of total freedom.

The bottom line is that UBI will, in almost all foreseeable cases, be introduced in societies that are capitalist to one degree or another.

Whether it would help to make those societies run more efficiently, or facilitate the emergence of some kind of radical alternative to capitalism, is more difficult to say. Perhaps it would do both.

One of the problems with the Leftist analysis of capitalism is what might be termed a form of 'reification'. In this context, the term means a tendency to conceive of capitalism as a 'thing' that can be changed only by being smashed, rather than as a complex of relations potentially subject to evolution into something else. Consequently, it becomes more difficult to see capitalism as being subject to possible transformation from within.

What does seem clear is that the present system – with its crippling poverty traps, baffling obstructions and marginalisation of large sections of the population, as outlined in Ken Loach's recent brilliant film *I, Daniel Blake* – is not an option.

Personally, I see UBI as part of a smorgasbord, a basket of desirables if you like, that would characterise a post-capitalist (or post-corporatist) society. These could include: a radical reassessment of the goals of economic growth and of full employment; the reduction of the working day/week/year; the valuation of currently unpaid work, often done by women; the development of workers' cooperatives, profit sharing in traditional firms, and mutuality in the financial sector; radical alternatives in the sphere of finance; changes in company law to compel corporations to take into account social and environmental factors rather than merely the interests of shareholders; the break-up of large corporations into smaller entities; enhanced public involvement in the ownership and control of industries; the radical redistribution of wealth at both a national and global level; the growth of ethical investment; worker (and consumer) participation in management; and of course UBI itself.

UBI would, in that case, be only a part of a package that would help to ensure the survival of our civilisation in the coming difficult times.

Dystopia might be defined as a 'bad' or 'negative' utopia. So one could say that, while the avoidance of dystopia is the main priority at this stage, the only feasible way to avoid it is not through reinforcing the present system, but through forging ahead with the construction of utopia itself.

You don't have to be a utopian, though, to endorse UBI. You just have to be persuaded that it would be an improvement on the ways things are done at present. This book attempts to make that case.

Of course, whether capitalism is capable of transformation into a qualitatively new system that would embrace new social, economic and environmental values is a crucial question, and one for which there is no easy answer.

I've mentioned already a balancing act that I'm trying to accomplish with this book. That is, I'm trying to make the ideas accessible on the one hand; and, on the other, not distorting them in the interest of simplification.

Another balancing act is that between trying to give an accurate overview of UBI (both historical and theoretical), and advocacy of basic income itself.

In terms of giving an account of the topic, I hope I provide an adequate indication of some of the difficulties and limitations of the UBI proposal, as well as its advantages. It should be made clear that it is not, and does not claim to be, a cure-all for everything that is wrong with society.

In terms of advocacy, while I'm personally in favour of one particular (Left) version of UBI, I hope I've made it clear that advocacy of basic income is not confined to the Left. While a Right-wing version might, arguably, have a serious downside, there is a certain scope for a political alliance on this issue, across the traditional Left-Right spectrum.

From the point of view of getting basic income established, tactical alliances may be appropriate between Leftist and conservative supporters of UBI. Nevertheless, it's incumbent on Left-wing supporters to urge the implementation of UBI in a way that benefits, in particular, the weakest and most vulnerable sections of the population – and certainly in a way that does not weaken them further, or make them less secure.

There is at the moment no well-established UBI system except in Alaska[14] (where a partial basic income has been in place for a long time). Nevertheless, in an extended piece of writing it's a lot less awkward to use 'is' rather than 'would' or some similar term, so I've generally preferred the former to the latter. If the reader bears in mind some future situation, or some parallel/alternative/imaginary reality where UBI actually exists, that will, I hope, make the discussion easier to follow.

Finally, I should add a note about capitalisation. In a political context, I use the terms 'Left' and 'Right' to distinguish them from the usage in more general (non-political) terms. Similarly, the word 'Green' as I use it denotes Green politics, whether parliamentary or otherwise.

I use 'libertarian' with a small 'l' to denote a person who holds liberty (whether economic or social or both) in high esteem, to distinguish such a person from a member of a Libertarian party.

1

UNIVERSAL BASIC INCOME: AN OUTLINE OF THE IDEA

INTRODUCTION

The traditional situation of a job for life is rapidly being eroded. Already, machines are replacing workers at supermarket checkouts and in banks, making life more complicated for customers and enrolling them as temporary, unpaid employees of the organisation.

We face a future where, it is projected, there will be massive displacement of humans by robots of one kind or another. In the near future, there will be driverless vehicles on the roads,[1] as there have been driverless trains for years. Jobs particularly under threat include those of cashiers, marketers, customer-service employees, factory workers, financial middle men (and women), journalists, lawyers, and phone workers.[2]

Medical diagnoses can increasingly be carried out over the Internet (either completely automatically or with a human professional online) and robots can do surgery. Higher education in its traditional form is threatened by the development of MOOCs (Massive Open Online Courses). Parents worry about how to anticipate the coming robot revolution in terms of their children's education.[3]

The subjection of the human being to the machine – so effectively satirised in Charlie Chaplin's film *Modern Times* – has been replaced by a new threat: the replacement of people by machines, as foreseen in modern films including the *Terminator* series.[4]

Even traditionally human-specific activities such as love and sex are being called in question by technology, with recent films such as *Her* and *Ex Machina*. In the future, the sexual partners of many people may be robots.[5] Whether you think all that is comical, sad, exciting or horrifying, it's difficult to see how such a future could be avoided, even if it were desirable to avoid it. There is too much money to be made.

Martin Ford projects that mechanisation will push people off the land where they traditionally made a living, and deprive them of the jobs they might otherwise obtain in the cities to which they migrate as a result. Machines threaten to make economic activity redundant at both the higher and lower ends of the scale.[6] Ford describes how recessions eliminate routine jobs: then organisations realise that, in the wake of recovery, technological advances permit them to operate without rehiring the workers.[7] While online activity is great for the corporations that prevail in the Internet, income for everyone else drops to the level of pocket change.[8]

Ford points out that the computer technology of today has roots in the taxpayer-funded, post-Second World War federal funding for research. It does not look as if this is leading to prosperity for the descendants of those taxpayers.[9] While the stock market soared, Wall Street banks got rid of tens of thousands of jobs.[10] Concerns about the effect of 'immigration' on jobs ignore the issue of 'virtual immigration' raised by electronic offshoring.[11] Higher education is also under threat, with the growth of online education.[12] Technology promises to shake up the area of healthcare as well.[13] In Ford's view, emerging industries will seldom be labour-intensive.[14] (Ford supports the idea of a guaranteed UBI as a means of addressing the problems he outlines.)[15]

Where the money is going to come from to buy goods, if nobody has a job to earn it, is not something that owners of businesses, or indeed investors, seem to have thought through to any great extent. In this sense, capitalism is not a 'rational' system: it does not necessarily work in its own interest. Things that are good for individual capitalists (such as cutting back on the number of employees) may be bad for the system as a whole. The 'invisible hand' of the market that is supposed to ensure the best possible functioning of the system breaks down here (as it does elsewhere, for example in regard to pollution and resource depletion).

While new jobs will no doubt be created by the growth of new technology, they will tend to be at the higher end of the scale, with a growing income gap between those with high and low skills.[16] The notion of UBI as a solution is now reaching the mainstream of political debate: in the context of discussions of the 'robot revolution', a *Financial Times* editorial called for 'data-driven pilot projects' to test the UBI idea in practice.[17]

The idea of a guaranteed basic income, citizen's dividend, national dividend, or UBI, is fairly straightforward. It involves the state paying a certain amount of money to all, without means testing or work requirement.[18] Those who argue for UBI usually want it to be enough for each person to live on, though basic income could exist in a partial form (as it already does in Alaska).[19]

In Ireland, for example, the government already pays a form of basic income to a sector of the population (in the form of child benefit, at €140 per month per child).[20] UBI would extend this principle to everyone.[21] For those who support UBI, it seems particularly important to defend any 'universality' that may already exist (for example in the form of child benefit or pensions) as they may form the foundation of a future UBI.

The goal of 'full employment' is a mirage. This is due to a number of factors, including the increased role of technology and the growing role of women in the workforce. ('Full employment' traditionally meant full male employment, with women remaining in the home.) Much of our current 'employment' is deficient in terms of the quality of the jobs available.[22] A (vulnerable and insecure) sector of the workforce, sometimes described as the 'precariat', is emerging.[23]

Insecurity is rapidly becoming a permanent part of people's everyday lives. Many workers in traditional jobs are unable to make ends meet. If someone is unfortunate enough to lose their job, they have to deal with an unwieldy welfare system that can have the effect of forcing them into poverty and subservience, despite the – often well-intentioned – efforts of those who administer the system.

The exaggerated importance attached to jobs and to 'full employment' means that the natural environment is, in a political sense, pushed to the sidelines: we are faced with the absurd choice between maximising job creation on the one hand, and preserving the future of the planet on the other. While deforestation and the overuse of fossil fuels threaten the future of human civilisation and indeed of the planet itself,[24] the spectre of unemployment seems easy to fix in comparison – it is simply a matter of rethinking how we distribute wealth in the society.

It should be emphasised that full-time employment in the traditional sense for all adults is not feasible and would be an ecological nightmare if it were. (This is not to mention the social nightmare many people endure already, which consists in spending all day working and commuting and seldom seeing their family.) Instead, it seems obvious that we need to find ways of redistributing income that detaches it from work, and ways of redistributing necessary work so that people have more free time.

In the meantime, the current system contributes to multiple problems. Certain types of legitimate work are invisible and devalued, including the activities of carers and homemakers (whether male or female) because they do not easily fit into the formal economy. For many people, the balance between work and life is hopelessly out of kilter. The authoritarian response to the problem is Soviet-style 'workfare' of one kind or another:[25] in other words, making income more dependent on work, rather than less.

Workfare, with its constant monitoring[26] and compulsion, is dependent on an unquestioning adherence to a traditional work ethic that is rapidly being undermined by social and economic developments. Meanwhile, massive inequality in terms of wealth distribution[27] threatens to destabilise society. In the United States, it was estimated in 2014 that the wealth owned by the top 0.1 per cent is almost the same as that owned by the bottom 90 per cent.[28]

The marginalisation of the 'precariat' means there is a potential bomb under industrial-corporate society, whose effects (xenophobia and possible new forms of fascism) are likely to make things even worse than they already are.

Guy Standing points out that the precariat are 'floating, rudderless and potentially angry.'[29] They are distinct from the proletariat in that they do not have the stability, or rootedness, of the latter.[30] They lack a sense of identity based on work.[31] They experience 'the four As – anger, anomie, anxiety and alienation.'[32] The precariat may regard trade unions negatively, as having looked after the interests of their own members to the disadvantage of the precariat.[33] To take an example from Ireland, a 'two-tier' pay disparity has developed, whereby new entrants to the teaching profession are significantly disadvantaged vis-à-vis their older peers.[34]

The precariat are subject to 'zero-hour contracts' and vanishing pension provision. Social immobility becomes intensified. On a global scale, the danger is that the precariat, exasperated by the inaction of traditional politicians, may follow demagogues, potentially supporting candidates of the extreme Right. In the culture of 'precarity', the widespread and increasing use of state surveillance leads to a lessening of privacy and freedom. In the UK, doctors are told to police the 'fitness for employment' of patients in receipt of disability benefits, undermining the traditionally confidential physician–patient relationship. How to establish a society that takes account of the rise of the precariat is a central question of our time. Precariousness affects the children of the post-war generation much more than it does their parents.[35]

Indeed, we have entered a dangerous time of ever-increasing surveillance, anticipated in novels such as Orwell's *Nineteen Eighty-Four* and Zamyatin's *We*. Every move we make on the street is recorded and may be analysed in future. Every time we log on to the Internet, our every move is subject to being stored and sold on for commercial purposes. Privacy is an increasingly valuable, and increasingly disappearing, commodity. In the future, it is not too far fetched to imagine that people may have to pay large sums of money to retrieve their privacy or prevent it being taken away, if indeed that will be possible any more.

College education is being simultaneously 'massified' and downgraded, with crippling debts for students, and 'internships' for graduates instead of jobs.[36] The 'internship' culture (unpaid work as an intended transition between education and employment), while it no doubt assists some people in getting valuable job experience or functions as a stepping stone to full-time employment, in other ways perpetuates a culture of under-employment and precarity.[37]

Machines threaten to make us free. Instead of seeing the prospect of freedom from coerced labour as something to be celebrated (as it might be in a rational society) we view it with a sense of dread. We have replaced the goal of 'being' with an ideology of 'having'.[38] Our lives are dominated by money (or too often, by the lack of it). Everywhere, we encounter a continuous maze of bureaucracy in terms of form filling, talking (or more often waiting to talk) to people in call centres, and other forms of (unpaid) time-wasting activity.

Continual demands for information force us to become unpaid government functionaries, whether we like it or not. Our brains are colonised by numbers – accountancy has supplanted poetry. Only children retain some measure of freedom from an administered and quantified culture, and those not for long and decreasingly – as the 'wired' young person with earphones, computer games and mobile phone ubiquitously indicates.

Our culture is dominated by economic and work-related values[39] characterised by economic rationality – quantitative measurement and the reduction of everything to money and accounting. Combined with this are the global dominance of economic growth as the main priority, whereby everything is assessed in terms of Gross Domestic Product (GDP), and the prime importance attached to technological progress.[40]

We allow labour to spill over into leisure (with constant demands for workers to be available via phone, text and email). Simultaneously, leisure spills over into work (for example, people spending work time on Web surfing or self-absorbed computer games) so that our life is taken over by a seamless web of cultural conformity. Consumption, the frantic desire for the latest model (whether in terms of clothing, cars or smartphones) takes the place of the desire for personal development.

Instead of learning how to expand our higher capabilities, we use our free time to engage in more and more sophisticated forms of consumption.[41] We celebrate the mundane, the banal and the trivial like never before. It's not enough to enjoy a meal: we also have to share a picture of it on Facebook before it's consumed. At one time, the cynical observation about the dominance of commodities in our society, was that cameras took people on holiday in order to collect images of scenery. Now, if anything, the process has intensified with smartphones. We don't enjoy the beauty of nature for itself: we fetishise images of it instead. We have long forgotten what it means simply to enjoy nature rather than seeking to wrap it up for a future consumption that, perhaps, never happens.

WORK

At this point it's worth saying something about the nature of work itself. There is a lot of mystification around the concept of work.[42] It's assumed that work is necessarily a good thing, regardless of its effects on the worker, on society, or on the environment. Job creation, like economic growth, is one of those ideals that conventional economists and their followers take as a 'given'. It's a value that is assumed, and that informs their discussions while seldom being seriously analysed. In fact, there are many different kinds of work, and (arguably) only some of them are worth preserving, or celebrating.

In considering whether a particular form of work is worthwhile, we might ask ourselves the following questions: (1) Do I like to do it? (2) Is it something that develops my abilities and positive qualities (creative, caring, intellectual, problem-solving, and so on)? (3) Does it help – or at least refrain from causing harm to – society or the environment? (4) This is probably the most revealing question: would I do it, or something like it, if I didn't have to rely on it for a living? If a person can answer 'yes' to all of those questions, then it seems clear that they are, in fact, fortunate enough to be doing the kind of work that is valuable in itself. But only a small fraction of work actually falls into that category.[43]

For example, in regard to question (1), suppose I enjoy digging holes on the beach all day and filling them in again, and I find someone silly enough to pay me to do it. In this scenario, the activity is certainly something that I like to do, but it's probably something I shouldn't like to do (because – for anyone over the age of three or thereabouts – it's a more or less time-wasting, unproductive, unhelpful and uncreative activity). Admittedly, it may have the side effect of keeping me physically fit and healthy, but there are probably better ways of achieving those goals – such as swimming, sports of various kinds, hiking and so on, which involve more varied kinds of muscular exertion, cooperation (football), and/or aesthetic enjoyment of nature (hiking).

On the other hand, suppose I work for a fossil-fuel company in an intellectually demanding job and enjoy my work. That may satisfy questions (1) and (2) (it's something challenging that I enjoy doing), but probably not (3) (since it's likely to be bad for the environment, contributing to pollution and global warming as well as using up finite resources). And even if it did satisfy all those conditions, I might decide to chuck in my job completely if (as per item (4)) I won the National Lottery, thereby being released from the necessity of working for a living.

A good question in regard to whether a particular job is worthwhile, therefore, is: would you do this job if your needs were otherwise met?[44] Many, perhaps most jobs would fail this test, and some of those who passed it would – as outlined above – pass for bad reasons. On the other hand, some of the most important work (for example raising children in the home, a task traditionally performed by women) is downgraded and devalued in our society, and effectively becomes invisible.

In crass economic terms, if the reproduction of the labour force – which people normally do without pay – were paid for at its full worth, the cost would be very large indeed. One estimate suggests the contribution of Britain's unpaid economy may be equal to the country's GDP (Gross Domestic Product). In 2010, unpaid childcare was worth £343 billion (for comparison, the financial services industry contributed about a third of that amount to the economy).[45] In Ireland, there has been furious controversy about the recent 'bailout' of Irish banks. Yet no one, so far as I am aware, has asked for a bailout for hard-pressed homemakers, some of them under threat of losing their homes as a result of the economic crash and the consequent 'austerity' which was imposed on the population.

The argument that as a society we should continue to place such an emphasis on 'jobs' in the formal economy is open to serious question. Arguably, only a minority of jobs are worthwhile in terms of job satisfaction (as distinct from the money they bring in for the worker and his/her dependants, or of the benefit they may be to society as a whole).[46] Jobs in the creative, cultural and scientific sectors come to mind: think of an artist, craftsperson, designer, scientist, engineer or inventor who works for the joy of it, to make the world a better place in some way, and to enhance his/her peer esteem without regard to financial reward, and without counting the days until retirement. (Work in higher education used to be like that, but not any more.)[47]

Higher education, whose aim could be to prepare students for a life-time of leisure, culture, social participation and self-development in a rational and humane society based on technological development and sensitivity to the requirements of the planet, is being turned into the opposite: a means of fitting students with transitory, 'practical' skills which may be outmoded before they are even used. The goal, insofar as there is one, seems to be for the individual to become the servant of the machine rather than its master.

Of course, there is much essential work that people do primarily for the money, without which society could not function. But the argument in favour of that kind of work should be from the point of view of soci-ety as a whole, rather than in terms of benefit to the worker, since his/her needs could be provided for just as easily through an unconditional distribution of wealth. (There is, of course, also much inessential work that people do mainly for the money.)

The ideal career plan is sometimes said to be to 'find something you like to do, and get someone to pay you to do it'. While that's no doubt a good idea in principle, for most people the two sets of things, 'what I like to do' and 'what someone would pay me to do', do not normally overlap to any great extent. (Even where they do, in a rapidly changing economy and society there is no guarantee that they will continue to do so throughout the employee's life – a job skill you learn today may be obsolete tomorrow.)

The idea that someone should spend 8 hours a day (excluding com-muting time) 5 days a week for 40 years of their life doing something that, by and large, they would rather not be doing,[48] is a fairly recent one, and is an effect of the rise of the middle classes over the last few hundred years.

Whether a more humane and rational society would need some form of socialism to bring it about, or whether it could happen under capitalism (or some variant of capitalism), is an important question. The difficulties are familiar enough. The problem with (state) socialism is that it needs bureaucrats and functionaries to administer it, and such individuals are notoriously averse to freedom (at least for others). The problem with capitalism, as it currently exists at any rate, is that it needs a certain amount of unemployment to maintain the demand for employment and help keep wages down: too few potential workers means pressure to raise wages.[49]

Until recent times at least, the aristocracy somehow managed to remain free of the pressures of the work ethic. Echoes of this may be found in the work of the great English comic writer P.G. Wodehouse, with his best-known character Bertie Wooster. (The aristocratic avoidance of work by Bertie and his peers has an enduring charm, though it might be punctured by a too-close examination of where his money actually comes from – a critical take that is, obliquely, suggested by Bertie's membership of the Drones Club.)

Historically, the rigorous, time-devouring work discipline of the nineteenth century contrasted with the leisurely life of the medieval peasant. The peasant of the Middle Ages could enjoy up to half a year's vacation: the modern US employee enjoys eight days.[50] This seems like something close to insanity on a mass scale.

The sociologist Max Weber famously made the connection between work ethic and Protestantism – specifically Calvinism. The Protestant valuation of work involved a sense of the 'calling': the notion that the onus is on the individual to do their duty in the everyday world. In the context of Calvinism, this was combined with a sense of anxiety around the certainty of one's personal salvation. The encouragement to engage in money-making activities – in contrast to the traditional (Catholic) religious valuation of poverty – was therefore strong, in order that it might function as a sign to yourself and others of your membership of the elect.[51]

Busy activity was regarded as the most suitable means to get rid of religious doubts and to impart the certainty of salvation.[52] In Weber's terms, the Calvinist creates the conviction of his/her own salvation.[53] Acquisition, and worldly diligence, became prime values in terms of the spirit of capitalism: waste of time became the deadliest of sins.[54] The acquisition of wealth as the result of labour in one's calling was a sign of divine favour. The valuation of hard work, combined with the limitation on consumption, was a powerful impetus towards the accumulation of capital.[55]

Many people in our modern societies who may never have been inside a church, and indeed whose families may have been non-religious for generations, are still unconscious victims of this particular mindset, and feel a sense of dread at the threat of unemployment.[56] This is not just because of the impoverishment and lessening of freedom that result from unemployment under our current system (admittedly a rational concern). It is also because of the idolatry of work[57] and the (largely irrational) anxieties that arise from it. Here, we may be looking at an inherent 'fear of freedom'[58] which, while it may have been useful at one time for the capitalist system (it helped to maintain a disciplined workforce), is rapidly becoming less so, even for capitalism. People need money to buy commodities, and if they can't earn enough, that's bad not only for them but for the economic system as well.

Because we can only think of 'jobs for all' as the ultimate goal worth striving for, the goal actually becomes even more difficult to achieve since we refuse to entertain alternative ideas, such as the direct redistribution of wealth with UBI. UBI, after all, might actually have the effect of increasing employment, at least for those who want it.[59]

The spectre, overshadowed by the historical failures of state socialism, of a planned economy with its dangers (real and imagined), operates as a strong deterrent to any project to humanise life and work. There are, however, other ways of helping to bring about a more rational society (or a somewhat more rational one at any rate). UBI is one of them.

As a rough distinction, we could highlight the difference between 'labour' (something to be avoided whenever possible, or minimised when it is not possible to avoid it) and 'work' (a potentially productive and fulfilling activity).[60] Hannah Arendt points out that the words for 'labour' in Latin, English, Greek, French and German denote elements of pain and effort (and also have reference to the travails of birth).[61]

The ancient Greeks possessed slaves because they wished to avoid the 'slavish nature' of the labour activities needed to maintain life.[62] Plato, in *The Laws*, wished to prevent citizens from engaging in trade or business, while Aristotle, in *Politics,* did not want citizens to be involved in mechanical employment or other basic forms of activity, in order that they might have the leisure for personal improvement and political activity.[63]

It is deeply ironic that, just as we are developing slaves of our own (machines) to do so much necessary work and take the drudgery off our hands, we regard it as a problem rather than a solution. ('Where are the jobs going to come from?')[64] The key point is that we need to emphasise forms of human activity in the productive sphere that are positive, freeing, creative and fulfilling, as distinct from those that are negative, inhibiting, uncreative and unfulfilling.

At the same time, we need to rationalise and – where possible – minimise necessary work, in order to provide as much free time as possible for the development of the creative potential that exists in all of us, and which currently atrophies under the illogical pressure to spend our days doing things that, ideally, we would rather not be doing.[65] How to bring about such a society (that is, through capitalism, socialism, or some variant of either) is a central question, to which there is no easy answer.

Perhaps a combination of technological development, ecological pressure and trade union organisation could help bring about the kind of society that rationalises, minimises – and, so far as possible – humanises necessary work. At the same time, such a society would maximise human freedom for self-development and re-engagement with nature, human connectivity and creativity.

Of itself, the chaos of capitalism/corporatism could not bring this about, any more than the potential tyranny of state socialism. In the scenario outlined, there would be a 'positive' blurring of the work/leisure distinction: leisure would ideally involve an element of creative endeavour, and work would ideally involve as much of an element of enjoyment as possible.

Such an impetus towards a radically different form of society would be diametrically opposed to the goal of 'full employment' which has traditionally preoccupied both Left and Right. It would be characterised by two main demands: the severing of income from work through UBI, and the reduction of the working day/week/year.

WORK AND RETIREMENT

The notion of 'retirement age' (retirement often being a euphemism for compulsory redundancy on grounds of age) is a fairly recent invention, with no specific biological justification. As is so often the case in public discourse, the concept often involves a mix-up of rights and duties: liberty (the freedom to retire) is conflated with coercion (the compulsion to retire).

There is sometimes a tendency to equate the two, so that the fear is that if you get rid of compulsion, you also get rid of freedom: if people are allowed to postpone retirement at will, the argument goes, it may be that they will end up with no choice in the matter and have to continue working whether they like it or not.

It has to be admitted that such a fear is not completely unjustified. There is a parallel with previous debates about women in the workplace. One of the arguments against removing the prohibition on women's participation in the workplace was that the freedom to work would turn into the economic compulsion to work. (At the least, it's easy to imagine such an argument.) This, to a considerable extent, is what actually happened.

Nevertheless, few people want to turn the clock back to the situation where women had to leave work once they got married (as was the case with the civil service 'marriage bar' in Ireland, until relatively recent times). In terms of the practice of compulsory retirement that still exists in some countries, 'congratulatory' retirement parties are held to celebrate something that people may not have wanted to happen to them.

While compulsory retirement has some apparent justification in jobs where physical strength, stamina and reflexes are crucial and where the safety of the public is paramount (firefighters, police and airline pilots come to mind), such jobs are in a small minority. Even in such cases, compulsory retirement should logically depend on the employee failing periodic physical (and mental) examinations, rather than on exceeding some arbitrarily defined age limit, since people do not uniformly lose their work-related abilities at one particular age.

41

There is a separate argument for compulsory retirement, particularly in coveted and/or publicly funded jobs, such as those in academia or the public service. The argument is that compulsory retirement favours new entrants to the job market, specifically younger people who may find it easier to get a foothold on the ladder, if older people have to leave their positions.

But even if that point were correct, compulsory retirement should logically, in that case, be determined by the number of years that a person has worked in the job, rather than by their chronological age. For example, those who started or resumed work late in life due to family or other commitments, should not – according to any reasonable concept of fairness – be penalised as a result, by being forced to retire at the same age as those who began work straight out of school or college.

A staged approach to retirement – whereby people step down gradually from work rather than leaving it all of a sudden having passed a particular age landmark – would, arguably, be more human-friendly than the psychological dislocation often caused by a sudden cessation of employment that happens at present in countries where the practice of compulsory retirement exists. While UBI might make that innovation easier, it will not solve this on its own – a full-fledged rethink of the role of work in our society is also needed.

WORK, LABOUR, LEISURE, PLAY

Writing presciently in the 1950s, Arendt described a society of labourers, which is soon to be freed from the chains of labour, but which no longer has any understanding of the higher forms of human activity that could take their place – a disastrous situation.[66]

Things haven't changed very much in the intervening half-century or more. The survival of an ideology of work at the same time as its material conditions have been eroded poses a serious social problem. The development of automation and the widespread participation of women in the workforce could, with rational organisation, have been the means of reducing labour time to a necessary minimum and expanding the sphere of freedom for everyone. Instead, we have done the opposite: work has expanded, while leisure time has contracted.[67]

In some cases, work and leisure have become increasingly hard to distinguish – though not in a positive way. We have the reports of Chinese workers who spend their working hours 'mining' for virtual gold in computer games, and who then spend their 'free time' playing computer games. Play itself is relegated to the sphere of childhood and disappears from our lives (replaced by organised and commercialised 'sports' and stereotypical 'fun' drinking activities such as 'hen' and 'stag' parties).[68]

The traditional Left critique of mass culture was of a culture based on technology and oriented towards entertainment, which functions at the same time to reinforce the values of the socioeconomic system and provide an illusory escape from them.[69] When you add smartphones, computer games and the Internet into the mix, this in some ways intensifies the situation of an alienated culture: it is increasingly difficult to escape from work, wherever you are; or, even in your free time, to escape from an administered culture.[70]

ADVANTAGES OF UBI

What, then, are the specific advantages of UBI? The most important element is that it breaks – to an extent at least – the connection between work and income. For people in conventional employment, it means that they have an increased sense of security. If they lose their job, the UBI is already there, an automatic support until they find full-time employment. The 'bag-lady syndrome' (the terror of being impoverished and out in the street)[71] in our atomised society is alleviated with UBI.

Once established in a society, UBI would be extremely difficult to dislodge in a political sense. Even the current welfare systems are politically hard to dismantle (which has, however, not stopped neoliberal governments from trying their best to do so). Unlike the situation with present social welfare systems, UBI is paid to everyone, in a relatively simple process – there is no argument to answer that it involves excessive bureaucracy or unfairness.

With the new system, the individual can supplement their UBI with part-time employment, without the encumbrances and pitfalls of current social welfare systems. UBI gets rid of the 'stigma' that may exist as a result of participation in the existing social welfare system (with UBI, everyone receives basic income, so no one is singled out as an 'undeserving' recipient who needs to 'get on their bike' and 'get a job').[72] For women in particular, UBI reduces dependency on the masculine 'bread winner' and makes economic independence a more achievable prospect. Dignity for everyone is increased – an important aspiration.

UBI is democratic because it is paid to individual citizens rather than to households[73] without the intrusiveness that current welfare systems involve. It has the potential to lessen sexual oppression, reduce dependency, and increase equality between the sexes.[74] UBI also functions as a means of support to small farmers, and as a way by which people who wish to live a rural lifestyle would be enabled to do so: instead of being channelled to agribusiness, the money would go directly to people living on the land.[75]

UBI fulfils (to an extent at least) the radical dream of 'to each according to his/her needs.'[76] It compensates for historical injustices by giving people a stake in the economy, of which their ancestors may have been unjustly deprived. For the descendants of an Irish family who lost their land and property as a result of the plantations of the seventeenth century or as a consequence of the later penal laws, or of an English or Scottish family who were historically deprived of land under enclosures or clearances, or the descendant of many African-Americans who were enslaved for generations, UBI reinstates their claim to a part of the social product of which their ancestors were dispossessed (whether or not that happened under the guise of legality) and goes some way towards recompensing them. Furthermore, it does it without 'affirmative action' or depriving anyone else, since, by definition, everyone gets UBI (not just those with a claim – however justified it may be – to redress for historical deprivation).

In a moral sense, there seems to be a much stronger argument for giving money directly to people whose ancestors have been deprived, than for the current types of unearned income which are unquestioningly accepted by our society (for example share dividends, inheritances, or intra-family gifts for purposes of tax avoidance) and whose recipients may benefit from the economic injustices perpetrated by their ancestors.

It would, of course, in many cases be a legal-financial nightmare to establish how much an individual is due as a result of some injustice that was inflicted on an ancestor. With UBI, though, you don't have to go down that road. Instead, the individual gets a direct share in the social wealth.

UBI allows unemployed people to take up work without losing out financially, since it does away with poverty traps – with UBI, it is always more advantageous to work than not to. Consequently, the negative psychological effects of unemployment are lessened.[77]

Furthermore, UBI gives unemployed people a greater sense of security than do the current systems of unemployment benefit or assistance. It means that they aren't forced to take up employment with which they might have a problem (for example a vegan being required to work in an abattoir). For self-employed people starting up a business, UBI provides something on which to fall back, in the event that the enterprise should turn out to be unsuccessful.

An advantage for employers is that UBI reduces bureaucracy and increases flexibility. Since workers have greater security with UBI, it may lessen the need for some forms of employment-protection leg-islation (though not, for example, in the spheres of health and safety).[78] Arguments for and against a minimum wage would, with UBI, have a dif-ferent context (though they would, no doubt, still take place).

In the US, a Leftist like the recent presidential candidate Bernie Sanders has argued for an increase in the minimum wage to $15 an hour, while a prominent libertarian like Peter Schiff argues against such a minimum wage level, on the basis that it would deter employment creation.[79] With UBI, such debates would no doubt continue, though in a different context where the basic security of the worker has been enhanced.

EMPLOYMENT AND FREEDOM

It seems that UBI appears both to favour the work ethic (it removes some problems, for example poverty traps that reinforce unemployment) and go against it (with UBI there is less pressure on workers to take jobs). At first glance, this seems to be something of a paradox.[80] What is actually going on with UBI, though, is an increase in freedom, whereby people who actually want to work are enabled to do so, while those who do not wish to work are not forced to do so.

UBI, through the reduction of bureaucracy that it involves, also appears to have the effect of making life easier for both employers and employees – another paradox. It goes against the current 'zero-sum' game in industrial relations whereby if one party wins in a negotiation, another loses.[81] UBI is, in some ways, a win-win situation. Freedom has the potential to benefit everyone.[82]

Traditionally, one of the promised benefits of socialism was to provide the security that capitalism had denied to workers. UBI offers that security without the downside in terms of coercion, stagnation, and institutional bureaucracy that have historically beset socialist (or would-be socialist) societies.

Of course, the struggle between Right and Left (in traditional terms between 'capitalism' and 'socialism') could, and no doubt would, continue in a society with UBI – though it would be a struggle between a capitalist system that worked more efficiently than before, and workers who were more secure than they had previously been. Whether that would be an improvement from a capitalist (or conversely from a socialist) point of view is a moot point. It would undoubtedly be a better situation from the point of view of human freedom.[83]

Under the current system, as already noted, many employees are subject to 'precarious' work. Their jobs may be temporary or seasonal, they may be working part-time or on short-term contracts with less legal protection than full-time workers have. Their working hours may vary (even to the extent of 'zero-hour contracts') and consequently may clash with their home and social lives (to the extent that a social life is possible for a precarious worker). Full-time jobs have been replaced for many people by the 'gig' economy of sporadic work (which is all right if that kind of work suits you, but not if it doesn't).

With the present system, people may not have enough insurance contributions to obtain full state benefits if they fall ill or become unemployed, or to receive a full pension when they retire. Furthermore, they may face difficulties when claiming benefits from the social welfare system.

Even if an employee has a conventional (or 'safe') job, that job may be an unsatisfying one, offering few opportunities for training or the fostering of skills, and the activity itself may be one that harms either the natural environment or society, or both. Because of the currently weak status of employees, the balance of power in negotiating pay and conditions favours employers. Part-time workers may work fewer hours than they want or need, while others in full-time employment may have to work longer hours than they wish, or than suits their home situation.[84]

The establishment of a UBI system, on the other hand, gives employees greater freedom to move out of a job that they find unsatisfactory for one reason or another, and provides them with extra negotiating power. It makes life easier for people in precarious employment by providing financial support when they are not working.

Since UBI does not depend on prior social welfare contributions, it reduces the bureaucracy and uncertainty that people would otherwise face. It makes it easier for the employee to work hours that suit him/her, to choose work that is socially beneficial, or to reject undesirable work. It facilitates people who choose to spend their time (for example) caring for others, growing food, or making objects (or repairing them). UBI also makes it easier to set up alternative structures such as cooperatives.[85]

For the self-employed or those who want to become self-employed, UBI provides something on which to fall back if their enterprise doesn't work out, particularly as such people may not be adequately provided for by current social welfare support, which may be intrusive, bureaucratic, time consuming, delayed and/or inadequate.

UBI makes it potentially easier to access credit and investor support. It alleviates the difficulties of income insecurity and the problems of cash flow that may occur while getting a business off the ground. It means that the effect of the failure of a business on the entrepreneur's dependants is softened (since they have their own basic income, which acts as a cushion). It increases the possibilities for 'social enterprise' whereby the entrepreneur is not exclusively driven to maximise profit, regardless of benefit to the community.

Sustainability, as distinct from making the highest possible profit, becomes a goal that can be achieved. By reducing short-term pressures, UBI makes it easier to plan long-term in regard to the business enterprise.[86]

It's a seeming paradox that UBI is potentially attractive both to entrepreneurs and salaried workers, sectors of society that are often seen as having conflicting interests. The common theme, though, is that UBI reduces bureaucracy and removes impediments to economic activity, whether that activity involves working for yourself, for someone else, or in a cooperative.

A NOTE ON SOCIAL WELFARE SYSTEMS

The current social welfare systems of the West were designed for a society of full, lifetime, male employment, with women largely relegated to the home, a system where the (male) worker entered employment in his teens or twenties and stayed in one job until retirement age (if he was fortunate enough to reach it).[87] The current social reality bears little resemblance to this picture (nor indeed should it – the participation of women in the workforce is obviously to be welcomed). We need to change the system to reflect the new reality, rather than trying to force new wine into old bottles.

The social state has its origins in the ideas of Lorenz von Stein (1815–1890). The idea was primarily to head off the revolutionary impetus of the nineteenth century – to stave off a radical change in the nature of society, not to help it happen. The social state was basically defensive in origin, from the point of view of the capitalist establishment. (This does not mean, of course, that aspects of the modern welfare state may not be desirable in themselves.) Elements developed in the Germany of Otto von Bismarck that took form in the modern welfare state (for example health insurance, laws on industrial accidents, old-age and invalid insurance) and later developments in the Weimar Republic in Germany, are vital to understanding the post-Second World War welfare state. Important also is the 'historic compromise' between capital and labour that was developed in Sweden in 1938.[88]

In literature, the weaknesses of what would become the modern welfare state were exposed most devastatingly in the writings of Franz Kafka, specifically in his novel *The Castle*, with its relentless account of its downside: the red tape and bureaucracy that trap the hapless client caught in its mesh. No matter how hard you look, no one appears to be actually responsible for the fate of the supplicant in *The Castle* (or of the defendant in Kafka's other major novel *The Trial*). Bad things just happen to them. As Arendt points out, the rule by 'nobody' that is characteristic of bureaucracy can be one of 'its cruellest and most tyrannical versions'.[89]

Anyone who has been caught up in the maze of tax, welfare, immigration, employment, pension and insurance regulations characteristic of the modern state would readily agree. It might be observed that the tyranny of bureaucracy is not so much the fault of 'socialism' or, indeed, of capitalism – rather it is a result of each mindset (that of the state and of business) trying to compensate for the deficiencies of the other, and in the process making things worse than they were before, or would otherwise have been.

Instead of giving us the security of socialism combined with the freedom of capitalism, the capitalist state ends up giving us the opposite: the security of capitalism combined with the freedom of socialism. Thus, we end up with the worst of both worlds: a situation which, particularly in large countries such as the USA, is now morphing into the corporate state, with virtually total corporate control of the media and government, and an out-of-control financial sector which operates for its own ends. This – as distinct from the Right-wing buffoonery that operates as a sham alternative to the corporate state – might be legitimately described as a form of fascism.

In a small country like Ireland, state bureaucracy may be mediated by a sense of social cohesion, a desire to balance complexity with efficiency, and humanitarian concerns ('small is beautiful' has some validity when it comes to the size of a community or a state). In much larger countries such as the US and the UK, such amelioration is less likely to occur. We all live in an 'iron cage' of bureaucracy, in the terms of Weber, to such an extent that freeing ourselves from it becomes difficult to imagine, and may indeed even appear as a threat.

The origin of the welfare state coincides with the Beveridge Report, published in the UK in 1941, with its 'cradle-to-grave' taxpayer-financed cover, including what became the National Health Service. Its main goals were the achievement of growth based on capitalism, and to make up for the deficiencies of the market, consequently guaranteeing social stability and the demand for consumer goods. The trade-off was that workers gave up any goal of workers' control, which had been a key socialist aim prior to the Second World War. In the current situation, weakening employment and the mass importation of goods from countries with semi-slave conditions have meant the undermining of domestic consumer markets. Criticisms of the welfare state (primarily from the Right but also from elements of the Left) include the argument that the welfare state removes incentives for work; that it is inefficient, leads to statism and high tax rates, and fails to compensate for the deficiencies of the market.[90]

The welfare state is also open to the criticism that it engages in too much control over people's lives and too much intrusion into their personal affairs, and that it involves high administrative expense. The crucial issue from our point of view, though, is that means testing results in the situation that there can be a cut-off of support when you get a part-time or low-paid job: a marginal tax rate of 100 per cent.[91] If and when an unemployed person takes up a new job, he or she may be faced with a period of irregular income (or none) without financial reserves as a support.[92]

To what extent the welfare state would continue in the context of a UBI system[93] is a matter of debate. On one side of the argument (the Left), one could envisage the preservation of the welfare state, with the sole (though significant) exception of the rationalisation that UBI would involve. At the other end of the scale (the Right) there could be arguments for UBI to take the place of many or most of the state provisions that currently exist (for example in regard to education and health).[94] In that scenario, the recipient would get an unconditional UBI, but would have to pay the (significant) costs of health and education him/herself.

In other words, in the context of UBI the Left/Right debate continues – the argument for or against UBI is not a Left/Right one in itself, though most of the input to date has probably come from the Left.

How this discussion would play out in political reality is a matter of conjecture. It is sometimes hard to persuade voters of the benefits of expenditure on, for example, health and education, since it is often unclear that the money is being put to the best possible use (for example focusing on front-line services, rather than paying high salaries to administrators). If, however, the money actually ends up in your pocket as a result of an increase in the level of UBI, the advantage is palpably apparent.

That could, conceivably, mean that there would be political pressure to cut back on expenditure on high-cost areas such as health, education, the salaries of politicians or (in some countries like the US) prisons and the military. Instead, the money involved would be distributed directly to the people. Such a development is not always easy to categorise in traditional Left/Right terms, but it might depend on the general enlightenment of the population. Ideally, they would say 'yes' to money ear-marked for wise spending on health and education, and 'no' to money spent on 'defence' (aka 'attack') or on locking up people for little or no reason.

The potential disadvantages (and/or possible advantages) of giving money directly to citizens that would otherwise go on state expenditure of one kind or another are obvious, but it is sometimes difficult to see how such debates would fall along the traditional 'Left-Right' spectrum. If I want more money in my pocket (and everyone's pocket) at the expense of the government spending it on health and education (or conversely on prisons and new military toys) does that make me a conservative or a progressive? Perhaps it calls into question – at least within the parameters of this discussion – the whole distinction between the two.[95]

YOUNG PEOPLE, CARERS, ARTISTS

For young people in particular, UBI opens up new horizons. It enhances security and independence. It gives them some breathing space to evaluate their life prospects in terms of study, personal development, relationships, reproduction and employment. It lessens the role of financial pressure in making decisions about a particular course of study. As a result, students are less likely to enrol in programs that, while promising to lead them to more lucrative employment, are unsuited to their interests or abilities. They may indeed end up dropping out from such courses, consequently wasting time, effort and money (whether it's their own money, that of their parents or the state, or some combination).

UBI makes it possible for students to factor in other issues (for example social, environmental, creative) to their choice of studies rather than purely financial ones. It eases the economic pressures that people often face while studying, and reduces – or eliminates – the burden of debt that they might otherwise carry over into later life.[96] In the US, 70 per cent of people leaving college with bachelors' degrees are in debt: the average debt of those graduating in 2015 was $35,051.[97]

While Sanders called for the abolition of student fees in public universities in the US, there have, contrariwise, recently been calls in Ireland to institute a system of student loans and fees. (The availability of loans will probably have the effect of causing a resultant spike in the level of fees – students in the UK can currently pay up to £9,000 per year in fees.)[98]

UBI, in contrast to the current situation of insecurity and precarity, reduces the pressure on younger people to emigrate,[99] so that if they do make that decision, it is more likely to be on the basis of a free choice, rather than the outcome of financial constraints. (There is, of course, nothing wrong with emigration *per se*, as long as it's something you want to do – for example to see the world, gain work experience that may not be available at home, expand your cultural horizons, or enjoy a varied lifestyle – rather than something you are forced into by economic circumstances.)

For carers, UBI provides a reliable and secure income. People can combine caring with additional part-time work. It gets rid of the 'care trap' that can face carers who take up paid work. It reduces bureaucracy, in that carers do not have to apply for allowances or credits. With the new system of distribution, there is no need to make a convincing argument to the authorities that someone is in need of care. With a system of UBI, those who receive care have a greater sense of empowerment, since they have an income of their own. UBI enhances the quality of life for both carers and recipients of care. Security and dignity are increased for everyone. (UBI does not, of course, meet the extra costs that care may involve – they would need to be provided for separately.)[100]

UBI supports artistic and creative activity by giving artists, designers, inventors and other creative people a financial basis on which to survive. Creative activity adds economic value to society, though such value may be difficult to quantify. The marginalisation of artists is hard to justify even in economic terms. How much foreign direct investment in Dublin (for example) by multinational corporations is due to the city's perceived 'vibe' as a culturally stimulating place to work, an atmosphere to which artists vitally contribute? This would be very difficult to specify exactly in economic terms, yet there is probably a significant element at work in terms of the influence of artistic and creative activity.

Of course, the economic element in regard to artistic activity is by no means the only one. There is a basic argument for artistic and creative work as being valuable in itself, regardless of the extent to which it contributes to economic development. We value the art and architecture of cities such as Florence and Venice[101] as a supreme achievement of humanity: indeed far more than the economic successes of the merchants and rulers who, through their patronage, made such creative achievements possible. It's true that the local Italian economies would, today, be much poorer in terms of their tourist trade without the works of Brunelleschi or Tintoretto that attract so many visitors – but that's a comparatively minor issue in the overall scheme of things.

Without their artists, architects, writers and composers, eras of history would be hard to distinguish from times of barbarism. Yet we continue to push artists to the margins of society, as we have always done.[102] Seven Greek cities reputedly fought for Homer's body after his death, cities in which he had to beg for food when alive. Van Gogh sold only one painting in his life and ended up killing himself, while today the purchase of his work would be beyond the resources of many major art museums. Despite the traditional picture of the artist starving in an attic, physical hunger is not a catalyst for good art, any more than it is for good accountancy.

UBI at least alleviates that kind of dismal situation to which artists have traditionally been subject, by giving creative people an economic floor on which to operate while they produce work that may not be of economic value, at least not immediately or obviously. It releases them from dependency on family assistance or grant committees, and frees them from having to produce work ('pot-boilers') tailored to the market, rather than the work being the direct expression of the artist's creative energy. The support provided by UBI also makes it easier for ordinary people to experiment with creative or artistic activity.[103]

SUMMING UP

UBI reduces inequality, in that it enhances the possibilities of opportunity for people who have been economically marginalised. It increases freedom, including the freedom to work (as well as the freedom not to work). It fosters economic functionality and efficiency in an era of increased mechanisation, while at the same time opening the door to the prospect of a life beyond mere functionality.

On the one hand, UBI facilitates the capitalist system in that, by giving people money in a way that is not dependent on work, it provides the means to buy the commodities it produces. It also makes it easier for businesses (particularly small businesses) to operate, by potentially reducing bureaucracy in terms of employment-protection legislation, and providing an economic floor for entrepreneurs. On the other hand, it makes it easier for workers to organise to defend their interests through trade unions, or to develop 'post-capitalist' alternatives (such as worker cooperatives).[104]

Perhaps a combination of technological development, ecological pressure and trade union organisation could bring about the kind of society that rationalises, minimises – and, as far as possible – humanises necessary work. At the same time, such a society would, ideally, afford maximum opportunity for self-development and re-engagement with nature, human relations and creativity.

It is unlikely that such a society would develop of its own accord, either through the chaos of capitalism/corporatism or the tyranny of state socialism. In a desirable scenario, there would be a 'positive' blurring of the work/leisure distinction: leisure would involve an element of creative activity, and work would involve as much of an element of enjoyment as possible.

Such an impetus towards a radically different form of society would be diametrically opposed to the destructive goal of 'full employment' which has traditionally preoccupied both Left and Right. As noted already, it would be characterised by two main priorities: the severing of income from work, and the reduction of the working day/week/year.[105]

Such a vision may seem utopian, but it is no more utopian than the (unachievable and undesirable) society of full employment (though the latter might indeed be regarded as more of a negative utopia or 'dystopia'). The obstacle in the way of such a positive form of society developing may not be so much the work ethic or ideology of work – which has clearly outlived much of its usefulness, even for capitalism. The real obstacle may be the development of a culture of passive consumerism, to give an illusory compensation to people for the control they have lost over their lives.

The prevailing mindset makes it difficult for many people to imagine the potential that freedom offers, beyond playing endless computer games or watching daytime TV. We have become both passive surveyors (of the couch-potato variety) and, at the same time, objects of universal surveillance,[106] both online and offline. Freedom is difficult to imagine, or maybe even to want, when you never had it in the first place so you don't know what it's like.

For trade unions – weakened by decades of neoliberal opposition – to play an active role in agitating for the desirable kind of society indicated, they will need to look beyond the conventional ideology of work, broaden their horizons to encompass part-time workers and the 'precariat' in general, and seek new horizons of freedom and equality of opportunity. The weakness of trade unions has been one of the prime reasons for the perilous state of the working class, particularly in the US. A commitment to UBI could be a factor that would help to give them a new life.[107]

2

A BRIEF HISTORY OF
BASIC INCOME PROPOSALS

In the history of political thought, UBI has been somewhat of a fringe idea until fairly recently. However, an impressive number of Left-wing theorists and intellectuals have, in recent times, lined up in support of the proposal. These include Michael Hardt and Antonio Negri, Noam Chomsky, Naomi Klein, Yannis Varoufakis, Paul Mason, Slavoj Žižek, and many others.[1] (Žižek refers to UBI as 'arguably the Left's only original economic idea of the last few decades'.[2])

UBI is also coming to the fore with writers who have focused on the implications of new technology for employment and for the health of the capitalist economy.[3] Discussions around UBI are also in the process of becoming 'mainstream' in the more thoughtful sections of the media.[4]

Historically though, the idea of UBI has not been prominent in political programmes of either Right or Left, though some well-known thinkers have expressed support for the idea at various times and in various ways. These have included Henry George, J.K. Galbraith, Erich Fromm, Peter Drucker, Marshall McLuhan, Martin Luther King, Jeremy Rifkin, Margaret Mead, Paul Samuelson, Buckminster Fuller, and Hazel Henderson.[5]

In the long-standing disagreement between (mis)interpreters of Adam Smith and (mis)interpreters of Karl Marx as to how society should be run, the idea of UBI has, up to now, been very much a sideshow. There are probably many reasons for this, but one problem may be that it appeals neither to the greed often associated with capitalism, nor to the envy often associated with socialism. It appeals neither to the desire for wealth on the one hand, nor to that for power on the other. Many people who support UBI do so not because it will make them any richer in a personal sense, but because it would be good for society as a whole. They believe that it would operate as a stabilising force, affording the maximum possibility for freedom and the development of human potential.

UBI promises to free people – to some extent – from the constraints of both market and state. It is an unfortunate fact that freedom itself may be a threat to those who believe they have a monopoly on what the future of society may (or should) look like, whether such people come from the Left or the Right.

While UBI is now in the process of becoming a mainstream proposal, due to the manifest failure of our current employment and welfare systems to offer adequate freedom and security to the populations of developed countries (never mind undeveloped ones), it has traditionally been marginalised in political debate.

Right-wing resistance to the proposal probably comes from the mindset that places a high value on the work ethic (at least for others, if not always for oneself). There is also the view (stated or more often unstated) that the working class needs to be kept in a state of regimentation in order for the system of industrial capitalism to run smoothly.

Left-wing opposition to UBI may originate in the fear that basic income would weaken trade unions, undermine the sense of community and camaraderie that work (supposedly) involves, and let the state off the hook in terms of having to provide comprehensive services for the citizens. There may also be some remnants of patriarchal role-playing, to do with the notion of a man's role as breadwinner – however much technology has called in question traditional forms of work, in particular the more macho, labour-intensive activities traditionally associated with male work.

At the extreme Left, (some) anarchists may have an issue with anything that depends on the state for its functioning, since UBI would require some form of centralised structure in order for it to work. Conversely, (some) Marxists may entertain suspicions of anything that proposes to diminish the necessity for the traditional recipe of state socialism as an interim measure on the road to communism. (UBI also calls in question the need for a power structure to organise work, and its remuneration, on a national basis – traditional conceptions of state socialism would necessarily require some such structure.)

Three roots have been identified to the idea of UBI without strings attached: the notion of a minimum income that first took shape at the start of the sixteenth century; the idea of a grant without conditions that came up towards the end of the eighteenth century; and the combination of the two in the concept of an unconditional basic income, which took place around the middle of the nineteenth century.[6]

The roots of the basic-income idea have been traced back to the humanists Thomas More and Johannes Ludovicus Vives, though – significantly – their ideas did not involve the divorce of income from work, so the link could be seen as being somewhat tenuous. Key figures in the history of ideas such as Montesquieu and Condorcet have also been cited, in terms of the prehistory of UBI. Their proposals, though, are based on entitlement, and they do not emphasise the issue of unconditionality. However, their ideas did feed, in important ways, into the development of social insurance programmes. In one sense, such ideas anticipated UBI proposals. In another way, however, they may have steered us away from them, in that they are based on an individual making enough contributions to qualify for payment, rather than the notion of a person deserving support by reason of being alive.[7]

The republican Tom Paine developed Condorcet's idea further, in an effort to compensate citizens for being deprived of the 'natural inheritance' that they might otherwise have enjoyed,[8] though Paine supported the idea of an endowment rather than an income *per se*. One could argue that this is a somewhat academic distinction as long as a person actually gets the money. However, there is an important practical distinction between the two: I can waste my endowment on a single gambling loss or unwise investment, whereas that is less likely with a regular income. (This distinction will be discussed later.)

The 'utopian socialist' Charles Fourier – drawing on the teaching of Jesus who supported the right to take one's means of subsistence when one is hungry – proposed a version of unconditional basic income, though not a universal one. Echoing Paine, Fourier proposed that the money would compensate the poor for their loss of access to natural resources.[9]

The latter argument is an important one in justifying the limitations of property rights: the idea is that everything that is made derives ultimately from things that at one time belonged to no one (or to everyone, which is much the same thing). Philippe Van Parijs traces this kind of argument back to Gerrard Winstanley and the Levellers' movement in seventeenth-century England. He also finds it in such English nineteenth-century reformers as William Cobbett, Samuel Read, and Poulett Scrope, and in the work of the twentieth-century philosopher Robert Nozick.[10]

Such a justification may also be found in the ideas of the Dutch humanist Hugo Grotius (1586–1645) according to whom land may be regarded as the common heritage of the human race. The idea of a basic endowment resurfaces in the writings of the French nineteenth-century philosopher François Huet.[11]

The work of the Fourierist Joseph Charlier contains the first fully fledged account of a basic income, though it quickly fell off the radar. His proposal for an unconditional basic income was based on the rental value of real estate.[12] The English liberal (or libertarian) philosopher John Stuart Mill referred to UBI in his favourable elaboration of Fourierism,[13] but it was only in the twentieth century that the discussion got going to any significant extent. Between the wars, there was talk of a state bonus or social (or national) dividend. The discussion was revived in the 1960s and 1970s in the US, in the context of debates about the 'demogrant' or 'negative income tax', and in Europe during the 1970s and 1980s.[14]

The first UBI scheme actually to be introduced was the Alaska Permanent Fund, which aimed to share the oil wealth of the state, and gave annual dividends to everyone in Alaska in proportion to their years of residence (though the latter provision was later successfully challenged). In 2008 the dividend reached the level of $2,069 per person[15] – enough to give something of a cushion to the citizens, though not enough on which to live.

In 1918, the philosopher Bertrand Russell argued for an intriguing combination of anarchism and socialism: everyone would get a basic subsistence regardless of work performed, and a much larger income would go to those doing socially useful work.[16] The problem, though (as always with such benevolent schemes) is that power tends to attract people who are hostile or indifferent to the freedom of others, so it's questionable how such a programme of enlightened, libertarian socialism could be either brought about or maintained in the real world of hands-on politics.

The engineer Dennis Milner also proposed the idea of UBI, and fellow engineer Clifford H. Douglas (popularly known as Major Douglas) put the idea forward as a means of combating the perceived problem of overproduction, and the lack of credit and purchasing power on the part of the population in a post-First World War situation.[17]

The fact that both Milner and Douglas were engineers has perhaps some significance, in that the instinct of engineers is (presumably) to solve problems and provide workable solutions, whereas economists are often – though not always – limited by given systems and conventional analyses.

The 'Social Credit' political movement that Douglas was instrumental in forming eventually foundered, perhaps due to a combination of the theoretical obscurities of his economic-political analysis, and the practical threat it posed to the establishment of both Left and Right, which led to its political marginalisation.

The idea of a UBI or 'social dividend' was also proposed by the British economist George D.H. Cole, who favoured it as a means of sharing the produce of the common heritage. It was also tabled by his fellow economist James Meade, who suggested it as a solution to the issues of poverty and unemployment.[18] However, the UBI proposal was politically marginalised by the emergence of the social welfare model.[19]

In the 1960s, the issue came to the fore in the US, in a report written by a group calling itself the Ad Hoc Committee on the Triple Revolution, which included the scientist Linus Pauling and the economist Gunnar Myrdal. The 'triple revolution' referred to is that of nuclear weapons, the civil rights movement, and cybernetic automation. The last mentioned of these, in the view of the Committee, promised to produce an economy where machines would largely replace human beings. The result, as envisaged, would be unemployment, social inequity, and the lack of purchasing power on the part of consumers. The Ad Hoc Committee proposed, as a solution, a guaranteed minimum income to replace the mishmash of welfare measures. The report was released to the media and sent to President Johnson. After a media flurry (largely critical) the issue faded into obscurity.[20]

The writings of Robert Theobald cited the negative effects of automation on employment. The neoliberal economist Milton Friedman in *Capitalism and Freedom* proposed a version of UBI in the form of a 'negative income tax'. On the face of it, this seems a delightfully subversive idea. However, the proposed subversion was in favour of capitalism rather than the population as a whole, and was envisaged as a transition to a 'pure' capitalist society where transfers would be obsolete.[21]

The notion of 'freedom' that capitalism supposedly offers from a neoliberal perspective tends to ignore the constraints on freedom that jobs normally involve: if I have to spend my day doing something that I wouldn't do if I weren't paid to do it, I am not 'free' in any meaningful sense.

This issue also highlights the tension or contradiction between the freedom of corporations on the one hand, and the freedom of individuals on the other. In the contemporary economic system and in its accompanying ideology, the two kinds of freedom are frequently in opposition. This is particularly the case since corporations are in a position to exert unprecedented power through their control of the media and – most famously in the United States – of the political system itself.

In contrast to the position of Friedman, James Tobin's notion of a 'demogrant' was a more generous proposal: each household would receive a credit dependent on the composition of the family, which could then be supplemented with (taxed) earnings.[22] Tobin, together with fellow economists Paul Samuelson, J.K. Galbraith, Robert Lampman and Harold Watts, called on the US Congress in 1966 to adopt 'a system of income guarantees and supplements'. This led to a political initiative (the Family Assistance Plan) of the Nixon administration, which verged on a negative income tax. The plan, prepared by Senator Daniel Patrick Moynihan, was decisively rejected in 1972. This was apparently the result of opposition both from those who felt it went too far, and others who believed that it didn't go far enough.[23]

The opposition from the former derived in part from the influence of the populist author Ayn Rand, and citations of the supposed negative effect of the nineteenth-century 'Speenhamland' experiment in income support in Britain. Under sustained political opposition, the libertarian possibilities of the Nixon idea morphed into their opposite. The result was the bureaucratic, and largely discredited, 'workfare' philosophy that has caused so much misery in subsequent decades.[24]

In Europe, the French theorist Michel Foucault offered an incisive analysis of the concept of negative income tax in 1979, relating the US proposal to developments in French politics in the 1970s. Writing dispassionately and without any obvious value judgement, Foucault points out that the negative income tax – which facilitates neoliberalism – offers a non-bureaucratic, non-socialist mechanism that encourages the individual to rise above the threshold, providing a solution to 'absolute' rather than 'relative' poverty. (That is, it fulfils what are regarded as basic needs, without trying to close the gap between the poor and the rich.) Foucault observes that negative income tax also offers increased flexibility of the workforce, with the abandonment of the policy of full employment: it would be up to people to work or not as they wished.[25]

Subsequently, in the US, ideas around UBI from the point of view of 'people's capitalism', a 'National Mutual Fund', and the distribution of dividends from universal share ownership emerged.[26]

The concept of 'people's capitalism' seems on the face of it to be a contradiction in terms. On the one hand, Leftists have always believed that capitalism and democracy are at odds. The more you have of the former, the argument goes, the less you will have of the latter. Indeed, there is a persuasive argument that we no longer live in a democratic society. Examples that are sometimes cited include the overruling of democratic decisions in Europe (for example in Greece) as a consequence of the recent financial crisis, and the inordinate influence of corporations on US politics and the media.

On the other hand, some Rightists entertain suspicions of democracy as promoting a politics of envy and governmental oppression, stressing (for example) the difference between democratic and republican conceptions of government, and the fact – as they see it – that democracy and freedom do not necessarily coincide.

Consequently, 'People's Capitalism' – a conception of capitalism that is combined with a proposal for widespread redistribution of wealth – has an odd sound since it suggests the possibility of joining, within the capitalist system, fairness with freedom – a possibility that may evoke an instinctive negative reaction from both Left and Right, though for different reasons.

After its political demise in the United States, the UBI issue resurfaced in Europe, in the work of Meyer *et al.* in Denmark and J.P. Kuiper in the Netherlands, who urged the decoupling of work from income. The proposal was taken up politically by the Radical Party in the Netherlands, by the Dutch trade union Voedingsbond, and in 1985 the Scientific Council for Government Policy in the Netherlands urged the adoption of a partial basic income.[27]

In the UK the idea got some traction in the Basic Income Research Group (BIRG) which morphed into the Citizen's Income Trust in 1998. In Germany, the idea was mooted in Thomas Schmid's book *Liberation from False Labour*.[28] Prominent academics associated with the notion of UBI in Germany included Michael Opielka, Joachim Mitschke, Claus Offe, and Fritz Scharpf. In France, the most notable proponent of UBI (initially supposed to be conditional on work but later proposed as unconditional) was André Gorz, a key figure in Left-wing discussions around an alternative future. Notable figures in France associated with the idea included also Yoland Bresson, Alain Caillé, and Jean-Marc Ferry.[29]

In Ireland in the 1980s, in the midst of a debt-related economic crisis with some resemblance to the one we have experienced more recently, the radical economist Raymond Crotty in his book *Ireland in Crisis* proposed a UBI or weekly national dividend of around £80 per week (in 1984 terms) as a result of a drastic reduction of government expenditure, among other measures. (Crotty's plan represented a somewhat strange combination of Right-libertarian anti-statism, with a radical plan for the redistribution of wealth.)[30]

In 1986 a group of researchers and trade unionists organised a meeting bringing together supporters of UBI in Louvain-la-Neuve, Belgium, out of which grew the Basic Income European Network (BIEN), which produced a regular newsletter and organised biennial conferences. To signal the growing global appeal of the idea, the acronym BIEN was subsequently redefined to signify 'Basic Income Earth Network'.[31]

Congresses took place in venues such as Antwerp (1988), Florence (1990), Paris (1992), London (1994), Vienna (1996), Amsterdam (1998), Berlin (2000) and so on. The first congress of BIEN as a global organisation was held in Cape Town in 2006,[32] and the 2008 congress was held in Dublin. In the United States, the US Basic Income Guarantee Network promotes the idea.[33] A journal, *Basic Income Studies*, offers a forum for in-depth discussion of UBI at an academic level.[34]

Prominent supporters of the idea of UBI in Ireland include the organisations Social Justice Ireland,[35] and, more recently, Basic Income Ireland.[36] The Green Party/Comhaontas Glas in Ireland has had a long-standing commitment to UBI, though with varying degrees of emphasis over the years. Indeed, most Green parties in Europe and North America have endorsed some form of UBI. On the other hand, social democratic parties have been less enthusiastic about UBI, tending to see it as potentially undermining minimum-wage legislation or the role of paid employment as a means of social coherence, or as being unjust to workers vis-à-vis non-workers.[37]

There are related questions regarding the continuing relevance of trade unions, if the issue of pay for work were to become less pressing. In response to this, one could point out that questions of pay and pensions will certainly not go away with UBI, and in any case the position of workers would, to some extent, be strengthened if they had a UBI on which to fall back – for example if they had to go on strike.

As noted already, the UBI idea has, until fairly recently at least, been marginal to mainstream thinking in sociology, politics and economics. Traditionally, the Left has tended to monopolise the concept of justice, while the Right has focused on freedom as its main goal. UBI, which (in most of its incarnations) aims for both justice and freedom, threatens to call in question the traditional, dualistic Left/Right mindset.

Because it puts forward a 'win-win' solution, UBI challenges both the traditional view of class struggle from the point of view of the Left, and confidence in the stability of the capitalist system as it presently exists from the perspective of the Right.

However, it might be argued that both responses are mistaken. Leftists can be assured that UBI does not claim to be able to resolve the class struggle: it will not of itself reduce the massive disparity between rich and poor, solve issues of economic growth, or end the debt crisis. Nor will it, of itself, realign the ownership and control of the means of production, distribution and exchange in favour of the working class (or of their self-appointed political representatives).

Rightists, on the other hand, can be assured that the freedom that UBI offers will not undermine the economy. The facile argument that, with UBI, 'no one would want to work' can be addressed by turning it upside down. Stated otherwise, what the argument really means is that UBI would abolish unemployment – or more specifically that it would abolish involuntary unemployment.

The main problem that the modern capitalist economy faces is not that there is too much work to go around, but that there is too little (or at least too little of the right kind). From a capitalist point of view, the issue is not that this involves inequity – capitalism has not traditionally been overly concerned with that issue (except insofar as it threatens its own foundations) – but that, if no one has a job, there will be no one to buy the goods that the system produces.

And that really *is* a problem from the point of view of those who own and control the means of production of such goods. (And that is to say nothing of the wellbeing of the masses of people who are unable to buy them.)

Of course, to argue that UBI would solve the unemployment problem is putting things too simplistically. With UBI, people may still not be able to do the kind of jobs they actually want to do. I may have to work in a restaurant or a call centre if I want to supplement my UBI, when I really want to be an astrophysicist or a company director. I may have to become a self-employed cleaner or make things to sell, if I can't find anything else.

UBI does not promise utopia or the Kingdom of Heaven (at least not by itself, or in the short term). What it does, however, is to allow me to live – while at the same time I am able to work either part-time or full-time – as a means of helping to support my life ambitions, whatever they may be. By eliminating poverty traps and encouraging additional flexibility in terms of industrial relations, UBI makes it easier both to create employment, and to gain access to employment for those who want it.

In a paradox that may be hard for those enmeshed in either/or thinking to understand, UBI potentially gives heart to people both on the Left and the Right. For the Left, it offers an enhanced level of income security, which should strengthen the hands of workers rather than weakening them. If you do have to go on strike, you won't be on the breadline while you're involved in the dispute – even if you are unfortunate enough to lose your job on account of it. It also means that the threat of extreme Right-wing reaction is diminished. (As recent developments in Britain, the European mainland, and the United States have shown, a working class that has been marginalised, impoverished and ignored may just as easily veer towards the extreme Right as towards the Left.)

UBI also gives additional energy to a more just and equitable distribution of wealth throughout society. Since everyone gets basic income, the arguments around distribution, in a society where UBI exists, will not highlight caricatures of 'welfare queens' or idle spongers. Rather, they will focus on whether it would be more beneficial to put the money in the pockets of the population as a whole, or to expend it on corporate welfare (or indeed on expanding the role of the state).[38]

For those who think in a Right-wing or traditionally conservative way, UBI offers the possibility of increased flexibility in terms of industrial relations (since workers have greater security through UBI and a job is not the only means of staying alive, it may become potentially easier to get rid of unsatisfactory employees). UBI offers enhanced security to entrepreneurs trying to get a business off the ground, or to business people trying to operate a small firm with – as is often the case at present – minimal state support, or compensation if anything goes wrong. It also addresses the traditional Right-wing bugbear of state bureaucracy.

However, UBI will not abolish the Left/Right tension.[39] It will simply redefine it in, arguably, more constructive terms. Paradoxically, UBI offers to make life easier for both employees and employers – as well as for those on the margins of society, including the currently unemployed. It will not of itself overcome the deep-rooted problems of contemporary capitalism – whether the latter are defined by the Left in terms of massive structural inequality, or by the Right as an out-of-control, bureaucratic state. But it may help to construct a more humane framework in which the traditional political struggles, albeit modified in some ways, will continue to exist.

The remarkable fact is that UBI seems to fulfil a certain kind of historical logic, in two ways that have traditionally been regarded as being in tension with each other.

In the first place, UBI seems necessary to deal with the issues of unemployment, underemployment and precarity that have beset the working and middle classes for some decades, and that threaten to get worse with technological development, as time goes on.

In the second place, some form of UBI also seems required from the point of view of the capitalist system itself, since – putting it in the crudest terms – people need money to buy goods and services.

It is the dynamic of capitalism to keep wages down in order for firms to compete with each other, and to maximise profits for shareholders. There is an economic logic (however perverse) for firms, whenever possible, to replace workers with robots – after all, the latter never get sick, take time off for maternity/paternity, or look for pensions. But what may benefit individual firms and shareholders is disastrous for the system as a whole, from an overall capitalist point of view.

A radical adjustment is needed, entailing – at least to an extent – the divorce of work from income. For the two main reasons outlined above, it seems that some form of UBI will be inevitable, at least in advanced industrial societies. However, it will need to happen sooner rather than later. The discontent of the marginalised working and middle classes has shown dangerous tendencies to nationalist extremism.

Authoritarian mindsets and entrenched interests will, no doubt, resist the implementation of UBI as much as they can, for reasons that are often illogical, even from the point of view of their own self-interest. However, the more the idea gains traction in civil society as a whole, the more politicians will find it unavoidable to grapple with the issue. We can only hope that this will happen before things fall apart in a political sense (or rather, before they fall apart more than they already have).

3

FREEDOM, JUSTICE AND SOLIDARITY: THE PHILOSOPHICAL BASIS OF UBI

In this chapter I will try to situate UBI in terms of some values, such as those of freedom, justice and solidarity, which are widely believed to be foundational to our modern society.

The slogan of the French Revolution ('Liberty, Equality, Fraternity') sums up three of the basic values of modern societies. Most people think liberty is desirable; many think equality is a good thing (at least in terms of equality of opportunity), and fraternity (in the sense of social cohesion) is something that is surely needed for a society to function properly. Admittedly, there are some issues with the revolutionary slogan mentioned above. The first issue is that it was born in bloodshed: the guillotine (though itself a more-or-less humane improvement on previous barbaric methods of execution) was a key factor in the birth of our modern societies – something which, as high-minded liberals or libertarians, we often forget.

There are other issues with the slogan as well, which I will look at below. It should also be noted that the three concepts (Liberty, Equality, Fraternity) are interlinked – discussing one often involves us in a discussion of another, with which it is entwined.

FRATERNITY

'Fraternity' sounds a bit odd to our ears. It reminds us of American student societies, with their weird 'hazing' rituals. For those who studied Latin, the word raises some obvious feminist issues: 'fraternity' literally means 'brotherhood'. (In a feminist-influenced culture, the question could be asked whether we should replace 'fraternity' with 'sorority', or 'sisterhood'. That would, no doubt, be equally dismissive of half of the population.) Perhaps 'solidarity' would be a better term for our modern usage than 'fraternity'.

However, if we take 'fraternity' to mean something like community, fellowship, cohesion, or indeed solidarity, it's not immediately clear why such a goal should be the concern of politicians (rather than, for example, of individual citizens, voluntary organisations, religious groups or whatever). But as a means of describing a society without the artificial divisions of the old (pre-revolutionary) regime, it works well enough. With the previous, artificial stratification dissolved, there would (or should) be a greater sense of community and togetherness.

However, fraternity seems to be undermined in a society that keeps the old class distinctions in one form or another, or allows very great economic distinctions to exist between the poor and the rich.

Put like that, fraternity seems fairly close to equality. A society without social stratification (or with less of it) would, ideally, also involve a greater sense of community for everyone. (You could, of course, in theory have a society of equality where everyone hated everyone else – so it may be that fraternity, or something like it, is necessary to complete the ideal picture of our social aspirations.)

David Graeber mentions the concept of 'baseline communism' – the many ways that, even in the most alienated of societies, people naturally help one another.[1] If someone falls in the river and you pull them out, you don't (normally) charge for your time or expertise. Similarly, if someone asks you directions, they don't usually have to pay you for your help.

Of course, the term 'communism' used in this kind of context has none of the negative connotations that the word has taken on in the last 100 years or so. Strictly speaking, 'communism' refers to a kind of society that existed in the dim and distant past, before slavery, feudalism, capitalism or socialism. It also refers to the kind of voluntary communism that exists in communes, religious communities and the like, or indeed to a – projected, envisaged – future society of free association, without money or a state. However, when people use the term 'communism' they usually have in mind the failed state socialist experiments that began with the Russian Revolution, and ended up with the Gulags, and various forms of oppression and tyranny. Consequently, I will normally refer to 'communism' (small c) when talking about the former – the neutral or positive sense of the word – and 'Communism' (large C) when referring to the latter, negative sense.[2]

The Irish tradition of 'meitheal' or mutual aid on the farm is another example of the concept of 'baseline communism'. Another instance may be found in the cultural sphere. In Ireland (and the UK), entry to both public and private museums and galleries is usually free, perhaps because of a consensus that culture should be available to everyone. In similar institutions in continental Europe, you normally have to pay.

If you get into difficulties while hiking in the Alps, you may have to pay (a lot) for your rescue. If that happens to you on the Wicklow mountains, for example, you won't. Mainland Europe is not always more enlightened than the islands on its fringe – it is sometimes too facile to differentiate between 'enlightened' social democracy on the mainland, and benighted neoliberalism on the insular fringe. (That said, you seldom if ever come across people sleeping in the streets in Vienna, while such sights are common in Dublin.)

Fraternity is something that we take for granted as a value, perhaps without always being conscious of this. It has a lot to do with the implicit willingness of human beings to help one another, by virtue of being part of the same human community.[3] A justification of UBI is that it would help to bring about a society of increased fraternity. Since it is itself an exercise in mutual aid, UBI embodies, to an extent, the goal of fraternity and solidarity in the society.

EQUALITY

Equality seems, on the face of it, to be a questionable concept. A society where everyone was equal in every way would surely be monstrous. It would be a community of clones: everyone would look the same, would be equally intelligent (or equally stupid) have the same tastes, and so on. Clearly, that's not what is meant by equality, in any reasonable understanding of the concept at any rate.[4]

But what does equality mean as a goal? Nietzsche taught that we can trace the doctrine of equality to the Christian teaching of the equality of souls in the eyes of God.[5] There is a long, tangled and contentious debate as to whether, or to what extent, Nietzsche – who endorsed the pre-Christian value of domination over the Christian value of compassion – influenced fascism, but we don't need to go into that here. We can, however, agree with Nietzsche that the ideology of equality played a key role in establishing our modern values. Unlike Nietzsche, most of us believe that equality (to some extent at least) is desirable.

Whether that belief is well grounded in a philosophical sense is a different matter, which I won't go into here. It may be that a belief in some basic principles (for example those of equality, freedom, the integrity of the human person and of nature, the avoidance of unnecessary suffering) is essential to the functioning of any desirable society, though this is not the same as proving their validity in some ultimate sense.

Assuming that we don't want a society of clones, the question then arises as to what kind of equality we do want. Clearly, we should aim for equality in terms of voting, and equality before the law, though our present arrangements often fall far short of that.

A petty shoplifter may have less chance of evading justice than a white-collar criminal who has, perhaps, seriously harmed millions of people, since the latter can afford good legal representation and avail of social prejudices that favour the class to which he or she belongs. (Such prejudices may, in the first place, have actually helped to frame the law to which the white-collar criminal is – supposedly – subject.)

There is also the goal of 'equality of opportunity'. In other words, the argument goes, if I have the potential to be a highly efficient plumber, and you have the potential to be an impressive oboe player, we should both have the opportunity to develop our abilities to the greatest extent possible. Such equality of opportunity should, according to this view, be independent of our family background, and the idea implies that we should have equal possibilities for educational and skills' development, independently of where we are coming from in social terms. (This is not as easy to bring about as it may seem.) The argument is that we didn't choose our family, and that we therefore should not be penalised for it.[6]

Equality of opportunity, then, arguably involves an emphasis on 'levelling up' rather than 'levelling down'. It doesn't necessarily mean abolishing elitism. You might even say that, in an ideal society, there should be as many élites as there are people. The key issue is that such elitism would be determined by ability and effort, not by the individual's economic circumstances, or background. Far from abolishing individualism, equality of opportunity would in that case give maximum opportunity for individualism to flourish. (It would, though, be an individualism of the mind or spirit, rather than of material acquisition and possession.)

As well as equality of opportunity, it's fairly uncontentious, in most developed societies, that there should be some kind of equality in terms of a floor. In theory at least, no one should fall through a hole in the ground in terms of food, shelter, healthcare or educational opportunity, simply because they were born into particular circumstances, or for whatever other reasons. We implicitly accept that people have basic needs that should be fulfilled, however much we may fall short of this in practice.[7]

The argument that there should also be a ceiling (as well as a floor) in regard to wealth distribution is much more contentious. One argument is that the existence of a class of super-rich people is bad for democracy, since they can attain political power out of all proportion to their status as citizens. A counter-argument is that it's none of the state's business how much money people make through their own effort. The rich will have no reason to work or invest if they face taxes at, or approaching, a confiscatory level. The argument goes that if I make a lot of money, whether through hard work, inheritance or winning the lottery, I should be able to enjoy the result in financial terms, to ensure that my children go to the best private schools, and so on.

Such enhanced educational opportunities, though, may have the effect of marking a particular group of people off from the rest of the population: people who enjoy private education learn how to talk, dress and behave in particular ways, and engage in customs and rituals that set them off from the rest of the society. (This is particularly the case in Britain, where class distinction has been brought to a fine art, but it is true in more subtle ways in countries such as the US and Ireland as well.)

Furthermore, such individuals are in a position to make social contacts that will be invaluable to them in later life, to the exclusion of those outside their privileged circle. This, arguably, reinforces inequality of opportunity in other ways as well: for example, through maintaining a mindset that helps to keep inequality going.

This is an example of how there is a potential clash between two of the key values we're talking about (equality and freedom), since certain types of freedom may undermine equality (and may possibly undermine other freedoms as well).

Furthermore, the ability to amass great wealth and to indulge in the opportunities for gaining power that it involves means that it is precisely the kind of people you would least want to have wealth and power (i.e. those who place a high priority on such things) who end up acquiring them. They then (through control of the media and in other ways) reinforce the system which gave them such privileges in the first place, and the feedback loop of inequality continues.[8] Eventually, if this goes on for long enough, it may endanger the system of democracy itself.

Finally, perhaps most damningly, the opportunities given to the social élite do not necessarily correspond to their abilities. The children of people of a higher social class may enjoy ample opportunity to develop potentials they don't have (or don't want to develop if they do have them) while those of a lower social class may have the abilities and the will to develop them, but not the opportunity.

Many a potential scientist is lost to a working-class family, through lack of economic opportunity and limited expectations on the part of his/her parents. What is less obvious, though equally true, is that many a potential plumber is lost to a middle-class family, through the misguided idea that mental work is necessarily more desirable, or satisfying, than manual. The irony, of course, is that a plumber may well end up making more money than a molecular biologist – so the argument doesn't hold water even in economic terms. (While I sometimes need to get my bathroom fixed, I seldom need to have my molecules rearranged.)

There is also an argument that the rights to wealth (whether acquired by an individual or his/her ancestors) should be weighed in the balance against other things that may be even more essential, such as protecting the environment, caring for children, and so on. Arguments in favour of a ceiling on wealth would take these into account as well.

Furthermore, there are arguments for forms of 'positive discrimination' that would seek to redress the balance in favour of groups that have been historically disadvantaged (such as African-Americans in the US, or Catholics in Northern Ireland).

If however, as a consequence of positive discrimination, I'm turned down for a job because I have the wrong skin colour or practice the wrong religion,[9] I might be aggrieved as well . There are no easy answers to this question, though UBI could contribute something by compensating people for the unjust treatment to which their ancestors were subjected, of which they may not even be aware.

The all-day surfer, enjoying his or her unearned UBI, may be the descendant of someone who unjustly lost their property centuries ago. Consequently, he/she may be deserving of an unearned income without even knowing it, at least as much as someone who has actually inherited the wealth in question. (Or, indeed, perhaps more than that person, if the latter enjoys wealth created by the exploitative activities of their own ancestors.)

There are, clearly, huge inequalities in the current distribution of wealth, inequalities that may give rise to massive political destabilisation as a result.[10] Some people, even in the high-income bracket, recognise that the present situation is both unjust and socially unsustainable.[11]

But by and large, such arguments are not heard. And in any case, the ultra-rich are highly mobile. If you detect the danger in time, it should be fairly easy to head off to that island in the Pacific (provided, of course, that it's sufficiently high above sea level to escape the ravages of global warming which industrial capitalism has created).

Thus, a new aristocracy is created and we even, arguably, have a new form of feudalism, marked by the favourable treatment of the banking and finance industries vis-à-vis the ordinary person in the street. ('Socialism for the rich, capitalism for everyone else.')

The argument is sometimes made that, even if there were a radical redistribution of wealth from the top down, it wouldn't make much difference to those at the bottom. However, what people get so indignant about is not so much that they have nothing (or less than nothing in the case of student debt or negative-equity mortgage debt) but that the rich have so much more, and out of all proportion to their deserts.[12]

Redistribution of wealth from the top down should, according to this viewpoint, be a priority from a psychological (and indeed from a political) point of view, as much as from an ethical one.

Of course, something that may be desirable from a psychological, political or ethical point of view may not always be possible in practice. It's difficult to tax the very rich, since they can, with the assistance of highly paid lawyers and accountants, adjust their personal circumstances so that their tax liabilities are minimised, or perhaps removed altogether, while at the same time manipulating the media so they look everywhere but in the right place for the cause of the problem of unequal wealth distribution. It is also the case that the rich, by definition, are more mobile than the poor – if you make things too difficult for them, they can just take off for more welcoming climes. This is another example of how wealth perpetuates inequality, in a self-reinforcing process.

Injustice is wrong, but it is also politically destabilising. And it is just as likely, perhaps more likely, that as a result of massive inequality society will lurch to the extreme Right rather than to the extreme Left. (Far-Left alternatives require deep thought and analysis rather than the knee-jerk reactions that characterise the far-Right.)

At this point we should mention the notion of fairness, closely allied to the concept of equality. On the face of it, there does seem to be a 'natural' instinct towards fairness. Children are likely to exclaim 'that's not fair' if one gets an ice cream and the other doesn't. (They are less likely to invoke the abstract notion of equality, unless they come from a family where those kinds of philosophical debates are actively encouraged.)

The parent, though, may point out that the reason why one child has been deprived of a treat while the other has not is that the first child has infringed the rules of the household in some way, and is therefore being sanctioned.

Thus, the parent – if in philosophical mood – might want to point out to the child the difference between equality and justice. Justice requires that someone who has behaved inappropriately should be treated differently from their peers. The most obvious reason is that it teaches them not to repeat the behaviour (whether in the context of the family or that of the society as a whole).

Justice may also require more intervention on behalf of the development of one child rather than on behalf of the other, for example if the former is not getting on as they should in an educational sense. A child coming from a deprived background where the interests of the family revolve around drink, sport and tabloid newspapers has much less of an opportunity for intellectual development and stimulation than the child of a university professor who takes a deep interest in its development – even though both children may be in the same classroom at school. The former child may need more effort from his/her educators to encourage the child's development to their maximum potential, than the latter. In this way, justice is different from equality.

Justice (if it's worth the name) assumes – as an ideal at least – the underlying equality of all members of the family (or the human family) in terms of their deserts. It also recognises, however, that intervention is sometimes needed to redress the balance, where the actuality falls short of the ideal.

In terms of society as a whole, the extent of what that intervention should be is a matter for debate. Reverse discrimination is sometimes proposed as a means to this end: for example to redress historical injustice, and to institute more diversity in terms of role models and decision-making.[13] Against this one could argue that two wrongs – historical and present-day discrimination – don't make a right. In political terms, discrimination of whatever kind can lead to widespread resentment (whether justified or not) that may be destabilising. In any case, there are other ways of redressing historical injustice than instituting reverse discrimination – UBI being one of them.

What should be the scope, or focus, of the redistribution that UBI would involve? We probably should, at the least, look for the fulfilment of basic needs and equality of opportunity at the level of the individual state. UBI seems to be an appropriate mechanism to bring this about, since it introduces a (currently missing) element of fairness in society.

However, whether that element of fairness should be extended to the world as a whole is perhaps a different (though related) issue. Equality of opportunity for everyone in the world might diminish the chances of many of us, while it increased the chances of others. Is that something that we should strive for? (On the other hand it might, conceivably, make everyone richer, as argued by Rutger Bregman.[14])

While we may implicitly accept, to some extent at least, the value of equality, in practice we concede certain limits to this, as the current debate around immigration illustrates. Whether I come from the leafy Dublin suburb of Foxrock on the one hand, or from gritty Darndale on the other, should not matter in terms of the fulfilment of my basic needs or the opportunity to develop my potential. Or at least, many people would argue along those lines. But it might well matter if I came from Timbuctu, or somewhere else outside of Ireland (or, at least, outside the EU).

While some believe that complete freedom of movement should be allowed for the world's population to live wherever they wish, most people do not believe that. The ideal of equality for everyone still has its limits, usually defined by national and/or supranational borders (for example the borders of the EU). Whether those limits *should* exist is a matter of debate, but (supposed) self-interest prevents most of us from taking up that issue. In that sense, the desire for equality has its limitations.

The recent 'Brexit' vote in the UK illustrates this point: many British people clearly do not want equality of opportunity, if it involves a large number of people from other countries availing of it. The issue is seldom framed in moral terms, but there is a moral question involved: should the inhabitants of one country have more rights in that country than others, and if so why? (It should be recalled that we are all the descendants of immigrants, if you go back far enough.[15])

In regard to whether UBI should be instituted at a national or global level, we could note here that, by one estimation, fossil fuels are subsidised globally to the tune of $5.3 trillion per year.[16] Put another way, the fossil fuel industry is keeping us all much poorer than we need to be.[17] And this is altogether apart from the damage that fossil-fuel subsidy causes in terms of climate change.

LIBERTY

This brings us to the third value, that of liberty or freedom. Again, like fairness, freedom seems to have a natural foundation, in terms of its being close to something that human beings naturally want.[18] In terms of what most people accept as being desirable, it's difficult to argue that freedom should be limited, except in cases of necessity.[19] A major argument for UBI is that people who have to work at jobs they don't want to do are not really free (even though they may not realise it).

Freedom is not, of course, an absolute value. It leads to a notorious paradox. If you have a society where everyone is free to make as much money as they can, the society will quickly become skewed, so that the freedom of others is put in danger (not to mention other desirable values such as equality and fraternity).

There are other limits to freedom. For example, the freedom to make money in capitalism is backed up by state coercion,[20] as anyone who breaks a contract or reneges on a debt may discover.

Different societies, and their accompanying philosophical systems, have different conceptions of freedom. In an economic sense, capitalism envisages freedom as the freedom to make (and keep) money.

Socialism places more of an emphasis on the importance of security, and freedom from the wants that economic injustice and insecurity bring about. Both capitalism and socialism may pay at least lip service to (non-economic) social and political freedoms such as freedom of speech, assembly, worship and so on, though they may define these in widely different ways.

In capitalism, economic freedom tends to expand to the extent that it undermines desirable social values such as justice (and can end up undermining freedom itself, since it enables a particular class, that of the wealthy, to become extremely powerful out of all proportion to their size, or merits). In socialism, the emphasis on economic security and equality means that freedom may be curtailed, not just at the economic level but at other levels as well.

Even the capitalist state, though, realises the negative side of economic freedom: if corporations become too large and dominant, they are broken up by the state, which recognises the danger inherent in monopoly. (Monopoly means that capitalism is no longer working as it is supposed to, since a basic feature of capitalism is that there should be competition in the marketplace, in order to keep prices affordable for the consumer.)

Of course, socialism would take economic restrictions much further than that. In its classic form, which envisages a key role for the state, socialism would take over ownership and control of the means of production, thereby severely curtailing (if not eliminating) economic freedom. (This is in the name, ultimately and ostensibly, of the complete democratisation of society.)

Socialism would, of course, not completely abolish private property: you would still own your toothbrush (if you could find one to buy). Money would still exist in socialism, and people would be paid for their work. Eventually, socialism would undergo a transition into communism, where everyone freely does what they can, and gets what they need.

This is of course a gross simplification, if not a caricature, of socialism. (It's hardly possible to provide more in a short space.) And indeed there have been many other forms of socialism suggested (for example socialism from the bottom up rather than the top down, market socialism,[21] eco-socialism,[22] and so on).

We have already noted some of the drawbacks of capitalism, the most notable being that the freedom to acquire and keep wealth may lead to the undermining of other values in the society (including freedom itself). But socialism as it has traditionally been envisaged, and practised, is subject to a number of obvious failings as well, not least in regard to the issue of freedom.

In the first place, you would probably need to restrict the freedom of the citizens, to an extent at least. If you spend a lot of time and money educating the population – as they did in East Germany – and they all want to move to the West to use the skills you have given them in order to be able to buy a Mercedes or a BMW, you have to build a wall to keep them in. You also (probably) need a one-party state, not to mention a flourishing secret police, in order to prevent people from organising to bring back capitalism.

Furthermore, whatever may be said of the market as a means of distribution, it is – under normal circumstances – a fairly efficient mechanism. If people want to buy something they will do so (if they have the money) and that will encourage others to make and distribute the goods in question. Most, if not all, attempts to put in place alternatives to the market, in terms of planning, have been dismal failures. Socialism involves a lessening of some of the freedoms found in capitalism. One of those freedoms is the freedom not to work if one doesn't want to – for example if one has an independent source of income. Another is the freedom to employ other people and engage in market transactions.

While experiments with various forms of socialism (or even communism, for example in communes or religious communities) are possible in capitalist societies, the reverse is seldom, if ever, true. It's not usually possible to experiment with capitalism in socialist societies. Such capitalist experiments that do take place in the interstices of socialist societies usually come about as a result of the failure of socialism, in one way or another. Socialism, at least as ordinarily envisaged, needs some form of state coercion if it is to survive in its earliest stages. (Why such forms should be inclined to 'wither away' of their own accord is anyone's guess.)

Socialism claims to extend democracy to the economy and society as a whole. But democracy itself has its drawbacks (which are not confined to socialist societies by any means). It is not necessarily compatible with freedom, as countries such as Algeria, Egypt and Turkey have found to their cost in recent times. Democracy may lead to forms of oppression that exceed those of non-democratic societies, if it results in the 'wrong' people (for example religious fundamentalists) getting elected.

An essential component of a workable democracy is a freedom-loving electorate. If you don't have that, democracy will just reflect the prevailing, authoritarian mindset. Freedom (of a kind) may be possible under an enlightened absolute ruler (Frederick the Great, for example). It is not possible in a society, however democratic it may appear, where freedom is not widely valued by the public.

The flaws of capitalism are obvious enough. They include – but are not limited to – massive and growing inequality, environmental destruction, resource depletion, unemployment and underemployment, the subtle but all-pervasive manipulation of the media, the dominance of an infantile mass culture that distracts people from political issues that really matter, the corruption of the political system by economic power, the inordinate power of the financial sector (and its apparent immunity even from 'normal' capitalist responsibilities), consumerism, commercialism, the mass propagation of gambling, alcohol and commercialised sex by the media, and the general dominance of an ideology of 'having' over 'being'.

At its extreme, capitalism (for example in the form of 'vulture funds') leads to the total overriding of the human values we normally take for granted.

It should be pointed out though that there is an argument – which has come to the fore in some libertarian and conservative quarters in the United States – that the current problem is not capitalism but a deformation of capitalism in the form of a bureaucratic state corporatism characterised by military adventurism, incursions on personal freedom, and the unjustified support of finance capital by the state.

The flaws of socialism are sometimes harder to see than those of capitalism, when one looks simply at the theory of socialism. (Traditionally, a view has been that socialism works in theory but not in practice, and that with capitalism it is the opposite. However, in recent times it has seemed clear that capitalism doesn't work very well in practice either.)

The flaws of socialism may be difficult to see in theory, but they have been all too evident in practice. They may have something to do with the desire for power in some of its adherents (sometimes an unconscious desire). People who wish to exert power tend to gravitate to positions where they can exercise it most efficiently, and those who desire it most tend to gravitate to the top, assuming that their abilities (political and otherwise) allow them to do so.

In psychological terms, we tend to hate most in others the negative tendencies in ourselves of which we are unconscious: the desire to destroy the power and wealth of others is, itself, often motivated by power hunger and greed, so that we end up with the replacement of one form of domination by another, perhaps worse. Those who end up with power are often the ones whom we should least want to have it: inside a revolutionary there is often a (secret) policeman trying to get out.

Of course, the tendency for the power hungry to thrive is an issue with the state itself (not just the socialist state). In non-socialist societies, however, the state is held in check to some extent by the multi-party system, as well as by the pressures of a free economy. While capitalist societies have sometimes been unfree (as in fascism of various kinds, as well as military dictatorships), free societies have usually been capitalist.

The pressures of a free economy may be a force for good as well as for evil, since they lead to scepticism about the ambitions of government, and the latter are not always benign. It's true that socialism has not always been of the horrendous variety found in Orwell's *Nineteen Eighty-Four*, or in Cambodia under the Khmer Rouge, but the dangers of such developments should not be underestimated. The state is not necessarily a benevolent institution – it can easily turn to tyranny if given too much leeway.

To sum up the preceding discussion in a nutshell: the drawbacks of both capitalism and socialism are probably inherent in the systems themselves, rather than simply in their application. That seems to indicate that one answer is to rise above the traditional, 'either/or', Left/Right duality, and to think in terms of an additional aspiration – that of UBI – that would help to mitigate the deficiencies to which both systems are prone.

In the case of a capitalist society, UBI would give increased security, and the kind of economic freedom that capitalism promises, but fails to deliver to a large section of the population, as well as increasing the vitality of the economy by providing money for people to buy the goods it produces, and making it easier for them to earn more on top of the UBI they receive.

In the case of socialism, UBI would, in a sense, jump directly to the 'higher' stage of society, defined in terms of people's needs being supplied, as distinct from all payment being as a result of work. In this way, UBI would overcome (to some extent at least) the crucial stumbling block of a self-interested bureaucracy controlling people's lives, and help to deliver both freedom and security directly to the population.

Both capitalism and (state) socialism are deeply problematic in terms of recipes for an optimal society. The problem with both systems is that they permit antisocial people to attain great power (in the case of socialism) and great wealth – and consequently great power as well – in the case of capitalism.

The kinds of people who are drawn to wealth and/or power tend not to be the finest kinds of people in terms of personal and social qualities, so they end up with a status out of all accord with their merits. Furthermore, they obtain increased ability to strengthen the structures that gave them power and wealth in the first place, thus encouraging the same type of individual to prosper within the system – and so on in a self-reinforcing process.

If capitalism and the state are so deeply flawed, why not get rid of both of them? This question brings us to anarchism, which, in its best-known form, as set out in the writings of (e.g.) Peter Kropotkin, rejects both capitalism and the state. Anarchism as an ideal has much to commend it, but as usual the devil is in the detail. Without some kind of organised state structure, how do you deal with criminals and invaders?

You could banish the former and arm the populace against the latter, but the experience of the US shows that an armed population raises its own problems.[23]

Also, in a complex modern economy you need some mechanism to guarantee contracts, and indeed to distribute the wealth of the community so that everyone gets a fair share. How that could be done in the absence of some kind of state structure is difficult to see. (There are also Right-wing variants of anarchism – or quasi-anarchism – that would keep capitalism and a minimal form of the state.)

Another problem with anarchism is that there are many people in our modern society who could be described as psychopaths[24] and who would make it extremely difficult for a completely free society to flourish. The widespread occurrence of clinical psychopathology in the population may, to whatever extent, have its roots in our authoritarian structures; but even if it has, it would probably take several generations to get rid of it. In the meantime, the survival of an anarchist form of society would be difficult to imagine, since psychopaths (and sociopaths) tend to take full advantage of liberation from social constraint.

What we end up with, then, is a recognition of the weakness of both untrammelled capitalism and unrestrained statism – not to mention the difficulties of abolishing the state completely – together with the recognition that elements of both capitalism and state power may be desirable for a free, fair and functional society.

Consequently, modern politics usually involves an attempt to negotiate a (more-or-less uneasy) relationship between capitalism and the state, giving rise to various political positions. These include, reading from Left to Right: socialism, social democracy, progressivism, centrism, neoliberalism, libertarianism, neoconservatism, paleoconservatism, and extreme Rightism. All of these are sandwiched between Communism at one end of the spectrum and fascism at the other (though their relative place in the line-up may be open to question).

The deficiencies of the Left-Right system of classification may be seen in the fact that, in the US at least, the views of (Right-wing) libertarians and paleoconservatives on some key issues – e.g. foreign policy, the 'war on drugs' and bank bailouts – may be virtually identical to those of

(Left-wing) progressives. (At the same time, the two camps may be diametrically opposed on other issues: for example gun control, socialised
healthcare, and reproductive rights).

On the face of it, there seem to be two main boxes that one has to
think in when considering one's political position: that of 'socialism' of
one kind or another, or alternatively 'capitalism' of one kind or another.
But if we try to think outside of the box (or boxes) we could try to imagine a society that combined the advantages of the two systems while
minimising the disadvantages. This is, in fact, what happens already with
forms of what may be called social democracy, which combines a free
market with considerable state involvement in (e.g.) education, healthcare, transport and so on.

Alternatively, we could try to think of a deformation of capitalism
(or of socialism as it is traditionally considered) that would minimise its
negative elements and emphasise its positive aspects. For example – and
leaving aside the issues as to how to get there – we could imagine a form
of capitalism that largely comprised workers' cooperatives instead of
traditional firms. (Or – without going the whole way down that road – we
could envisage a society where firms were characterised by profit-sharing
to a considerable extent, and substantial worker involvement in management.) We could imagine changes in company law so that corporations
were required to embrace (e.g.) social and environmental values as well
as the responsibility to make a profit for shareholders, and where large
corporations would be routinely broken up into smaller ones.

Whether, or to what extent, 'exploitation' would continue to exist
in such economies is a moot point, but it would arguably be lessened.
However, a society of cooperatives (or of capitalist firms purged of some
of their negative elements) would, probably, still need a robust state
structure to guarantee their survival, as well as to guarantee shorter working hours (since that is certainly desirable) without loss of workers' rights.

One could also envisage alternative forms of taxation – for example
land tax, resource tax, energy tax, a tax on financial transactions, wealth
tax and so on – which might de-emphasise (or even eliminate) income
taxes. And, in constructing our imaginary market-based utopia, we could
also imagine radical changes in the spheres of banking and finance, so as

to lessen the role of debt and its influence on the constant pressure to maximise economic growth, with the environmentally negative effects of the latter.

Nevertheless, in spite of all this, what would still be lacking is a means of distributing wealth that benefits the whole of the population – which is where UBI comes in.

Similarly, of course, one could envisage a form of socialism, distinct from the 'top-down' variety, where voluntary forms of economic and social organisation existed at the basic level, and from which elected representatives – subject to recall at short notice – made decisions affecting the wider community.

How to balance the central concerns with those of the periphery would be a key issue for such a socialist society. In the absence of a market, planning would be needed, which would seem to go against the possibility of 'bottom-up' decision-making at the lowest level. It's also not clear how work, and income distribution, would be organised in such a society – assuming that it still used money, at least in its initial stages. Again, it would seem essential that such a society would have some form of centralised wealth distribution, at least until it shook off the vestiges of capitalist thinking and practice.

However – whether fortunately or unfortunately – such a form of socialism is a remote eventuality as things stand. The issue of the transformation of capitalism into something more humane (as well as more environmentally sustainable) seems both more immediate and more practical, specifically in regard to facilitating the values with which we started out: liberty, equality and fraternity. UBI would be a key component in bringing this about.

UBI AND A DESIRABLE SOCIETY

At this point, having articulated the three values of liberty, equality and fraternity and noted some of the complicated political issues that they involve, we can go on to show how they may be used to make a case for UBI.

There is a considerable academic literature on the issues of freedom, justice and equality with regard to UBI. The issue of fraternity (or solidarity) is mentioned less often, but it is often (at least) implicit in the discussion. It's not proposed to critique this literature here in any detail. Even to try to summarise it would be a daunting prospect. Instead, I will try to pick out a few of the central issues, in a very general way. The reader can delve into the source material in more detail, by following up the endnotes and bibliography.

Despite the complexity of the literature on the subject, the central question is fairly straightforward: is it right for people to receive money they haven't earned? Erich Fromm writes about resistance to UBI as arising from the abolition of the principle 'He who does not work shall not eat'.[25] Much of the defence of UBI seems to revolve around agreement with Fromm's position of opposition to that principle.

For a variety of reasons outlined in this book, some mechanism to distribute wealth in addition to the wage mechanism seems to be called for, if the values of freedom, equality, and fraternity are to flourish in our society. The most influential argument is that of Philippe Van Parijs. As I largely agree with it, I will briefly outline it here, together with some of the issues it raises. (Objections to the argument, and some general arguments against UBI, will be dealt with later.)

The argument runs as follows. UBI is a very effective means of implementing what Van Parijs calls 'real libertarianism', or 'real freedom for all'. That is, we should try to bring about 'the greatest possible real opportunities to those with least opportunities' subject to a regard for everyone's liberty. Van Parijs argues that there is no essential difference between 'real freedom for all' and social justice. Consequently, freedom and social justice are closely intertwined. For him, justice is about the distribution of freedom rather than the distribution of happiness.

Being free, for Van Parijs, consists in being at liberty to do whatever a person might want to do (not just what he/she actually does want to do, or ought to want to do according to some prescription we might have).[26] Priority should be given to the freedom of those with the least freedom.[27] Real freedom consists in 'security, self-ownership and opportunity'.[28]

Van Parijs puts forward 'real freedom for all' as a conception of social justice. In other words, there is no basic conflict between freedom and equality from this perspective: the issue is how to distribute freedom in the most egalitarian way.

As a consequence, he argues for the highest income for all (an income without conditions) that would be compatible with security and self-ownership.[29] In a situation of job scarcity, a person who has a job enjoys an advantage, for which he/she should compensate by paying a tax to raise the general level of UBI.[30]

Since some people who are unemployed wish to work, a job is an asset whose value should be shared.[31] Certain people possess a higher degree of talent than others, which improves their chances in the job market. It is the benefits of these talents that are to be taxed as a means of funding the UBI.[32]

Van Parijs argues that it is not the surfer who spends all day on the beach who is taking an unreasonable share of the wealth produced by society, but those who enjoy the advantage of an attractive job.[33] The latter situation is massively affected by issues such as ethnicity, gender, citizenship of a particular country, looks, and talents in numeracy and literacy – these are determined to a great extent by our family environ-ment, something over which we had no control. They are 'undeserved gifts' of which the community as a whole deserves a share.[34]

Furthermore, he argues – in terms of discussing what amount might be seen as 'due' to work – there is the difficulty of defining work (does it include housework?) There is also the problem of comparing differ-ent kinds of work in terms of distributing wealth in proportion to work. Should work which is effort intensive, dangerous, useless, be compared to work which is relaxed, safe, useful – and if so, how?[35] Van Parijs rejects the argument that a person's income should be '*strictly proportional*' to their work, in favour of the position that it should be '*positively affected*' by their work (his italics).[36]

For Van Parijs, crucial issues for the future have to do with the intro-duction of an unconditional basic income, redistribution of wealth on a supranational basis, and the fostering of social solidarity, rather than a fixation on the capitalist-socialist struggle.[37] Van Parijs sees UBI as a

radical reform comparable to the abolition of slavery, or universal suffrage. It can even be seen as a means of bringing about the kind of radical
need fulfilment summed up in the well-known phrase 'a capitalist road
to communism'.[38] (Of course, as mentioned already, 'communism' is here
envisaged in a positive sense as a descriptor for a realm of freedom,
rather than the opposite stereotype, attached to various failed attempts
of the past.)

A different, though compelling, argument arises from the work of
Hillel Steiner. According to this position, a tax based on natural resources
is appropriate, since these resources were not originally the property
of anyone, or any group of people. Accordingly, one can justify a redistribution of the part of the global income corresponding to the value
deriving from natural resources. From this 'libertarian' viewpoint that
offers a justification of UBI, we can also defend the taxation of inheritances and genetic endowments. To approximate what is naturally due
to the world's inhabitants, Steiner suggests a single tax at a level based
on land rent.[39]

From an egalitarian perspective, Baker argues that people are entitled
to the satisfaction of their basic needs, to be compensated for their
work, and to an equal share of what is left over. It follows that in an
egalitarian society, everyone, whether working or not, would have a
right to something. Within existing, unequal societies, UBI would promote equality by raising the standard of living of the worst-off.[40]

Bill Jordan wants to take the egalitarian case further, in arguing for the
common good, for a sense of membership in the community[41] – invoking,
it might be observed, the value of fraternity in addition to those of liberty
and equality. UBI, he argues, would particularly assist the 'underclass' in
Britain, including people with low earning power; those with handicaps
and those who care for them; black people; people in depressed and
deprived areas, and women and young people who live alone or are single
parents.[42] His argument highlights the values of 'sharing, co-operation, and
democracy' as well as communitarianism.[43]

UBI, in Jordan's view, would enhance the sphere of autonomy, political participation, and association: 'free association' would replace 'full
employment' as an ideal.[44]

It can be seen from the above that the arguments for UBI in terms of liberty, equality and fraternity are strongly intertwined: from the point of view of adherents of the idea of UBI, the prospect does not involve a clash of values (such as that between freedom and equality for example) that might appear in more traditional political recipes.

Raventós, arguing from a 'republican' perspective, writes that the independence that property gives is of fundamental importance in a political sense as well as in a private sense, since it facilitates freedom, self-government, and independence.[45] A guaranteed material base of life makes it possible for a person to grow in civic virtue and to function as an independent citizen.[46] UBI would offer much greater freedom to workers in general, and women in particular, than they currently have.[47] It would, in his terms, be a 'frontal assault on the feminisation of poverty'.[48]

From a more conservative perspective than most of the foregoing, Charles Murray also endorses UBI. In his view, the main drawback of the welfare state is not its inefficiency or counterproductiveness (though it manifests both of these) but that it weakens the family and community by depriving them of many of their 'functions and responsibilities'. UBI redresses the balance, making it easier for people to find satisfaction in their lives.[49] (Murray's perspective might be said to offer a particular, specifically conservative, take on the concept of fraternity, or solidarity.)

From the opposite end of the political spectrum, Michael Howard points out how UBI helps to deal with the issue of alienation criticised in Marxist theory and is a step towards the 'realm of freedom'.[50] We might observe that a commitment to freedom is one of the things that unite both Left and Right (apart, of course, from the extremes of both), though they may disagree radically on how freedom is defined or on how it should be implemented.

The above arguments illustrate the ways in which the common values of liberty, equality and fraternity may be interpreted – even from diverse political perspectives – and how UBI offers a means towards implementing, and consolidating, some or all of them in the society.

The foregoing discussion focuses around a very specific question. Who really owns money? In a legal sense – as things stand – the answer is fairly simple. You own the money you possess: as long as it's been acquired without breaking the law, you've paid your taxes, you've paid off outstanding debts, and so on.

But in a moral sense the question is much more murky. The Right argue that you have a moral right to the money you have obtained through work, and that anything else is (more or less) robbery by the state. In some extreme versions of this, the objection is to most taxation (or even all of it). However, the Right tends to have different attitudes to unearned income obtained by poor people vis-à-vis that obtained by the rich (for example through share dividends, capital gains, inheritances, intra-family transfers and so on).

But, one might ask, where did the money come from in the first place? Most money is created by commercial banks making loans.[51] So – it might be argued – at one point the money must have belonged to the banks, since they created it. (If I create a poem or a piece of music, most people would agree, I have a moral right to it.) Does that mean that the banks have a moral right to the money they create? It's difficult to see any justification for that – it is by no means clear whence such a right would derive. Most people, whether on the Left or on the Right (or in between), would have little time for the argument that banks should own all our money simply because they created it out of nothing in the first place.

The argument, then, might be made that money belongs (as of right) not to those who create the money itself (whether digital or in the form of notes and coins), but to those who earn it after it's been created. There is some intuitive appeal in that argument. After all, if I spend most of my day toiling in a coal mine, a factory or an office, it seems that I have more of a 'natural' right to the money I earn than someone who could devote their time to such activities, but chooses instead to spend all day watching TV or surfing on the beach instead. Why should my money go to support that person's lifestyle?

However, the issue becomes more complex the more one examines it. For example, the coal in the coal mine originally belonged to no one (or to everyone, depending on how you look at it). The machinery in the factory is the result of a process of industrial invention going back, perhaps, hundreds of years. The computers in the office where I work may have resulted from decades of state (that is, public) investment in computer development. Much of our technological and scientific knowledge is part of a common cultural inheritance.

Furthermore, the coal mine where someone is working may be the source of carbon gases which are bad for the health of the population and the wellbeing of the planet, with negative economic effects that are not normally factored in when assessing the costs involved.

There is also the situation where my wages may be influenced positively by a strong trade union acting on my behalf – or indeed negatively by a weak trade union. I may be paid a high minimum wage put in place by a worker-friendly government, or a low wage that is the result of the opposite.

So the objects that I produce, or the services I provide, already incorporate much more than my labour. Furthermore, the profits I produce, and the wages I earn, are dependent on the free input of those who bring up children, whether on a full-time or a part-time basis. No business of any size would be able to make money without a toilet-trained workforce – people who can converse with each other and tie their own shoelaces.

In our capitalist system it's not just the worker who is rewarded, but those who profit by the worker's labour as well, most notably the shareholders of the firm. Whether, or to what extent, unearned income is justified has been vigorously debated for many years. It suffices to say that most people in our society believe that money received through (e.g.) share dividends, deposit interest, inheritances from one generation to another, or large intra-family gifts, is a valid form of income.

If it's justifiable for rich people to live off the labour of those who create goods and services in this way, it seems – on the face of it – a little odd to condemn the surfer (or video game player) who wants to do the same. It's very difficult, if not impossible, to establish how much money is 'rightly' due to the individual recipient of a wage or salary.[52] Consequently, the argument that any particular individual is 'undeserving' of an unconditional basic income is difficult to sustain.

In this chapter I have discussed three of the basic values of modern society – liberty, equality and fraternity – and looked at how these values have been used, in varying ways – explicitly or implicitly – to construct more-or-less persuasive arguments for UBI.

There are strong arguments, it seems, for UBI in terms of sharing out the wealth of society, both that which is produced by human labour and that which derives from nature – though it may be difficult or impossible to disentangle the two. The argument that work, and work alone, is deserving of reward is much more tenuous than it appears to be on the surface. There are, however, a number of objections to UBI from a variety of perspectives. These will be outlined and addressed in the following chapters.

4

POLITICAL ISSUES: THE IMPLICATIONS OF UBI FOR FEMINISM AND THE ENVIRONMENT

This chapter will focus on a number of issues arising from two major thought systems: feminism and ecology. There are some important links between the two. Most obvious is the rejection of 'domination' by both. There is also the emphasis on horizontal, networked communication rather than top-down control. For example, in her book *The Death of Nature*,[1] Carolyn Merchant examined the historical connections between the ideology of domination as applied to nature on the one hand, and to women on the other.

It would be wrong to suggest that a person who supports feminism must necessarily have an ecological outlook (or indeed viceversa). While there is a flourishing school of thought that might be described as 'eco-feminism', there is also a long-standing suspicion within the feminist movement of anything that might be seen as 'essentialism'.

In this context, essentialism involves the view that women and nature are in some way similar. (This is the counterpart of the view that men are in some way equivalent to culture.)

Conversely, not all people with an ecological outlook necessarily have a feminist perspective (though many do). Feminist and ecological viewpoints often overlap, but they sometimes do not. For every environmentalist who celebrates the 'nurturing' role of women, there may be a feminist who would prefer such women to be out there competing with men in the workplace.

I am taking it as a given that, as a general principle, feminist and ecological politics are to be endorsed. The questions asked in this chapter will focus on the implications of UBI for both.

However, it would be too easy to take it for granted that UBI is good for both feminist goals and for the wellbeing of nature. From a feminist viewpoint, what happens if UBI simply makes it easier for women to stay in the home and mind the children?

On the one hand – assuming that there are some women who already want to stay at home, but can't do so due to economic pressures – UBI would increase their freedom to do something they want to do. At the same time, though, it might lessen their desire to do something that many feminists think they ought to want to do – go to work in the formal workplace. Doing what one wants to do is one thing. Doing what one ought to want to do according to some viewpoint is something else. Sometimes the two kinds of activity coincide, and sometimes they don't.[2] There is an alternative feminist perspective that emphasises freedom of personal choice (despite the ongoing influence of social gender norms).

Of course, we must admit the opposite argument as well: UBI might make things easier for some women who currently want to join the formal workforce, but can't. It might also facilitate some men who currently want to be full-time homemakers, but aren't able to do so – thus making it easier for their female partners to join the workforce, should they wish to. Insofar as contemporary feminism emphasises the importance of choice, it would appear that the logical conclusion of such an emphasis would be in favour of UBI.

In regard to ecological issues, UBI gives rise to some similar concerns. Would UBI facilitate a 'Green' society, or would it work against it? The answer is that it might do both. UBI may allow people to escape from the 'jobs' treadmill and thus help to make formal employment less important in the society. As a consequence, it could lessen the impetus towards the overriding goal of economic 'growth' with (as Greens see it) its environmentally damaging results. In particular, UBI could reduce the pressure towards wasteful and environmentally undesirable forms of economic activity, which are currently justified on the basis that they 'create jobs'.

On the other hand, UBI could conceivably contribute to economic growth. This is because it would free people for employment who are currently unable to work, due to the constraints of the social welfare system.

We need to be honest about this: increasing human freedom may not necessarily bring about the results that some may want in terms of key issues such as women's participation, or a more ecological society. On its own, UBI may not necessarily increase women's participation in society outside the home. On its own, it may not necessarily work against the growth fetishism that, according to many, currently threatens the future of the planet.[3]

FEMINISM AND BASIC INCOME

We could briefly state the feminist arguments in favour of UBI as follows. UBI offers women a financial base that does not depend on their partaking in the wages of men. As a result, it allows them greater scope to live independently of men, at whatever stage of their lives.[4] Since UBI is paid on an individual basis, it potentially reduces women's dependency on men, making it easier for them (for example) to get out of abusive relationships. It does not exclude caring and reproduction. Even if one partner is unemployed, with UBI it is worth the while of the other to work.

UBI also reduces the current intrusion of the welfare state into the personal affairs and lifestyles of women.[5] It means that women are not forced into working outside the home if they don't want to, or indeed forced into working in the formal economy if they don't want to do that.[6]

The current benefit system normally assumes that a person has a life-long work history, so women who take time off from paid work to raise children lose out. UBI would not suffer from that drawback.[7] UBI could reduce the negative financial results of divorce for women.[8] It means that work that is currently assigned comparatively little value – i.e. homemaking and raising children – is given the recognition it deserves.

However, there are also some arguments pointing to the potential downside of UBI, from a feminist perspective. Ann Withorn argues that UBI begs the central question of whether it is possible to transform the patriarchal capitalist state. While UBI might do away with a massive bureaucracy and discrimination based on gender, there are also questions to be asked as to what government programmes will be replaced or altered. (Some programmes might be relegated to the realm of the market if everyone had a basic income.)

The 'individualistic bias' of UBI proposals might also interfere with women's ability to maintain relationships, on which their sense of security is often based. Withorn's overall argument is that UBI is not of itself enough: there also need to be wider discussions of how society should provide for itself.[9]

Ann S. Orloff raises more stringent objections. She concedes that UBI may make women's financial situation easier and increase their freedom of choice. However, she argues that the main problem is women's almost exclusive responsibility for domestic work. In her view, a more effective way of dealing with the main problem would be a programme of challenging the way work (of all kinds) is structured. UBI, according to this argument, might simply end up offering subsistence-level payment for women to continue in traditional caregiving roles. Rather than challenging the difficulties encountered by those who want to combine wage work with caregiving, UBI offers those who choose to devote their time to nurturing a way out of committing themselves on a full-time basis to paid labour.[10]

Orloff argues that jobs offer many more benefits than unpaid labour in the home (even if the person is in receipt of a basic income): they offer social networking, and an opportunity for developing a sense of self-worth and peer esteem.[11]

The question arises, of course, whether self-esteem and the demonstration of competence are adequate in themselves. The work should also, surely, be stimulating, challenging, fulfilling and worthwhile. Few workplaces offer that, to either male or female employees. Many jobs in our contemporary society could be described as 'soul destroying', unrewarding and lacking in intellectual stimulation. (The exception, perhaps, is the area of the creative industries – but even in that case, there is often a tension between how a worker would ideally like to tackle a project on the one hand, and the demands of the client and the market on the other.)

Orloff also notes the political resistance against 'handouts' in a US context. However, she also supports a 'generous' cash grant for the poor who are not in work (something of a contradiction, perhaps?) This, together with programmes that make it easier to combine work and caregiving, would, in her view, be better than cash grants of the UBI kind. Programmes are needed to make it possible for both men and women to combine work (in the formal economy) and nurturing. This would raise the relative status of women vis-à-vis men, and help to undermine the current domestic division of labour.[12]

Citing a small number of studies,[13] Ingrid Robeyns surmises that UBI would result in a decrease in the labour supply of women, though probably not an overwhelming one.[14] Robeyns argues that if a group of women withdraws from the labour market, this will result in an expectation that women have looser ties to it. The result would be increased discrimination on the basis of gender.[15]

What appears to be free choice is, in a domestic context, influenced by 'gender related structures and constraints' which would still operate in the context of UBI.[16] While she favours UBI, Robeyns believes it needs to be supplemented by adequate provision for children, childcare facilities, and economic protection of women in the event of marital breakup.[17]

Tony Fitzpatrick points to a number of objections to UBI, from a feminist perspective. While UBI offers freedom from the labour market, this is not necessarily the kind of freedom that would benefit women. They may, in fact, already be free from the market, and need rather to be free from constraining family structures. Having to pay tax on wages above the UBI might encourage low-paid workers (most of them women) to withdraw from the job market altogether. This could have a substantial class and racial dimension as well, with women from ethnic minorities more likely to decide not to participate in the labour market.[18]

Fitzpatrick concludes that, while UBI could lead to the sharing out of caring responsibilities between the sexes, it might on the other hand strengthen the gender division of labour. While it could make it easier for women to gain access to the public sphere and for men to access the private sphere, it could also do the opposite.[19]

However, an opposing argument would be that many women who work for a minimum wage may need to work at several jobs just to survive. On top of that, they may have childcare responsibilities. There is consequently a strong argument for encouraging low-paid workers to withdraw from the job market. UBI could free up time for such women to improve their skills and education, and assist their children with their education as well, thus helping to break the cycle of poverty.

It is probable that low-paid service industry jobs will soon disappear in any case, so UBI will be essential for this demographic. It is surely important to broaden the focus from that of middle-class women to those at the lower end of the economic scale.

Carole Pateman, questioning traditional gender roles within the household, sums up the position of some feminists, who, in her view, fear that a basic income 'without having to engage in paid employment' would provide a stronger incentive for women to undertake unpaid household work, and also a greater incentive for men to free-ride. (This is in the context of women's current place in the labour market and linking concepts about gender roles.)[20] Pateman herself does not reject UBI, but believes that the terms of debate need to be widened to encompass feminist politics.[21]

In response to such discussions (which for some reason tend to focus on examples based on traditional male-female, child-rearing couples to the exclusion of non-traditional living arrangements) it should be pointed out that UBI is not a panacea. It does not claim to solve every problem that women face. It will not, of itself, bring about the overthrow of capitalism or patriarchy. It does not present itself as an alternative to other social policies – such as changing the traditional gender-based division of labour and the associated mindset – but as a potential complement to them.

With UBI, there could well be a necessity for increased vigilance in defending, in addition, welfare measures that already work. From a feminist point of view, the need to agitate for maximum participation of women in the world of formal employment (for those who want it) would remain unchanged. This would be made easier by a reduction in the working day/week/year, and by more flexible working arrangements for both men and women. That would help to lessen gender-based constraints, and consequently would be of potential benefit to everyone.

It would be wrong, however, to argue that UBI is devoid of potential downsides, from a feminist point of view. Freedom is a two-edged sword: it gives a person the liberty to act in ways that diverge from the consensus, whatever the consensus may be (provided, of course, that one does not harm others in the process).

Some of the objections to UBI from a feminist perspective, however, seem contradictory. With its individualistic bias, UBI is seen on the one hand as potentially undermining women's security in the family structures they already have. On the other hand, it is viewed as potentially weakening women's status in the sphere of employment, by making it easier for them to retreat to the home, with the consequent loss of their foothold in the world of paid employment.

However, the question should be asked as to how many women in well-paid, or fulfilling, jobs would actually want to sacrifice their careers for family. It seems intuitively obvious that most would want both, as indeed men do.

There is no easy consensus on the issue of the desirability of 'home' versus that of 'work'. The point, surely, is that the tension between 'traditional' and 'progressive' views regarding the role of women would not end with UBI, just as it would not end for society as a whole. It would certainly continue, though in a different context (a context wherein freedom had been enhanced).

Some objections seem to be a version of the 'work is good' argument that is sometimes applied to work from a more general point of view: such a perspective regards UBI with suspicion, as potentially undermining the work ethic.

Of course, we cannot deny that, for many people, work in the sphere of formal employment offers a sense of community and self-worth that they might not otherwise have.

We could ask the deeper question, though, as to why such opportunities are not available elsewhere than in the world of formal employment – and whether the dominance of paid work in our lives helps to maintain such an undesirable situation. (If jobs were such a wonderful thing, people would surely want to do them without being paid!)

In any case, since UBI offers freedom to everyone (of whatever gender) it potentially makes things easier than before for people who want the social and personal advantages that, they believe, paid work involves. This is for the simple reason that it makes it easier for them to get a job. Whether that job would be part-time or full-time is another matter, but in any case we probably need to start looking at a radical reduction of the full-time workday and/or workweek.

That is not to say that, in a society with UBI, people who enjoy working eighteen hours a day on – for example – software development wouldn't be able to do it. The point is that they wouldn't have to spend the bulk of their time working in the formal economy, if they didn't want to.

Of course, we could point to work in the voluntary sector and to various forms of creative and educational activity as (currently) offering similar opportunities for people to develop, feel a sense of self-worth, and shine. UBI could greatly increase the role of the voluntary and cooperative sectors, since those who felt the need to participate in the work world would find it easier to do so.

But a more radical point is that UBI offers the opportunity to restructure society in order to make activities of all kinds more fulfilling and engaging, not just those that involve constraint and necessity. (As an old saying goes: if work were a good thing, the rich would have found a way to keep it all for themselves.)

In some ways, the arguments around UBI seem to recall those around women's suffrage a century ago. It's worth pointing out here that not all arguments against 'votes for women' came from conservatives or reactionaries. For example the anarchist Emma Goldman – a woman of impeccable Leftist and feminist credentials – argued against the suffragist position on the grounds that it was irrelevant, that it distracted from more vital issues, and that it ran the risk of strengthening the conservative vote.[22] Such arguments have strange echoes of some of the current arguments against UBI.

Indeed, we may agree that Goldman was not necessarily wrong in all of her arguments. On balance, though, in the light of history, most people believe that the achievement of female suffrage was a positive development (though – like everything else – it may have had its downsides in particular instances). Future historians will, perhaps, say the same about UBI.

An argument that sometimes seems to underlie feminist objections to UBI might be stated as follows: increased economic freedom (through UBI) could make women less free than they already are. If you make it too easy for women to stay at home, many will do so, and the position of women as a whole will be undermined. This kind of argument is not very different from the argument that men, too, need to have to work in the formal economy, as otherwise they might spend their time playing video games, watching TV or surfing (whether on the Internet or the beach).

The answer is twofold: it's your business what you do with your freedom, and if I think you should be doing something else, it's up to me to help change public attitudes in ways that make that more likely to happen.

As in other areas of life, freedom of choice doesn't – by definition – mean you necessarily have to take one path or another. It means you have the freedom to choose the path you want to take.[23]

BASIC INCOME AND ECOLOGICAL POLITICS

The discussion around UBI in the context of Green (or ecological) politics focuses on what is called 'post-productivism'. This involves the idea (a) that ecological concerns should be crucial to social policy; and (b) that we need to move away from the notion of paid work as a central element of society.[24]

Claus Offe notes the disruptive effect of economic growth on the natural environment. The fact that social dependency needs growth to support it means that employees will tend to favour growth at the expense of the environment. For Offe, UBI makes it politically easier to make a critique of industrialism from an ecocentric perspective. He argues that UBI would offer workers increased flexibility and an opportunity to obtain additional qualifications. This in his view – combined with a reduction in working time – would potentially assist in (re)establishing full employment.[25] (Though whether full employment is any longer possible, even if it were desirable, is a moot point.)

Tony Fitzpatrick argues that UBI offers a means of slowing down the process of economic growth. UBI undercuts the ethic of employment, and consequently challenges the 'productivist' mindset that gives it credence. The most desirable kind of UBI would slow down growth to the extent that environmental and economic priorities would be in balance.[26] (One could observe here that the whole issue of economic growth is one that increasingly needs to be unpacked: growth of what? For whom?)

Fitzpatrick, however, cites a number of problems. Echoing the feminist debate, he states that UBI might simply reinforce existing values and habits.[27] He points out (with reference to Andrew Dobson) that there are tensions between the 'anti-materialism' of ecological thought and the fact that UBI needs to be financed by material wealth.[28] He notes that there is no guarantee that free-time activities financed by UBI would be environmentally helpful.[29]

However, a riposte is that people do not necessarily spend their money on flashy material goods such as cars or expensive watches – young people of the 'millennial' generation may display status by spending money on experiences, music, travel, fair-trade foods, craft beers, artisan coffee, vintage bicycles, and vinyl collections.[30]

Fitzpatrick, however, endorses UBI as part of a 'policy package' including land and energy taxes, the shortening of working time, and the growth of informal exchanges.[31] He also notes Jan Otto Andersson's suggestion of the possibility of combining a small UBI for all with a Citizen's Wage paid to people who are engaged in activities judged to be socially and environmentally desirable.[32] (The drawback should be pointed out of the inevitable bureaucracy that the latter would involve – and who, in such cases, makes the 'judgement' as to what activities are desirable?)

Van Parijs rejects the idea that UBI is based on Green ideas. In his view, moving away from an emphasis on economic growth might have negative effects on employment, but that situation could be addressed with (for example) employment subsidies and/or the reduction of working time, rather than UBI. Being 'Green' and being in favour of UBI have, in his view, a common cause: that one supports free time. In line with his philosophical support for UBI outlined earlier, Van Parijs argues that we should defend UBI, not on ecological grounds, but as a means of escaping the rat race.[33]

However, while Van Parijs makes an overall very convincing case for UBI, it's not entirely clear why support for eco-politics should depend on a support for free time. Some people who support Green politics might equally be concerned about the loss of biodiversity, or about leaving a livable planet for their children and further descendants. Perhaps the reason that so many ecologically minded people support UBI is that the preference for individual freedom and for the wellbeing of the planet are both indications of a particular mindset which places needs before wants, values before material desires.

André Gorz, who resisted the idea of UBI for much of his career, finally came down in support of it (with the proviso that it should be sufficient to live on rather than a means of forcing people to take up unpleasant jobs – which, in his view, would happen if it were paid at less than subsistence level[34]).

In Gorz's opinion, the ultimate goal of a UBI is a society in which work is no longer experienced as a necessity. In the future he envisages, everyone from childhood onwards will be involved in, and attracted to, a range of activities encompassing the areas of art, sport, technology, science, politics, philosophy, and 'ecosophy'.[35] (The last-mentioned term, originating in the writings of Félix Guattari, means an overall mindset with ethical dimensions, which would link together the whole range of ecologies, from science and the environment to politics and society.[36])

In such a society, in Gorz's view, the exchange of knowledge would replace the exchange of commodities. The expansion of free time would enable people to develop creative capacities, which would in turn enhance their productivity to a massive extent. This sphere of freedom offers the ability to create unlimited wealth, while a minimum of time and energy is spent on it. In Gorz's view, the full development of the forces of production makes full human employment unnecessary. Production could then become a secondary activity: the overriding goal would be to maximise free time.[37] The distinction between 'freedom' and 'necessity' would be blurred to vanishing point: freedom would permeate the whole society.

Gorz's view, surely to be endorsed, is an optimistic one where UBI is seen as facilitating a 'utopian' society. In such a society, the goal of free time and individual creative development is combined with the development of an ecological perspective on a widespread basis. This is the opposite of the pessimistic viewpoint: that UBI could lead to a society of lazy parasites, feeding from an out-of-control industrial-capitalist system that is devoted to the production and dissemination of environmentally dangerous, and socially damaging, products.

The important issue, as in the case of feminist views of UBI, seems to be the development of a desirable (ecological) mindset. Such a mindset would help to facilitate the human and ecological potential opened up by the possibility of freedom from economic constraints.

UBI may be a necessary condition for a good society, but no one claims that it will be enough on its own. In order for society to make the best use of the positive effects of UBI, it will need to be accompanied by a change of consciousness. Such a change would not only foreground the value of freedom, but also highlight the positive opportunities that accompany it. These include not only increased opportunities for the participation of women in the formal workforce, but at the same time an enhanced role for men in homemaking and child rearing.

Furthermore, in the interest of the wellbeing of the planet, UBI will need (urgently) to be accompanied by a critique of the ideology of economic growth, and of the fetishism not just of commodities, but of work itself. While UBI offers a considerable degree of increased freedom, the offer is not enough if there is no desire to take it up in ways that benefit the individual, society as a whole and the planet. Fostering that desire is a political project. It will accompany the struggle for UBI, and will no doubt continue after it has been won.[38]

5

ANSWERING SOME OBJECTIONS

In the previous chapter, we looked at some of the problems that various commentators have mentioned about UBI. In particular, we considered whether it might reinforce women's traditional role in the home, rather than challenging it, concluding that there is some force in that objection. The answer – for those who believe that women should play a stronger role in the formal workplace – is to agitate for change in terms of gender roles in society, and a more equal division of labour. This would be better than resisting UBI, with its possibilities for enhanced freedom for women.

We also looked at the question as to whether UBI might encourage an alternative mindset to that of economic growth as the dominant goal in our economic system of industrial capitalism. Again, we concluded that, while it might do this, it might also have the opposite effect of encouraging growth by making it easier for people to get employment. (In other words, with UBI, people who don't want to work wouldn't have to. On the other hand, people who are currently not permitted to work would be allowed to work. So there might be an element of balance involved.)[1]

The discussion around economic growth itself is a separate issue, and will no doubt continue after UBI is established. People will continue to argue about whether, or to what extent, we should redefine growth. They will discuss different ways in which to count it. They will argue over whether we need to pay attention to it at all. They will debate whether we should maximise it, ease off on it or minimise it. (Or whether, indeed, we should consciously aim for a society of 'degrowth' in the interest of the environment.[2])

The deeper question in that context is whether a society that downplays the importance of growth would be compatible with capitalism, at least as we know it. Is the pursuit of growth an essential element of capitalism, or only of the form of capitalism that we have, that depends crucially on debt for its functioning? If growth is essential to capitalism and we want to get rid of growth, with what would we replace our current economic system – and would it be a case of 'out of the frying pan, into the fire'?

To explore the issue of growth vis-à-vis capitalism in any depth would be beyond the scope of this study, but it does bring up the important question as to whether ecological politics is compatible with capitalism, in the long term at least. (If, indeed, there is a long term to speak of, given the prospect of climate catastrophe.)

WORK AND INCOME

A further argument that is sometimes raised against UBI is that it has the negative effect of reducing the importance of paid work in the economy. Paid work is seen by some as being of value (apart from its role in production) in that it gives workers a sense of purpose, reinforces their feelings of identity and self-worth, offers them a network of colleagues and contacts, and provides them with an opportunity to shine in the workplace.

The answer to this objection is firstly to admit that UBI would, in one sense, decrease the role of paid work. (That is, for those who don't want to work, or don't like what they are doing.) In another sense, however, it would increase it (that is, for those who do want to work and currently can't). It would do so by making it easier for them to get a foot in the door of work, by giving them increased opportunities for further education and training, and by removing current 'poverty traps' (at least in Western cultures). To what extent the increase in work would balance out the decrease remains to be seen.

But let's concede, for the sake of argument, that UBI would, indeed, on balance, reduce the importance of paid work in each individual's experience. Is that a bad thing? We could ask ourselves why we place such importance on paid work, when the most privileged sections of society, both in ancient and more recent times, have always tried to avoid such activities.

We could question why we accept the situation where an individual's sense of identity and purpose, their social life and personal development, are linked so closely to employment in the formal economy, at the expense of activities outside the factory or office. Perhaps we need to re-emphasise those latter kinds of pursuits. These could include activities to do with family and social life, creativity, personal and cultural development, voluntary work, political activism, or what is currently known as 'leisure'.

Is it really an ideal social goal that people should have to spend 40 hours a week (excluding commuting time), 50 (or whatever number) weeks a year, for 40 years of their lives, doing something they have to be paid to do? And this is at the expense of their family lives, personal development, and freedom to do what they wish with their lives.

Certainly, for much of recorded history the rich tended to avoid involvement in the formal work force, regarding money-making (as distinct from money-receiving) as being beneath them. The extent of work fetishism in our society may be seen from the fact that, today, even many rich people have succumbed to the mirage as well – it is not enough to have money, you must also be seen to be making it.

SOME THEOLOGICAL ISSUES

One of the most important sources of the 'work ethic' (the valuation of work for the sake of it) is, of course, the Bible. We should start by pointing out that scriptural texts often function as a kind of Rorschach test: religious people tend to project their socio-economic-political preferences unto the writings in question, rather than simply deriving them from the biblical sources (as they often believe they do).

To begin with, there is the well-known and very influential admonition of St Paul that if anyone refused to work, that person should not eat.[3] This sentiment has, historically, permeated both capitalist and socialist thought and practice.[4] Western culture is heavily influenced by the biblical story of the fall of man, particularly the condemnation of Adam to a sorrowful and laborious relationship with the earth. (This is the counterpart of Eve's subjection to (sorrowful) reproduction.)[5]

Just why the consequence of 'original sin' should become something to celebrate is never entirely clear – revealingly, the rich have always tried to distance themselves from those consequences while urging them for the poor, at least as regards engagement in physical toil.

Just as we do our best (rightly) to alleviate childbrith problems for women, we should surely do our best to alleviate toil-related problems for men (or rather for both sexes).

As a counter-argument to this gloomy and negative ideology of work, which is supposedly rooted in biblical teaching, we could cite various counter-examples from scripture. There is, for instance, Jesus' reference to the lilies of the field that neither toil nor spin, his commendation of the 'idleness' of his follower Mary vis-à-vis her busy sister Martha, and his dismissal (in a parable) of the notion that working time and income should necessarily be connected.[6]

The parable of the talents (from where we get the word 'talent') urges the importance of developing our gifts rather than letting them atrophy,[7] which arguably justifies giving people the freedom to do precisely that, thanks to UBI. The Old Testament certainly condemns idleness, but it also casts a scathing glance at 'busyness'.[8] Far from being a blueprint for capitalism, the New Testament in one place endorses a kind of voluntary communism.[9]

As with so many other things, the attitude of the Bible to work seems to be a matter of interpretation, and perhaps also of the unconscious biases that people bring to biblical interpretation in the first place. It is an oversimplification that 'fundamentalists' interpret scripture literally, while more sophisticated religious people interpret it metaphorically.

Adherents of both schools interpret scripture both literally and metaphorically, depending on the text in question, and the appropriate interpretation on which their advisors have decided. There is no 'transparent', objective interpretation of scripture (if indeed there is such a thing as non-metaphorical language at all, which is open to debate).

Objective interpretation of scriptural texts may be difficult (if such a thing is even possible). It is obviously much easier to interpret scriptural authority selectively, so that it is in accordance with one's class background, interests or preconceived views (as in the film *Twelve Years a Slave*, where a slave owner uses a Bible verse, Luke 12: 47, to justify the beating of slaves).

Without going too deeply into theology, it seems clear that the Bible (or at least one interpretation thereof, which emphasises the work ethic) has had a crucial influence on our contemporary valuation of work. However, a completely different interpretation is possible, as briefly suggested above, which downplays the role of the work ethic and highlights the importance of freedom and self-development.

The work ethic then (in the sense of the valuation of work for its own sake, regardless of the good it does to the worker or the planet) may be seen to have a questionable basis even in Jerusalem, let alone in Athens.[10]

As one might expect, however, there is no explicit endorsement of UBI in the Bible[11] (or indeed of capitalism or socialism or any other 'ism'). Even slavery, an integral part of the socioeconomic system of the time, is not specifically condemned in the New Testament – though presumably the 'golden rule' or ethic of reciprocity (behave towards others as you'd like them to behave to you)[12] implicitly condemns slavery: since few, if any, people would want to be slaves.[13]

However, there is certainly an implicit drive towards justice, economic equality and indeed freedom, particularly in the Gospels: giving is commended, and we are to treat others as we would want to be treated. Presumably, if everyone practised the socioeconomic virtues outlined in the New Testament, we would have a much more equal society than exists at present (since charity and voluntary redistribution would be universally practised). Such a society would also be a society of enhanced freedom, since poverty is a serious constraint on freedom.

The key question does arise as to whether, or to what extent, biblical-influenced redistribution should be compulsory or voluntary: whether, for example, it should be the province of the state or of private charity. This is a matter of ongoing political debate between progressives and conservatives respectively, particularly in the US.

Without going into the details, it could be pointed out that (with the exception of the anarchists among us) we already endorse the role of the state: at least at a minimal level of defence, security, and the guarantee of contracts. Since money itself would have no validity without the state to endorse it, we could, arguably, defend the role of the state in being involved in its distribution as well.

But even from a point of view (the argument for the 'minimal state') that is antagonistic towards the role of the state, or wishes to reduce it to a minimum, it is also possible to endorse UBI. This is because UBI actually offers to reduce the role of the state from its present level. It would do this by cutting down radically on state bureaucracy, constraint, and intrusion into people's lives.

In this sense, the argument for UBI goes beyond the usual Left/Right divisions, on a platform of freedom that is common to both perspectives, however much they may normally differ in regard to the definition or implementation of freedom.

However, there is an important distinction to be drawn when discussing support for UBI – between Right-wingers on the one hand and Left-wingers on the other. On the one hand, we have Right-wingers (like Friedman) who endorse UBI[14] as a stepping stone to the reduction, or elimination, of state support. On the other, we have Left-libertarians who see UBI as a means towards a society of increased social justice as well as freedom (often drawing little distinction between the two goals). The issue of the level of UBI is key to such discussions – as is the question of what, if any, other forms of state support should be retained.

THE ARGUMENT AROUND LAZINESS

At this point we need to take up a related objection: that people wouldn't work if they had their basic needs supplied. Consequently, the argument goes, the economy would collapse and there would be no money to pay the UBI. How can we deal with that objection? For a start, it is true that UBI permits people who don't wish to work not to do so. On the other hand, it allows people to work who currently can't, as a result of welfare restrictions. (Arguably, to some extent one tendency would offset the other – though we don't really know how the balance would work out in practice.)

Put another way, the objection is that UBI would – in a sense – actually solve our current unemployment problems (since with UBI there would, supposedly, be too many jobs for too few people, or at least for the numbers of people who would want to do them). UBI might, of course, introduce the opposite problem: too many jobs for too few people. Against that, you could make the point that wages would rise as a result, so that people who formerly resisted the temptation to work would finally give in to it.[15] (We should also recall, of course, the increased role of technology in the economy and the reduced demand for human labour as a result, which would counter this argument to some extent.)

The above objection is also related to the level of UBI. Few people who have become used to a comfortable lifestyle would, one imagines, be content to subsist on a basic income that was around the equivalent of the average social welfare payment. (Raventós points out that the argument that UBI encourages parasitism is based on the – erroneous – premise that the human psyche has no need of stimulation.[16])

On the other hand, if the amount were to rise enough, more people might be tempted to drop out of the formal economy, or at least out of full-time employment.

In honesty, we need to admit that there are many imponderables in regard to UBI. These will need to be addressed by studies of situations where something like UBI has already been introduced, and by the implementation of pilot schemes in specific instances. There could also be the gradual transformation of existing welfare systems to incorporate the goal of universality – though without giving too much of a jolt to our current systems.

POLITICAL RESISTANCE

We may anticipate, though, that governments will resist UBI for a number of reasons. These will include a visceral, though perhaps unconscious, fear of increased freedom for the population. Governments tend to attract people who are interested in power, and power often comes at the expense of the freedom of others. Consequently, it often comes more easily to governments to erode freedom rather than to increase it (whether this is done consciously or, as often seems to be the case, unconsciously).

An example of this is the present phenomenon of growing surveillance. It's the natural tendency of police authorities to want to know as much as possible about everyone – information gathering is, after all, an important part of their job. If left unchecked – for example by a free, vigorous and unbiased media – the logical outcome of that is totalitarianism.

There is also the inherent tendency of bureaucracies to increase complexity rather than to reduce it. The more bureaucracy exists, the more work there is for civil servants, lawyers and accountants – not to mention the ordinary citizen who must struggle daily with a growing mass of increasingly incomprehensible, and unpaid, paperwork.

There is, furthermore, the tendency for ideologies (in this case the fetishism of work) to outlive their usefulness. In other words, even if our current welfare systems were shown to be a drag on capitalism itself (since they keep people poor and unable to buy the things it produces) many people might still continue to support such systems, since they worked at one time in the past. (Or, at least, they worked better than they do now.)

There is also the difficulty that politicians tend to be people who are extroverted and who have little leisure time for reading up on policy matters – neither of which lends itself to the study of radical alternatives to our current creaking systems. One can envisage, then, that many politicians may be the last to concede the ground on UBI, and in some cases may be among its most vigorous opponents. There is some truth in the saying that 'the right thing is what governments do when they've done all the wrong things first'.

There are also important issues to be addressed such as the redeployment of people who currently work in state bureaucracies, administering the current welfare systems (not to mention the trade unions that represent their interests). Such employees could be reassigned to assisting people of limited means, or who suffer various social-economic problems, towards finding a useful and fulfilling place in society, rather than concentrating on policing the system as at present.

They could also be reassigned to work in revenue collection, thus helping to plug the holes in our revenue systems (particularly in countries where, to one extent or another, tax evasion has become a national sport).[17]

PAYING FOR IT

What about the crucial issue of costing? Could our modern societies afford UBI? We will look at this in more detail later. At this point it's enough to say that – in principle – this is really a non-question. Any society where people already have, more or less, enough to live on, would also by definition be able to provide them with enough to live on with a basic income, since there would be the same amount of money to share around.

The difficulties arise when one considers the level of UBI, and the complexities that a new form of redistribution might involve. Obviously, a very low level of UBI would be easy to afford, but would probably not be of much use to anyone. A very high level of UBI might be unaffordable.

A level of UBI where everyone enjoyed the same standard of living as they do at present would by definition be possible to afford (since such a situation already exists, though it is currently bound about with restrictions). It might, though, be very complicated, thus defeating the goal of simplicity that UBI aims for. (This, of course, is a separate issue from the question whether UBI might have negative effects after it was introduced.)

The complications would arise from a number of factors. These include the question of what, if any, current welfare benefits (for example disability support) are to be retained in a society with UBI. Furthermore, we would also want to try to keep complexity to a minimum – since one of the virtues that is claimed for UBI is that it cuts down on unnecessary bureaucracy.

There would also be political difficulties involved in trying to avoid making things worse for anyone than they are under the current system.

There are two reasons for wanting to avoid this. The first is that, in many cases, it may be undesirable in itself. (Though not, however, in all cases – some rich people actually argue that they themselves should be paying more in taxes.[18])

The second reason is that, if a significant number of people would lose out with UBI, it could make it very difficult to establish, particularly if such people had a strong influence in the society – as the rich by definition do – and were in a position to exert political sway. (Whether or not they ought to lose out is a separate issue – we are talking politics here, rather than morality *per se*.)

In terms of defining UBI, and particularly for political reasons in helping to get it implemented, it's important to keep the discussion of UBI separate from the discussion around the redistribution of wealth – otherwise the two issues tend to become conflated.

UBI is itself neutral in terms of its redistributive possibilities. We could conceive of a high UBI where people who are currently on low incomes would be better off than they are at present. On the other hand, we could conceive of a low UBI where they would be worse off, as a result of the abolition, or reduction, of benefits that they currently receive. We could also imagine a situation where things remained unchanged in a redistributive sense. (In the last-mentioned case, the sole difference would be the removal of poverty traps and of the current weird combination that exists of prohibition/compulsion in regard to work.)

A person does not necessarily have to cease being a conservative, a neoliberal, a libertarian or a socialist in order to support UBI. As we have seen, they may support it for widely different reasons. What tends to unite people across the political spectrum, when it comes to support for UBI, is a desire for increased liberty – though the latter may be defined in widely different ways.

In political debates about the details of UBI as well as the numbers involved, people's individual preferences will, necessarily, feed into the discussion. But – while most of the contemporary debate takes place on the Left – it's important to remember that UBI is, to some extent at least, politically neutral when it comes to the key issue of the overall redistribution of wealth in society. As a consequence, for political purposes, tactical alliances are conceivable on the issue of UBI, across the (traditional) political, Left-Right spectrum. People may differ widely on UBI in regard to their motivations, the form they want it to take, and how they want it to be introduced.

WEALTH CREATION

There is, of course, also the crucial question of whether a state with UBI would continue to create enough wealth to pay for it – even given the massively increased role of technology in our contemporary world. If it didn't create enough wealth, it might have to borrow to support the UBI (or borrow in addition to what we do anyway, to support our current welfare systems). Such a situation of (additional) borrowing would probably not be desirable.

If the level of UBI collapsed, or threatened to collapse, as a result of the lack of a desire on the part of many people to work in the formal economy, there would be considerable political pressure to increase taxes of all kinds to support it (indeed also to institute taxes on things we don't currently tax).

If the level of UBI collapsed to a sufficient extent, it would become impossible to survive on it. As a result, those who could work would have to go out and work in order to live, whether they wanted to or not.

Whether there would then be enough work for them is a question that is difficult to answer, and perhaps could be adequately addressed only with a complicated computer model.

On the one hand, it could be argued that there would be a lot of jobs available, arising from the fact that people originally didn't want them, since they were able to survive on their basic income instead. On the other hand, firms that originally offered them might have collapsed in the meantime, since they were unable to obtain employees. (Or they might have replaced the workers with machines – though they might have done that anyway.)

However, it would of course be possible for most people (legally) to top up their basic income – even if it fell below subsistence level – by casual self-employment, which then might turn into more established enterprises in the formal economy.

Whatever about the complexities, it seems clear that, with UBI, there would be a certain amount of self-adjustment involved, even if the UBI fell below the level that was viewed as necessary for subsistence. In a society with UBI, people are of course allowed to work rather than prevented from doing so – so there is a certain self-sustaining dynamic in play.

However, if the sustainable level of UBI collapsed, there would obviously be problems for those who (for reasons such as mental or physical disability) were not able to work in the formal economy. Such people would, therefore, probably need to be provided for independently (as indeed they usually are at present, at least in countries with a functioning social welfare system). The rest of the population who relied wholly on UBI would have to find some means of subsistence in addition to it (at least until the economy recovered sufficiently for them to retreat to the study, the living-room couch or the beach).

The main difference between a basic-income society and our own is that a basic-income society would solve many of our current employment problems. With UBI, no one has to work who doesn't want to, and those who want to can. If you can't find a full-time job, you can work part-time.[19] If you can't find a part-time job, you can earn money, in addition to your basic income, by casual self-employment.

However, in a basic-income society there are, still, obviously many people who are not in the kind of work in which they want to be. For example – and no doubt rightly so – you can't become a rocket scientist or a brain surgeon without many years of training. Some jobs would continue to be low paid compared to others.[20]

So there would still be some kind of unemployment, affecting a section of the population whose skills and abilities do not correspond with their aspirations. A basic-income society might, then, have some problems of its own, but they would be different problems than ours, and perhaps easier to solve.

There seems, then, no difficulty in principle in affording UBI, as long as we concede that it might not always be possible to maintain it at a sustainable level for everyone. The difficulties involve the balancing of (a) a desire for non-complexity with (b) the issue of overcoming opposition from entrenched interests. The latter would include some who might see themselves as negatively affected by UBI (depending on its level, and the adjustments in tax and expenditure needed to pay for it).

It should be pointed out that such redistributive arguments do not necessarily fall along Left/Right lines. For example, it might be seen as a Left-wing move to combine a high UBI with a rise in the tax rate, particularly for those on higher tax bands. On the other hand, the question arises as to whether it would be a Left-wing or a Right-wing move to cut down on government expenditure – for example on education, health, or defence/offence – in order to raise the level of UBI for everyone.

Such imponderables, while they exist, do not obscure the fact that Left/Right issues would continue to exist with the introduction of UBI, and they might be of particular relevance when discussing the level of UBI to be paid to each citizen. A basic income of, say, one unit of currency (euro, dollar or pound sterling) a year would be easily affordable by any country, but would hardly be worth instituting. When it gets to higher proposed levels, the political difficulties kick in.

Putting the objection to UBI in a nutshell, the argument is that, with UBI, there would be too many jobs for too few people willing to do them. While this would certainly raise a problem, it would be the opposite problem to that which currently bedevils our societies. With UBI, we would have the problem of overemployment rather than unemployment (or underemployment). While that would certainly raise an issue, it could be an easier issue to resolve than the problem of unemployment (or disguised unemployment, when people are working in jobs that do not reflect their ability or fulfil their desires).

THE STATE

This leads us to the role of the state, and the objections that might be raised around it. In the first place, the goal of UBI diverges from anarchist ideals of a stateless society in that it depends on some kind of centralised structure to distribute the UBI. (It also depends on a tax structure to collect it and a financial system to create the money in the first place.)

It is indeed possible that UBI might appeal to some anarchists (or at least anarchist-leaning libertarians) in promising to reduce the role of the state (though not eliminating it). On the other hand, it could simultaneously raise the hackles of some Leftists who might oppose a reduction in the role of the state.

Conversely, anti-statists might regard UBI in a negative light, as entrenching the role of the state and making it indispensable. With UBI, people are dependent on the state for their subsistence (though possibly not much more than they are under our current social welfare systems, and certainly with more freedom than with the latter offer). Consequently, with UBI there would be political pressure to maintain the UBI system and to raise it to a level that makes the poorer better off.

The reason for this is that 1,000 euro, dollars or pounds extra – or less – in the pocket of a poor person feel a lot different than the same adjustment would to a rich person. A wealthy individual may see multiples of that figure being added to, or subtracted from, their investments every day, without being too concerned, and without perhaps even noticing. On the contrary, a poor person is all-too conscious of the level of their wealth, or lack thereof. It would be in their interest to organise, agitate and vote for the level of UBI to rise.

We could therefore envisage that, with UBI, there would be a certain pressure towards social equality: pressure that is greater than that which exists at the moment. This is because arguments against paying more to the 'undeserving' poor would be weaker (after all, everyone would get UBI, whether rich or poor).

Since UBI is paid to everyone, the argument to hold back on raising its level is less persuasive in a political sense, since everyone becomes richer by the same amount. However, the rich may be affected negatively by corresponding tax increases – consequently they might have to think up other reasons why those should not take place.

The final point to note here, in regard to the role of the state, is the issue of whether UBI should be paid at a national level, at a supranational level (for example the EU, for those countries that belong to it) or at an international level. Taking the last-mentioned, you could argue that it would be most appropriate for everyone to receive the same amount, by virtue of being a human being.

Against that, a northern European person might make the argument that he/she should be rewarded by the effort their ancestors made to travel to that region of the earth in prehistoric times, rather than staying in Africa, where (according to anthropologists) we all originally came from.

Such an argument, however, doesn't hold much water: no one proposes going through genealogical lists to establish whether your ancestors arrived in the country a generation ago or a hundred generations ago, in order to establish your right to a basic income. Furthermore, the African could reply that he/she is actually owed more than the Westerner, to make up for past colonial depredations of Europe on Africa.

On the other hand, there is the argument that it's colder in northern Europe than in Africa, so you need more money for heat, insulation, clothing and whatever. The indigenous peoples of the Amazon rainforest – assuming it continues to exist in the future, under the pressure of deforestation – would presumably not need UBI, since they are economically self-sufficient. If, on the other hand, there was an argument that they were missing out on the wonders of modern civilization due to their 'primitive' lifestyle, then the argument for UBI, in addition to other provisions such as modern healthcare and education, might arise.

Such discussions (about the morality of a global UBI), however interesting they may be in a philosophical sense, are destined to remain in the realm of speculation for some time to come. Discussions around the implementation of UBI will, for the foreseeable future, take place at a national level (or at most a supranational level, perhaps involving the EU). It has to be admitted that the reasons for that are political rather than ethical – once UBI has been established at a local level, it will become easier to talk realistically about bringing it about at a global level as well, in whole or in part.[21]

IMMIGRATION

A related issue involves immigration, a question that is currently to the fore in Europe, the UK (specifically with Brexit) and the United States (with the recent presidential election). For example, what happens if you set up a basic-income system in Ireland, and Ireland immediately becomes a magnet for all the lazy people in the rest of the EU, who just want to chill out and watch daytime TV while drinking beer and smoking dope? Such a situation would, perhaps, strain the system to breaking point.

There are a number of answers to that objection. In the first place, it may be possible for many people already to indulge such a lifestyle under the welfare system of the country where they live, since our current welfare systems are good at maintaining idleness, but bad at encouraging work. Secondly, immigrants may already qualify for welfare in the country they enter. All UBI would do would be to ease the pressure on them to find a job – and conversely, ease restrictions on working.

Of course, prospective immigrants may already be subject to welfare restrictions in the prospective country of entry: the question of easing off on such restrictions is, then, a separate issue.

You could, for example, address the difficulty by paying UBI at a fractional level to recent immigrants, or by limiting it to those who had been in the country for a set number of years. (This, for EU members, is to make the assumption that such restrictions would be compatible with EU law.)

For the UK, one of the (very few) advantages of Brexit is that it may make UBI at a national level more conceivable, since the immigration problem may not arise (depending on the level of Brexit and the agreement that may or may not be achieved on the free movement of people, in the coming years and decades). Conversely of course, if UBI were introduced at an overall EU level, then the UK would lose out on UBI as a result of Brexit.

Politically, the UBI argument could conceivably become a useful tool (for both sides) in the debate about the future of the EU. For those who support UBI, the argument would be that the EU should either institute UBI at a supranational level, or allow individual states to go down that road with whatever (economic, political and/or social) consequences may accrue, in terms of their relationship with the EU itself.

A further response is that there is a limit to the hedonistic possibilities of a subsistence-level UBI. For example, the temptation to earn some extra money (if only to afford more beer or recreational drugs) might become irresistible even for a person determined to pursue a lazy lifestyle, and people might become sucked into the world of formal work without even realising it.

We should not assume that UBI necessarily leads to the avoidance of work. Raventós points out the high number of people who already do overtime or work extra hours, either to earn more than they already do, above and beyond the fulfilment of their basic needs, or to perform the job better than they otherwise would. He notes that many people who have taken early retirement continue to work in the job market, even though their early retirement payments may be higher than a basic income would be.[22]

Finally, there is an argument that we should get rid of national borders altogether. Rutger Bregman cites an estimate that the removal of all borders to labour at a global level would boost wealth by $65 trillion.[23] Bregman cites a study that shows that immigration leads to increased earnings on the part of the domestic workforce.[24] Billions of people have to sell their labour at a fraction of the price it would fetch otherwise, because of international borders, which Bregman cites as the single largest source of discrimination in history.[25] To take an example, he notes that sixty-two individuals currently own more than the poorest half of the world population.[26]

It seems though that the aspiration to remove national borders, however desirable it may be, must remain in the realm of utopia, at least for the time being.[27]

CONCLUSION

Having spelled out the advantages of UBI in earlier chapters, I have tried here to give due weight to some objections that may arise to UBI. In some cases the answers to those objections are clear, in others they are less clear, and in yet others we have to admit that UBI may have some negative consequences. As far as we can tell, however, the negative consequences would be much less severe than are the negative consequences of our present welfare systems.

In any event, it is worth repeating that UBI is not a panacea. Though it will certainly solve some of our socioeconomic problems, it will not solve all of them. Some existing problems may become worse, and UBI may indeed introduce some problems that may not currently exist and that we may not, perhaps, even have anticipated. What does seem clear is that, given the direction in which our socioeconomic system is heading, our present way of doing things is not an option. UBI is the most obvious alternative to current welfare systems that have become unworkable and outmoded.[28]

There is a 'Right-wing' approach to UBI and a 'Left-wing' approach. The Right-wing version would use the idea of UBI as an excuse to cut back on state spending. This is not necessarily a bad idea, as long as the cutbacks are confined to a (dangerous and counterproductive) military-industrial complex, to corporate welfare, or to wasteful and futile forms of bureaucracy.

Where such cutbacks could become destructive is where they endanger forms of state spending that actually benefit the population as a whole: for example in health, education, or support for people facing mental or physical challenges. A low level of UBI, introduced too radically or drastically, could, conceivably, be used to force people into the workforce, since it would be impossible to live on it.

For those who support the idea of UBI, it's important to ensure that the concept is not used to erode the position of the most vulnerable in society, or to erode services that may be essential and that are better provided by the state rather than by private enterprise.

The 'Left-wing' version of UBI, which is obviously the one that I support, would see basic income as a means of radical redistribution. Money currently wasted on militarism, corporate welfare and financial redistribution, which benefits mainly the rich, would be redirected to the whole of society instead. Whatever services and institutions were needed to benefit society in general, in particular its most vulnerable members, would be retained and enhanced.

Crucially, UBI would be combined with an overhaul of attitudes to work, to make it easier for people who wished to work a shorter day, week, and/or year, to do so – while allowing workaholics to indulge their work fetishism. (Some people may actually enjoy working 18-hour days against a deadline, and it is, arguably, not the business of the state to stop them doing so if they want to.)

Tactical alliances are sometimes appropriate, for people who may support a particular proposal, though for widely different reasons. In Ireland, strange bedfellows agitated amicably together on EU-related referendums, while parting ways to oppose each other (vigorously) on issues such as marriage laws and reproductive rights. The same may happen in regard to UBI, with its supporters from both Left and Right.

In the same way, it is quite possible that an organised opposition to UBI may emerge, comprising some kind of alliance of visceral authoritarians and people who feel that their interests are, in one way or another, under threat. Since the present system is quite obviously not an option, it would be up to such an opposition to frame a better alternative to UBI. Such an alternative would need to compete with UBI in terms of the values of freedom, social justice, solidarity, simplicity and user-friendliness. That would, I suggest, be quite a difficult task.

To sum up, it is vital that UBI acts as a vehicle for social liberation, rather than as a Trojan horse for assisting a dysfunctional system. Both of these are possible outcomes. Those of us who want to make the world a better place – as distinct from fashioning a system of exploitation and inequity that would work more smoothly – should take the former route.

6

IMPLEMENTATION: MAKING UBI HAPPEN

Up to now, we have looked at some historical, philosophical, ideological and political issues around the idea of UBI. At this point it's time to take a more practical look, and to consider how it might be implemented, in one form or another.

In principle, the issue of costing is not a problem. In a society where everyone has, more or less, the means of living, the question is already answered. There is already enough money to go around (leaving aside the murky question of how money is created in the first place). The problem lies in readjusting the structure of distribution to make it simpler and less of a hindrance to people in their ordinary lives, than our current (outmoded and counterproductive) systems.[1]

We could also reconsider our priorities in terms of how we allocate money. Should we give priority to bailouts of banks and bondholders, to making the rich richer through quantitative easing and corporate welfare, and to destructive military adventurism with its tragic and socially disruptive consequences? Or might the money be better expended on direct redistribution to the population?[2]

Unfortunately, the corporate and media interests that control the mindset of the population make it difficult or impossible for the vast majority to think outside of this particular box, even when it might be in their interest to do so.

In theory, UBI could be instituted without making anyone better or worse off than they are at present (though it could become extremely complicated to do that). While wealth-redistribution is an important priority, in a sense it's a separate issue from that of UBI. The fundamental point here is that UBI should not be seen primarily as a means of equalising the distribution of wealth, but as a way of lifting burdens off people's backs and making their lives easier. (You can argue in favour of greater wealth equalisation and also in favour of the principle of UBI, but it's important – at least for theoretical clarity – not to get the two arguments confused.)[3]

It would be fairly easy for a society to introduce a form of UBI at a very low level. This could then be gradually increased until it became the main form of distribution – problems that developed in the course of this could be dealt with as they occurred. At the same time, other forms of already-existing support would be reduced, or eliminated, to make up for the amount distributed through UBI. To what extent this would (or could) be done is a political issue for the country involved.[4]

The problem, of course, is that it is the natural tendency of bureaucracies to increase complexity rather than to reduce it. This would need to be countered in some way – though so far attempts at simplification, for example with regard to tax systems, have had very limited success. And the institution of UBI, while it might reduce bureaucracy, would not eliminate it.[5]

In terms of the amount of UBI to be paid, in the context of developed countries we could think of a (very rough) figure at which to aim, of perhaps 1,000 dollars/euro/pounds a month (in 2017 terms) for each recipient. This would be reduced for the very young, and increased for those past retirement age.

Such a figure would, no doubt, be contested on an ongoing basis along political lines: the Right perhaps arguing for a lower figure, the Left for a higher. (However, some people might argue for a high UBI, at the expense of state expenditure in other areas. Whether that would be a Right-wing or a Left-wing position is a moot point.) In any case, UBI will certainly not end political debate, or struggle.

The main form of UBI proposed is a periodic (say monthly) direct distribution, paid into the individual's account by the state. There are, however, various other forms that a UBI (or something like it) could take.

The best known of these is a negative income tax, whereby the individual earning less than a given amount receives a subsidy from the state.[6] The advantage of a negative income tax is that it makes use of a system that exists already – the system of tax collection. There are a number of downsides though, as compared to the purer form of UBI.

Negative income tax relies on self-reporting; there may be a delay in payment if there is a sudden change in the individual's circumstances; and the income tax system, probably by its nature, is complicated, demanding and intrusive. Furthermore, negative income tax entrenches income tax as a system at a time when we should, arguably, be looking at alternatives to taxing work as a means of raising revenue.

Negative income tax may also be subject to political pressure by those at the lower end of the scale to skew it to their advantage – or indeed by those at the higher end of the scale (who normally have more political clout) to change it to theirs. In this way, though, it is no different from UBI (or indeed from current social welfare arrangements). In practical terms, negative income tax is similar to UBI: the two systems can be structured in such a way that the result for the individual citizen is the same in each case.

In both cases, you have to pay tax on money you earn over and above a certain level. With UBI you would, presumably, pay tax on any money you earned over and above your UBI (assuming, of course, that the income tax system is retained). With negative income tax you pay tax when you earn an amount in excess of a given level. Negative income tax is a more complicated way of doing the same thing as UBI does. (Depending on the culture in question, however, it may be more politically feasible.)

The discussion around negative income tax is overshadowed by the fact that its best-known advocate, Milton Friedman, is something of a *bête noire* for the Left. Indeed, his main goal was to abolish the ragbag of social welfare schemes (as he saw them) and solve the problem of poverty by giving money directly, and unconditionally, to people who need it. However, Friedman seems to have seen negative income tax as a transitional measure on the way to a minimalist neoliberal state of full employment. With the growth of technology and the effects of globalisation, this prospect appears much less likely than it did some decades ago.

Since full employment seems increasingly unlikely, and since people at the lower end of the economic scale may agitate strongly in their own economic interest, negative income tax may indeed turn out to function in socially equitable ways that Friedman may not have intended, or wanted.

There is also the proposal of a lump sum paid to citizens on reaching maturity. Such ideas, as mentioned already, go back several centuries, but a particularly intriguing form, in a US context, is suggested by Bruce Ackerman and Anne Alstott. On reaching the age of 21, the person receives a lump sum ($80,000 in 2004 terms) paid over four years in annual instalments. This would be paid for by a wealth tax of 2 per cent on each individual's wealth over $230,000 and would be clawed back, with interest, on the recipient's death (assuming that his/her estate has the capacity to meet it).[7]

This would no doubt provide a field day for lawyers and account-ants on the demise of the recipient. A more fundamental issue, though, seems to be that of unfairness: by its nature, such a stakeholder's grant is generation-specific. Older people would, understandably, feel aggrieved at being excluded.

Another idea is that of a time-limited income to be paid over a fixed number of years.[8] A variant is a 'sabbatical grant', from which the indi-vidual could draw throughout his/her life.[9] These are variants on the underlying notion of UBI, and may be given more or less consideration depending on the circumstances of individual countries. There is no 'one size fits all' proposal in regard to the form that UBI will, or should, take.

There are also various notions of diluting the concept of 'unconditional-ity' to make UBI payable not on the basis of means, but on condition of some form of participation in society. (This, however, runs up against the usual problems of bureaucracy and infringement on freedom.)[10]

We could pay for UBI out of income tax, and/or other forms of taxation such as land tax, energy tax, 'cap and share', VAT, wealth tax, transaction tax[11] and so on. UBI could also be paid through dividends from a dedicated fund; this would make everyone a shareholder and thus, in a sense, extend capitalism to the whole society, rather than to a select group as at present.[12]

More radical ideas include 'helicopter money' paid directly to the populace rather than to financial institutions as at present.[13] Though the issue is outside the scope of this study, we could also consider how UBI might be funded in the context of a rethink of how money is created in the first place.[14]

Of course, as with everything else, the devil is in the detail. Should we compensate for the fact that it's cheaper for two (or more) people to live together than separately? Should UBI be paid at an individual level – as most supporters argue – or at a household level?[15] (The latter would seem to undermine an important principle, that of unconditionality. It is also the case that UBI encourages people to live together rather than apart, which is surely a plus in a social sense, if we want to avoid a fragmented and atomised society.)

How, though, do you stop people having large families just to get free money from the state? Is UBI paid only to residents of the country in question, or more narrowly to citizen-residents? Does a person who goes to prison forfeit their UBI for the term of their imprisonment? Do you forfeit your basic income if you go abroad? If so, how long are you allowed to stay out of the country before the payment is stopped – a weekend, a week, a month, a year?

Such questions may, indeed, raise the issue whether 'universality' is an appropriate term in regard to UBI. As we saw already, however, if UBI is confined to a national level and does not encompass the whole world, the meaning of 'universality' is already limited in some way.

Of course, in many cases the issue of eligibility already arises in the context of current welfare systems, but it would need to be addressed specifically in the process of designing a workable UBI system. This would mean broadening the kind of scrutiny that we normally apply to social welfare recipients to the population as a whole. Assuming that we already have too much scrutiny of the population, this seems an inevitable drawback, though perhaps a somewhat minor one. (Something like this, however, already happens in a tax context, when questions may arise for the individual taxpayer about residency issues.)

These kinds of issues seem to indicate that UBI should be brought in gradually, rather than all at once – so that any unforeseen problems may be dealt with as they arise.

There is also the question of how UBI would intersect with current social insurance, work-related and contribution-based forms of income.[16] For political reasons if not moral ones, we don't want to make anyone worse off than they already are – particularly those at the lower or middle of the economic scale. However, there may be political difficulties, particularly in cultures where the traditional work ethic is strong, in giving people who haven't obviously earned it the same reward as those who have.[17]

Furthermore, rich people tend to have political influence out of all proportion to their numbers, so any proposals to reduce their wealth are fraught with difficulty. (Arguments for greater equality between rich and poor may be persuasive, but it can lead to confusion if we conflate them with arguments for UBI *per se*.)

The question of the domain of UBI also arises. As noted already, there is a moral case for paying UBI at a global level. However, there are practical arguments against it, not least of which is the question of who would collect and distribute the money. In the short term at least, UBI is unlikely to be instituted at a global level, for all kinds of political and logistical reasons. (However, a persuasive argument has been made for the payment of UBI on a global level, in the form of a 'Global Resources Dividend'.[18])

In the short term at least, the most likely forms of distribution would be either at a national level (the individual nation state) or at a supranational level (for example the EU, if indeed it continues to exist in its present form).[19]

At the time of writing, the future of the EU itself seems somewhat problematic. Problems include the Brexit situation; the pressures of globalisation and immigration; instability in the financial sphere and questions about the viability of the euro; a bureaucracy that is apparently insulated from social and economic reality; the growth of dissident and secessionist political movements throughout Europe; meddling by Russia in international affairs; and the apparently isolationist tendencies of the new government in the United States.

However, a radical step such as UBI could be part of the glue that would aid in holding the EU together. It could help to counteract the tendency of alienated sections of the population to opt for nationalist remedies.[20]

Conversely, of course, if anti-EU movements were to adopt UBI as a goal for their individual countries, they could also use it as ammunition for their own cause. This situation could arise in the event that the EU was reluctant to implement it – or, indeed, if a country-specific UBI was seen to be incompatible with EU policies in regard to welfare, immigration and so on.[21]

However, since the concept of UBI is based on expanding the realm of liberty, it is unlikely to be embraced eagerly by Right-wing authoritarians (or, indeed, by Left-wing authoritarians either).

In a US context, UBI could be instituted at the level of individual states of the United States, and might become part of the platform of a rejuvenated Left in that country. (Of course, support for UBI is by no means confined to the Left, and the fact that a form of UBI already exists in Alaska may give hope to supporters in other states of the Union.)[22]

UBI, however, is unlikely to be set up at a federal level any time soon (except perhaps in the form of a negative income tax, reviving the ideas that were gaining traction some decades ago in the US). And some states may be more sympathetic to the idea than others: what is thinkable in Vermont may be less so in Texas.

Some 'pilot schemes' in regard to the implementation of UBI have already been tried, or are being tried.[23] Various schemes of greater or lesser complexity have been suggested for different countries, for example South Africa and Brazil.[24]

The charity GiveDirectly, as its name suggests, operates on the principle that the best way to solve the problem of poverty is to give money directly to people who need it. It thereby provides, perhaps, a useful (voluntary) precursor of future, more generalised and institutionalised, UBI systems.[25]

In a UK context, Malcolm Torry proposes a costed citizen's income that would be established incrementally, and that would make minimal changes to the current tax and benefits system.[26] In the United States,

Charles M.A. Clark proposed a basic income for all children and adults which would take them above the poverty line, funded by a flat tax on all incomes, with the abolition of income tax deductions, and reductions in local and state taxes.[27]

BASIC INCOME AND IRELAND

In the final section of this chapter, I will look briefly at the situation with which I am most familiar, that of Ireland, since it exemplifies many of the issues that arise on an international level as well. Ireland is a small, relatively prosperous, developed country with an open economy and not much colonial baggage (except in a negative sense, as the recipient of colonialism[28]). It has, nevertheless, recently undergone a traumatic experience of debt and austerity as a result of the economic crash, and may offer a useful model for other countries in this regard.

The most prominent organisations proposing UBI in Ireland are Social Justice Ireland (www.socialjustice.ie) and Basic Income Ireland (www.basicincomeireland.com). In political terms, the most notable advocate of UBI has been the Green Party/Comhaontas Glas, though other political parties – most recently Fianna Fail – have shown interest in the idea from time to time.

The first UBI proposal for Ireland was developed by Brendan Dowling in 1977, though it received little discussion. A non-taxable grant was proposed for all citizens, with extra supplements for particular categories. The scheme was to be financed by a tax of 34 per cent on employee incomes, and by a payroll tax of 9 per cent on employers.[29] A number of studies since then have discussed the pros and cons of the idea.[30]

The most recent proposals were outlined by the organisation Social Justice Ireland in their book *Basic Income: Radical Utopia or Practical Solution*? Michelle Murphy describes five different roads towards the implementation of a basic-income scheme. These are: (1) all at once; (2) by groups; (3) one step at a time; (4) partial basic income; (5) gradual implementation. Her proposal for Ireland is to bring in a basic-income system over a 5-year period. This would, in her view, give enough time to ensure proper development of the system, and also to iron out any anomalies that might arise regarding the current tax and welfare systems.

In year 1, Murphy proposes introducing a universal pension for all citizens over 66. At the same time, work would begin to set up the UBI system separately from the current tax and welfare systems, ironing out any anomalies in the tax and welfare systems that might be thrown up. In year 2, refundable tax credits would be introduced for all employees. In year 3, one third of the UBI scheme would be introduced, with corresponding adjustments to the tax and welfare systems. In year 4, two thirds of the UBI scheme would be introduced, again with corresponding changes of a tax and welfare nature. In year 5, the remaining one third of the UBI system would be brought in, and concluding changes made to the tax and welfare systems.[31]

A number of issues arise with Murphy's proposal, in the specifically Irish context. In the first place, combining the introduction of the UBI system with the simultaneous dismantling of no-longer-needed elements of the tax and welfare systems may be more complex than it appears. In the short term it could introduce even more complexity into a situation that is already alarmingly complex.

In the second place, the staged introduction, while it appears on the surface to offer a solution to the difficulties that a 'short, sharp' introduction of UBI would face, would be problematic in Ireland. Governments in Ireland have been extremely inconsistent in regard to taxation issues, most recently with a debacle over the imposition of water charges.

This inconsistency is, in part, due to the PR (proportional representation) system that operates in Ireland. PR tends to throw up weak governments that are inordinately responsive to pressure by interests of one kind or another. Of course, proportional representation has its advantages, and arguably has been positive for Ireland on the whole. For example, it gives minorities (such as Greens) a political voice that they lack in other countries, in particular the UK with its 'first-past-the-post' electoral system.

PR, with its complicated and closely watched system of electoral calculation, also plays a cultural role in offering a kind of blood sport for the Irish population every few years, as they watch candidates being sacrificed, in excruciating detail, on the altar of mathematical calculation. (Such a satisfying indulgence, perhaps comparable to the appetite for bullfights in Spain, is not readily available to those in the UK with its more mundane electoral system.)

However, the political situation that exists in Ireland, largely as a result of PR, does not bode well for the long-term planning that a staged introduction of UBI would make necessary. A '5-year plan' would be subject to 5 years of attack and destabilisation from everyone who felt that their interests were under threat, not to mention from the prevailing ideology of opposition to 'something for nothing'. At the very least, it would seem necessary for there to be a strong groundswell of support for the idea of UBI, across the political spectrum, before it is implemented politically.

Eamon Murphy and Seán Ward, using 2015 figures, propose a costed UBI for Ireland. This would replace all tax credits and reliefs. It would also replace nearly all weekly social welfare payments: though with some exceptions such as carer's payment, disability allowance, fuel allowance, rent supplement and some others. Residency in Ireland would be a condition of payment. All other income would be subject to tax at a single rate of 40 per cent.

Under the proposal, the employee PRSI rate is abolished, while the employer PRSI rate is raised from 10.75 per cent to 13 per cent. (The authors point out that the current employer PRSI rate in Ireland is below half the EU average.) Tax credits and tax reliefs are abolished in the proposed system. The authors calculate that this would permit a payment of €150 per week for working age adults between 18 and 65 (less for children, more for older people). A supplement of €38 per week is paid to those between 18 and 65 who are actively looking for jobs.

They conclude that (apart from the abolition of tax reliefs) UBI would have a broadly positive effect, particularly among lower-income groups. High-income earners would face a marginal rate of 40 per cent, instead of over 50 per cent as at present. The authors also point out that there would be savings from the reduction in administration costs and welfare fraud.[32]

One question that may arise, particularly in an Irish context, is the cost of housing. Rents in Ireland have skyrocketed in recent years due to a combination of factors, including the lack of social housing as a result of 'austerity' politics arising from the economic crash of 2008 and following years, and an (inexplicable) resistance to the notion of building upwards, with resultant suburban sprawl through Dublin county and beyond. Consequently there would need to be some kind of payment either in addition to UBI, or on top of it, to compensate for the distortion in the housing market.[33]

There is also a strong case, in an Irish context, for the retention of a minimum wage, in order to avoid any tendency towards a 'race to the bottom' in which UBI might allow employers to engage – particularly given the freedom of movement in terms of labour that membership of the EU permits.

EU membership has undoubtedly been a cultural boon for Ireland in many ways. To take one example, within a 20-minute stroll from my apartment in the centre of Dublin I can avail of perhaps thirty different kinds of ethnic restaurants, and Dublin is now one of the most multicultural cities in the world, to the benefit of many. Anti-immigrant feeling seems less prevalent in Ireland than in other European countries, but this could change, particularly if Ireland comes under increased pressure of immigration as a result of Brexit. (It is conceivable that there could be an influx of immigrants from Eastern Europe who want to live in an English-speaking country and are no longer able to enter the UK freely, or to remain if they are already there.) A substantial minimum wage would seem essential if Ireland is to avoid becoming a low-wage dumping ground for neoliberal capitalism.

Michael Taft argues for UBI in an Irish context in terms of integrating it into other mechanisms, as part of a progressive, decommodifying package. These include the radical reduction of the working week to 30 hours, and lifting the social wage to average EU levels by raising the rate of employers' social insurance from 8 per cent to 20 per cent of direct wage. Basic income – introduced initially on a partial basis – would facilitate these reforms, while giving its own benefits as well. It would be instigated in the first instance through the transformation of personal tax credits into a direct payment to all adults.

Taft estimates that, factoring in the loss of personal credits, increased taxation and the payment of partial basic income, a casual worker would come out with €1,444 extra per annum, and a part-time low-paid worker on €13,000 per annum would be €700 better off. An average earner on €36,000 would neither lose nor gain. This would be of obvious benefit in terms of redistribution, but would also help specific categories such as students, and those caring in the home.[34]

Once the principle of desirability of UBI is established, a lot of work will need to be done, both in Ireland and elsewhere, on the practicalities involved, both economic and political. UBI may take different forms in different circumstances. Given the conditions (both economic and political) of a particular country or state, it may take the form of a coming-of-age grant, a lifetime sabbatical, or a negative income tax – or indeed of a regularly paid income to each individual member of society.

UBI could be funded through taxation in the traditional way, through new forms of taxation, or through universal participation in a national wealth fund (arguably extending capitalism to the population as a whole). More radically, it could be funded through a reconsideration of the application of existing mechanisms such as quantitative easing – or through a reanalysis of the whole process of money creation.[35]

The process of money creation is traditionally shrouded in fog – perhaps, to some extent, deliberately created – one result being that major disagreement exists among economists as to where money actually comes from in the first place. An analysis of how money is created, and how it might be reconsidered in the context of providing a basic income for the population, is beyond the scope of this book – here, we can only suggest it as a desirable undertaking.

CONCLUSION: SUMMING UP AND LOOKING FORWARD

ACADEMIC ISOLATION

Too often, academics have divorced themselves from the lives and concerns of ordinary people. This is part of a broader split between the political and intellectual 'élite' on the one hand, and the mass of the people on the other. In the United States, the derogatory term 'the flyover' denotes the broad swathe of the country that, according to people who live on the east or west coast, you have to traverse to get from one oasis of civilisation (for instance New York or Boston) to another (for example Los Angeles or San Francisco).

The liberal élite stereotype – or a parody of it at least – is that in between the coasts there lives a huge mass of people who are culturally, socially, economically and politically challenged.

They are divided, according to the stereotype, into two main categories. On the one hand there are people who go to church, are opposed to science, a prey to all kinds of conspiracy theories (from JFK to 9/11 to vaccination) and who homeschool their children to keep them from the evils of modern life. On the other hand there are people who live in trailer parks who have tattoos, mistreat their partners, abuse alcohol and drugs, are a prey to racist and sexist attitudes, and are probably involved in crime of one kind or another.

The Trump phenomenon – and the Brexit phenomenon in the UK, not to mention whatever will transpire on the European mainland – is in a sense a riposte to this, from ordinary people who resent being stereo-typed or flown over, at least in a metaphorical sense. Their vote is their weapon of last resort.

When citizens have nothing else left, they will often use their vote (whether in an election or a referendum) to make their feelings felt about those who they believe, correctly or incorrectly, have given them a raw deal.

In Ireland, it has often turned out to be the case that people use a referendum about issue A to voice their negative feelings about issue B or C. Similarly, they may use an election to give the government a good drubbing over one area of concern or another which may not even have been to the fore during the election. This is no doubt the case in other jurisdictions as well. Democracy can be a dangerous tool.

Within academia and in the humanities, the situation of isolation from the broad mass of the public has two major roots. On the one hand, there are the (often brilliant) insights of the Frankfurt School (prominent members of which included Theodor Adorno and Max Horkheimer[1]) and their followers. Unfortunately, these writings are couched in (often difficult) philosophical language, which makes them inaccessible to many people.

On the other hand, French philosophy (for example the writings of Jacques Derrida) and psychoanalysis (the work of Jacques Lacan for instance) have helped to make academic discourse much harder to understand than it has to be. Particularly in the case of psychoanalytically influenced theory, many students spend a long, frustrating and intellectually humiliating time trying to understand writings that, it turns out, are not capable of being understood by anyone but their author.

One wit summed up the two areas of thought that have dominated the humanities in recent years in the term 'Frankfurters and French Fries'. Politically, the effect of the domination of these two thought systems has been that of 'quietism', a term used to describe what happens when intellectuals stop trying to change the world and retreat instead to the study or the library.

The 'public intellectual' has become a vanishing breed, at least in the English-speaking world. (Individuals such as Noam Chomsky are rare exceptions, but even such a foremost intellectual as Chomsky is not given adequate attention by mainstream media – by and large, the mass media do not encourage trenchant in-depth reflection on political issues, at least if such reflection deviates significantly from the agreed consensus.)

Generally speaking, the radical energies of anti-establishment thought were, since the student upheaval of the 1960s, largely tamed and confined to academia, where they could do little harm in a political sense.

There were some exceptions, for example the anti-globalisation movement that developed around the turn of the century/millennium.

However, after 9/11 and the subsequent wars (including the 'war on terror'), the anti-globalisation movement seemed to vanish without trace – to emerge once again in more recent years in a Right-wing form. As far as I'm aware, little attention has been paid to this strange phenomenon: the political skewing of anti-globalist sentiment from Left to Right over the past 15 years or so.

What we have seen, to a great extent, is the evacuation of radical Left-wing thought from public debate. The gap has been filled by the Right, whether in the form of neoconservatism, neoliberalism, protectionism, or the far-Right.

Practical solutions by the Left to the problems of contemporary capitalism are hard to come by,[2] though apocalyptic prophecies abound.[3] One of the reasons for this lack has been the traditional reluctance of people on the Left to design workable solutions that might be implemented as an alternative to capitalism, or at least as a radical modification thereof.

This is, in part, the result of an antipathy towards 'utopian' thinking, presumably because the latter is regarded as unscientific. The study of capitalism, after all, deals with facts. The study of utopia deals with non-facts – it is more concerned with values, with what kind of society we would like to live in, as distinct from that which already exists.

The question whether politics (Green, Left, libertarian, feminist or whatever) should be based on facts or values is a relevant one. To take one example, I would prefer to live in a society where humane and ecological practices predominated, rather than the society of extreme inequality and environmental destruction that exists at present. Such a desire is value-based rather than fact-based. My desire to live in a Green, equitable world is founded either on something that doesn't (yet) exist, or on a rejection of a current situation on the basis that it falls short of what should exist. In both of those cases, my political attitude is primarily value-based, not fact-based.

A plurality of diagnoses exists of our economic, social and political problems, but – with the notable exception of discussions around UBI – there is often a lack of practical proposals for their solution. (Putting it another way, political theorists tend to be good at descriptions of problems, but less so at prescriptions for their remedy.)

This kind of failure is, of course, by no means confined to the Left. Conventional economists were, by and large, so caught up in their economic models that they failed to see the approaching train wreck of the recent economic crash.

Another, though related, issue is that Left-wing academics, where they do pay attention to politics, have tended to focus on the minutiae of identity politics, at the expense of issues involving social class, economic injustice and environmental destruction.[4] The result, again, has been the alienation of large sections of the population and the inflow of Right-wing ideology to fill the gaps.

Politically speaking, class politics are, arguably, much more crucial than identity politics. Class politics include issues around the inequality of wealth, growth and the environment, ballooning debt, the destruction of the social state, the threat, or reality, of unemployment and under-employment as a result of technological development, and the negative effects of economic globalisation.

As a result of the above situation, the allegiance of the working class and sections of the middle class have, in recent times, swung to the isolationist Right. The Brexit phenomenon in the UK and the Trump phenomenon in the US are symptoms of this, not to mention various forms of nationalist extremism on the European mainland. The rise of what has been termed 'authoritarian populism' is a major cause for concern, for those who value liberty.[5]

This is not to argue that identity politics, focussed on issues of race and gender for example, are not relevant. Indeed, the politics of race and gender are closely linked to those of other kinds of politics, class included. But when the issues of social class and wealth inequality are marginalised, then you have a problem.

The supporters of Trump and Brexit, and their counterparts on the European mainland, no doubt include racists and other antisocial individuals and groups, but they also include many ordinary people whose lives have not been improved by the economic situation in recent decades, and have even been made worse in many ways.[6] For example, in Greece, Spain, Croatia and Italy, youth unemployment in 2016 was estimated to be between 40 and 50 per cent.[7] This is not a recipe for political stability.

When you get to a political crossroads – as many ordinary people have done in recent times – it's just as easy to turn Right as to turn Left, and may often be easier. This is the case particularly as the Right-hand turn is wide, offers simple, or simplistic, solutions, and slopes gently downwards – albeit with a whiff of sulphur from off in the distance. The Left-hand turn, on the other hand, is narrow and difficult.[8] It appears to be crowded with indecisive people, bickering with each other over matters that do not seem to be of central importance to large sections of the population.

The traditional Left will tell you that the country of socialism is worth getting to, but will refuse to describe what it looks like: whether the climate is pleasant, the government congenial, what it's like to live there, how long it takes to make the journey, or the cost of getting to it.

As a consequence, it often doesn't sound like a particularly enticing prospect. Authoritarian nationalism and economic protectionism seem to lure voters more compellingly, since they hark back to a past that may not have existed, but that feels as if it ought to have.

THEORY, POLITICS AND THE ENVIRONMENT

When it comes to ecological issues, until recently the natural environment itself was marginalised by those involved in the study of culture and society (including by many whose main focus was on social class).[9] This was for a number of reasons, including the suspicion of the concept of 'nature' (it was regarded as 'essentialist') and the relegation of environmental issues to 'externalities' in economics.

In this context there has also been the historical split between the sciences and humanities (described most famously in C.P. Snow's essay 'The Two Cultures'[10]). The threat of global warming, highlighted for decades by climate scientists, took a long while to penetrate the minds of sociologists and cultural theorists as an issue to be considered. (However, the fact that London, for example, may be under water in decades to come is not something that can be ignored indefinitely, even by the most resolute relativists.)[11]

At the same time, the very notion of a knowable objective world, outside of language, was called in question in the academic sphere by the intellectual phenomenon which has been variously described as relativism, perspectivism or postmodernism, and which has challenged 'realism' as an explanatory view of the world.[12]

It is probably the case that realism gives us a better basis for political action than does relativism or postmodernism. If there is no knowable reality outside of the terms we use to describe it, then there is no knowable society to save from tyranny, or world to save from a polar-ice meltdown.

However, we should not base philosophical theories about the nature of the world on politics. Issues of truth inhabit a different sphere from those of ethics and politics, and so they should.[13]

We should, then, not base our theories about the nature of the world on the consequences that might flow from those theories, for social or political action. (If a child believes in the tooth fairy, it may make the prospect of losing their milk teeth less traumatic, but such a desirable result has no bearing on the existence, or otherwise, of the tooth fairy.)

In other words, the fact that we want to improve the lot of our fellow human beings, or to save the natural environment, is not a sound basis for the 'realist' view that such external entities have an existence, independent of our perceptions or linguistic constructions.

It's not an argument in favour of a particular belief that such a belief provides a useful basis for constructive action in the world. There may (or may not) be a real world 'out there' but the fact that belief in such a world gives meaning to social, or ecological, action is not a good reason to subscribe to it.[14]

A person who believes that reality either does not exist or is unknowable if it does may indeed come to the logical conclusion that it is, therefore, pointless to try to make the world a better place. Nevertheless, if the life of a family member were in danger, most of us would try to help that person rather than sitting around wondering if the individual in question actually exists, independently of thought, perception or language. Such philosophical musings have their place, but they should follow, not precede, whatever practical action seems necessary to save the situation in an immediate context.

Similarly – and this is the main point – in a world threatened by neo-fascism on the one hand and climate catastrophe on the other, it might reasonably be expected that intellectuals would make such political and ecological issues their immediate priority, and park for the moment the (admittedly very interesting) questions raised about what, if anything, we can ultimately know, or say, about the world.[15]

The point at this stage in history is not so much to understand the world; it is not even to change it for the better, but rather to save it from destruction.

Such pressing issues as the danger from the authoritarian Right and drastic climate change call into question the survival of our civilisation, if not of humanity itself. They are the matters, among others, that the movement for UBI attempts to address. Its impetus is underpinned by the determination of a group of academics, some of whose work we have touched on here. Such theorists took their social and political responsibilities seriously, even when – for much of the time – UBI was considered to be very much a fringe idea.

NEOLIBERALISM, MANAGERIALISM AND BUREAUCRACY

An issue relevant to the problem of academic isolationism described above is the pressure of neoliberalism on academics of all kinds. As Bregman points out, in academia 'everybody is too busy writing to read, too busy publishing to debate'.[16] The university – as well as schools, hospitals and media networks – has become like a factory. Quantity replaces quality.[17]

If the potential of radical thought has been undermined by institutionalisation, quietism and postmodernism, it has been undermined also by neoliberal managerialism. Under the pressure of neoliberal 'accountability', academics tend to spend their time writing papers that nobody reads, in order to tick the boxes that will help to get them the permanent jobs that no one enjoys doing once they have them. (Any time not spent on such research is devoted to paperwork, much of it focussed on assessing the teaching that no one has time to do, largely because of the paperwork.)

This is a problem for the world of work as a whole, of course, under the pressures of neoliberalism and the lore that is disseminated through MBA degrees.

A simple exercise in algebra will demonstrate the futility involved. If you have x hours to make widgets, and you have to spend y hours accounting for that activity, that means that you now have $x - y$ hours for widget production (resulting in fewer widgets, and/or widgets of lesser quality). Alternatively, you may now have to spend $x + y$ hours at work, which means more stress and – as a result – fewer widgets again, and/or widgets of lesser quality.

In the everyday world, managerialism and bureaucracy swamp our lives with form filling and box ticking. (The promised 'paperless office' as a result of the digital revolution has long been laughable.) As a result of the attempt to make work more efficient, the opposite actually happens. Capitalism in its present form does not, as is sometimes suggested, cut down on bureaucracy. Its tendency is actually to increase bureaucracy and decrease efficiency.

The great thinkers of the nineteenth century – people such as Schopenhauer, Mill, Darwin and Nietzsche – produced their work as a result of the spirit of intellectual enquiry. Such individuals were, often, untrammelled by entanglement in academic professionalism or managerial goal-setting. One of the potential benefits that UBI holds out is that it may help to make such commitment possible for future thinkers, scholars and theorists, by giving them economic security and a basis for survival. It would thereby assist in freeing writers and thinkers from the constraints of the academic bureaucratic machine, a machine that – as in so many other areas – stifles that which it is supposed to foster.

UBI may also help to make complex ideas more readily accessible to the public, since the tendency for academics to form an isolated élite, speaking to each other and to no one else, might thereby be lessened.

The misnamed 'neoliberalism' (it is neither new nor liberal) permeates every aspect of our lives, in the supposed service of making systems run more efficiently. With its mania for quantification, it not only swells the ranks of a professional managerial class but more insidiously, it turns everyone into a part-time bureaucrat or accountant, taking up large swathes of our time and sapping our creative energy.

It is no longer enough to struggle with your university studies: you first have to burden yourself with debt.

In terms of health, and in countries without a proper national health system, you have to negotiate complex health insurance products, amid the bewildering multitude of similar-seeming offers. (That is, assuming you are able to afford the right health insurance plan in the first place.) If you get a serious health problem, you have to worry not only about the problem but about the details of insurance coverage as well.

The complexities of planning for such an event as retirement daunt even seasoned accountants.

When we go shopping, we are everywhere beset with offers of 'loyalty cards'. Even ordering a cup of coffee can turn into a major exercise in introspection and communication. More 'choice' in our society often equals less freedom.

Everywhere, there is the pressure to waste time. When we use a computer or switch on a smart phone, we are constantly nagged about updates and 'apps'. The proliferation of information and the passwords (and various security devices) that protect it swamp us with layers upon layers of burdensome complexity.

Technology may have become an extension of the human nervous system, but at least the pre-industrial writer with a quill pen did not need periodically to go into his/her brain to make some adjustment in order to continue their work. As with so many other things, what starts out as a liberatory prospect ends up entangling us in its chains.

Admittedly, this is an issue with technology rather than neoliberal managerialism *per se*, but the latter has seamlessly interfaced with technology to ensure that there is no time when we can actually 'switch off' work, and escape from the endless demands of texts and phone calls, or from the Augean stable of the email 'in' tray. (The longer you ignore it, the more there will be to deal with, when you finally have to.)

On the Internet, we need to employ time-consuming, labyrinthine, and possibly futile methods to preserve some remnants of privacy from the prying gaze of corporations, the state, or some future totalitarian version of the latter. More immediately, uninhibited party pictures taken by a young person and posted on Facebook may, years later, ruin his/her career chances. And increasingly, we need to take care that some chance remark on Twitter about the private life of the King of Ruritania may not come back to haunt us the next time we try to cross the Ruritanian border.

The artist Andy Warhol famously prophesised that 'in the future, everyone will be famous for fifteen minutes'. On the contrary, in the future the longing of many people may be to be forgotten. That longing, however, is one that it may be impossible to fulfil.

In the previous century, novels such as Zamyatin's *We* and Orwell's *Nineteen Eighty-Four* warned people of this pressure towards a totalitarian surveillance society, but it seems as if the complexities of technology, the interests of corporations, and the tendency towards total knowledge and control by the corporate state have exhausted any efforts people might otherwise make to resist this tendency.[18]

In the neoliberal state, bureaucracy is externalised. In our ultra-capitalist society, life for the ordinary individual becomes more bureaucratic, rather than less. Contrary to Rightist claims, the bewildering complexities of the income tax system are not – or not merely – a function of a domineering state.

They are, largely, due to the fact that the capitalist system will not accept the idea of alternative forms of taxation (such as, for example, land tax, resource tax, energy tax, wealth tax or transaction tax, that might lift the burden of accountancy off individual citizens). The notion of a radically different financial system is equally anathema.

Corporations, as a consequence, spend much time and energy negotiating complex exceptions and allowances for themselves. This, in turn, makes the tax code more and more complicated and burdensome for the ordinary businessperson, or citizen, just as it provides a lucrative source of employment for lawyers and accountants.

In the area of social welfare provision, something similar happens, under the pressure of an outmoded work ethic. We have seen, particularly in the UK, the growth of a surveillance and 'sanctions' culture. This culture has the effect of giving people too little to live on, on condition that they don't earn any more. At the same time, they are under constant pressure to demonstrate their availability for jobs that may not exist in the first place. It's hard to say whether this insanity is reflected better in the works of Kafka, or of Lewis Carroll.

UBI will not abolish all these negative features of our society, but it will be a step on the way towards a society which functions for the sake of its citizens, rather than the situation we have at the moment: citizens who function, by and large, for the sake of the corporate state.

One exception to the neoliberal stranglehold is, of course, the financial sector. It seems that the 'hands-on' approach by the state to the ordinary citizen is counterbalanced by a 'hands-off' approach to finance, as exemplified by the relative immunity of the financial sector after the crash of 2008, compared with the ravages of 'austerity' for ordinary people.

It can be something of a struggle to describe the system that seems to be taking over our societies. 'Plutosocialism' is one possible term (derived in part from the Greek term for 'wealth'): socialism for the rich, capitalism for everyone else.[19] The triumph of the billionaires that has transpired with the phenomenon of Trump's election seems to be as much a consolidation of this process as a reaction against it.

CAPITALISM, TECHNOLOGY AND THE STATE

To make matters even more complicated, it is true that some supporters of free-market capitalism, such as Peter Schiff,[20] are as outraged at (for example) bank bailouts as are (some) Leftists. From this perspective, there is an argument that state corporatism is not real capitalism at all, but a monstrous deformation thereof. Real capitalism, the argument goes, would involve much more freedom for everyone than does the present system.

Capitalism, though, can work only if people have money to buy the goods it produces. Stagnant or falling purchasing power militates against this.[21] Through poverty, unemployment and underemployment, technological development threatens to make it impossible for consumers to obtain the commodities that the system produces, simply because they won't have enough money to do so.

It is therefore likely, if not inevitable, that some form of UBI will appear at some stage in the relatively near future, if only to fill the gap in purchasing power that has developed over the last decades. The political imperative is to make that happen sooner rather than later, and in a way that favours the values of freedom, justice and solidarity – rather than those of domination, inequity and alienation.

The growing contradiction between the push to maximise employment on the one hand, and the interests of the environment on the other, will no doubt hasten this process. The need for UBI is as much environmental as it is social or economic in nature. By lessening the power of the work ethic, UBI potentially alleviates the pressure for 'job creation' at the expense of the environment. (At the time of writing, this pressure threatens to roll back, under the Trump regime, much of the progress that has been achieved in the US in recent years in terms of environmental protection.[22])

However, even with UBI there will be a crucial element of choice (in a positive sense), on the part of the individual citizen. We can use it either to develop our creative abilities and expand our cultural horizons, or else to become more deeply enmeshed in mindless consumerism. No one can be forced to be free.

It would, however, strain credulity to imagine that, once the advantages of UBI are thoroughly explained, institutions such as governments, bureaucracies and trade unions will rush to embrace it. There are logical reasons why such institutions may be less than enthusiastic about UBI. Some civil servants who administer current welfare systems may feel their jobs to be under threat, a situation that the unions that represent them may regard as a matter of concern.

Trade unions themselves may feel (wrongly) that UBI will weaken them by making jobs less important than they currently are. Trade unionists should remind themselves that, by strengthening the security of individual citizens, UBI makes it potentially easier for workers to stand up against exploitative employers.

Furthermore, the rationalisation that UBI will involve could free up civil servants to be more constructively helpful and proactive in maximising the welfare of the citizens who approach them for assistance – particularly those people with challenges such as specific mental or physical needs. Other civil servants could be usefully redeployed to swell the ranks of revenue officials involved in policing tax evasion.

This is in addition to the need to regulate more closely the aggressive forms of tax avoidance ('tax avoision' to use the ingenious neologism) that currently do so much to keep sections of our societies impoverished, and our services underresourced. In that way, the current situation of an overpoliced citizenry, combined with an underpoliced corporate sector, might be reversed, at least to an extent.

There are also, of course, less rational explanations for the resistance that UBI will probably meet. These include an unconscious 'fear of freedom' either for oneself or others. More freedom for the individual, for example, may involve increased leisure to consider the meaning of life. Such meditations may not always be pleasant, and much of our obsession with irrational 'busyness' and mindless consumerism may be due to an unconscious flight from the prospect of such existential considerations.[23]

Some people, who are deeply constrained at an unconscious psychological level, may also be envious of the possibility that others could obtain the freedom that they themselves do not understand, or desire – a freedom that they may (perhaps) deeply fear.

There is also, of course, the tendency for ideologies of one kind or another to outlive their usefulness: a work ethic that may have been functional for the capitalist system at one time might no longer fulfil its role, but may yet survive as an irrational, though unconscious, prejudice.

As we have seen with Weber's analysis of Calvinism and of its lingering effects, the ordinary person in the street is often the victim of some long-defunct theologian.

CAPITALISM, SOCIALISM AND VALUE SYSTEMS

There is a tension in our society between two opposite sets of values. On the one hand, we have the values pertaining to ethics and aesthetics: the pursuit of the general good, of freedom, justice and solidarity, of beauty and creativity. On the other, we have the values specific to economics: the creation and acquisition of wealth.

On the one hand, we have the humane values of generosity and unpretentiousness. On the other, we have the desire to acquire goods and to obtain wealth and status through self-aggrandisement. On the one hand, we have altruism and mutual aid, on the other, materialism and consumerism.

The tension in capitalism is between adherence to the notion of the 'invisible hand' of the market (the idea that individual selfishness results in the good of the society as a whole) and the values of selflessness and reciprocity, propagated in particular by religions of one kind or another.

There is often a conflict between these sets of values, though in our society it is often an unconscious one.

The latter values – whether consciously or unconsciously held – permeate our society to one extent or another. They may be summed up in the golden rule ('do as you would be done by') to which many in disparate cultures (though not all) adhere.

In some parts of the world, such values may act as a counterbalance to the values of capitalism itself – for example in northern Europe, where a (relatively) strong social-democratic mindset prevails.

However, this is not universally the case. For example, in the 'Bible belt' of the United States, with its inheritance (both psychological and economic) of slavery, there is little social-democratic sentiment to speak of. We might surmise that a society where the ethics, rather than the theology, of religion prevail (even at a largely unconscious level) tends to be more humane than one where theology outweighs social morality.

There is, then, an inherent tension between the values of capitalism and those of what might be termed 'reciprocity' – the desire to treat others as you would like to be treated, which forms the basis of our Western, Christian/secular society.[24]

Of course, without wealth creation, the values of ethics, morality and aesthetics would be irrelevant, since there would be no one around to pursue them.

However, wealth creation that ignores ethics and aesthetics is self-destructive. It is self-destructive in ecological terms (it wastes resources and destroys the environment) and, more specifically, also in economic terms: people don't, and increasingly won't, have enough money to buy the goods that the system produces. Without social justice, wealth creation is undermined as well.

The crucial priority is to get the balance right between the two sets of values: those of wealth creation on the one hand, and of reciprocity on the other. In the effort to pursue this, Western societies have striven for some kind of accommodation between capitalism and the state.

When the balance is weighted largely on one particular side – that of mutuality and sharing – this tends towards socialism. Socialism has its own, inherent kind of tension. On the one hand, you have a profession of the ideals of freedom and social justice. On the other hand, there is the notion that socialism (at least of the state variety) requires some form of (supposedly temporary) dictatorship, even in theory. In practice, state socialism has led to widespread forms of tyranny that are so familiar that we don't need to rehearse them in any detail.

When the balance is weighted towards the capitalist side, you have the contradiction between private wealth creation on the one hand, and on the other the cultural beliefs (stressing the value of altruism, charity and sharing) that otherwise permeate the society, often in uneasy tension with the economic mindset that prevails as part of the capitalist system.

One of the things that crosses the various divides, whether they be those of Left versus Right, nationalist versus internationalist, growth versus de-growth, is the question whether the individual should think primarily in terms of the totality to which he/she belongs, or primarily in terms of his/her own interests.

This is an issue not only for those who belong to a Christian (or 'post-Christian' secular) tradition. There is an argument that opposition to self-centred thinking is the basis of the majority of the moral teachings of humanity, whether implicit or explicit: from Confucius and Buddha to Moses and Marx (with notable exceptions such as Nietzsche and Ayn Rand).

Of course, regardless of our stated views, we are all prisoners of self-centred thinking, to one extent or another. For example, an individual might take a considerable risk to save the life of a family member, but be less inclined to do so to save a stranger – still less an anonymous stranger in a far-distant country. We may even prefer to save the life of someone close to us rather than the lives of two (or more) people whom we don't know, if faced with an 'either/or' choice on the matter.

Thought experiments based on these kinds of dilemmas can be the source of lively philosophical debate, but they have the merit of exposing the fact that we are often more self-centred than we believe ourselves to be.

The issue is not confined to the human sphere. We may be in favour of animal rights, but perhaps more so for those animals who share our attributes of emotion and intelligence, or possess the quality of 'cuteness', than for others that do not. Most people prefer dogs and horses to crocodiles and snakes, while baby seals attract more compassion than do laboratory rats – though the rat may be subject to no less stress and suffering than the seal. (Beauty gives – undeserved, or presumably undeserved – advantages to animals, just as it does to humans.)

Nevertheless, despite these kinds of implicit (and often unconscious) hierarchies that we apply, the ideal of giving the same kind of consideration to others that we do to ourselves is an important one – and not just in regard to humans, but to animals and nature as well.[25]

From the point of view of wealth distribution, a society where UBI exists is one that maximises for others those opportunities that we would want for ourselves. To the extent that it stretches beyond the limits of national borders, UBI potentially strengthens further the value of reciprocity that underpins our civilisation.

This value is currently under attack from all sides, from neoliberalism to religious intolerance to neo-fascism. Such opposition to the value of reciprocity includes not just elements of the Right, but also of the institutional, liberal Left that has succumbed so catastrophically in recent times to the priorities of corporatism and the military-industrial complex.[26]

In recent decades we have seen rampant, out-of-control, futile foreign adventurism that benefits only the élite, and tends to cause mayhem where it operates. This has needlessly stirred up resentment in the Middle East, a factor that in turn causes terrorist chaos in the West, consequently feeding into the growth of the far-Right in Europe and elsewhere. The pressure of immigration to the West from Middle-Eastern trouble spots, and from Africa through the failed state of Libya, is a considerable factor as well. The result is a threat to the stability of our institutions, including the EU itself.

To put it in a nutshell, various forms of authoritarianism and high-handed interference in other people's lives – whether from Left, Right or the political centre – seem to comprise much of the underlying problem.

An important way to undermine these forms of authoritarianism is through the enhancement of freedom itself. Politically, this may call for a tactical alliance among freedom lovers across the political spectrum. One of the things that may unite them is a commitment to UBI.

Of course, UBI will not guarantee happiness, any more than wealth itself does. Nevertheless, as any wealthy person will tell you, it's better to be rich and unhappy than poor and unhappy.

Of course, UBI will not of itself make anyone rich, nor should it. It will, however, provide the basis on which individuals can pursue wealth, either of the material kind, or – perhaps more valuably in the long term – of culture, creativity and the human spirit.

CRYSTAL BALL GAZING

Let us take a moment to look into the future, and ignore for the moment the most pessimistic scenarios (for example runaway global warming and/ or a resurgence of totalitarianism). It's possible to discern some signs in the present that point to positive future directions our societies may take, in socioeconomic terms.

In the financial sphere, Bitcoin and digital currencies promise to make it easy to conduct transactions free of the threat of bank bail-ins (the situation where the depositor's funds are at risk if the bank goes pear-shaped). Digital currencies may also function as a means of paying UBI, free from the vagaries of the banking system.[27]

At the same time, information, the basis of the new economy, struggles to be free. Information is currently in a straitjacket. Outdated copyright laws make life absurdly difficult for many creative people, in particular for creators of films, videos or music. Information may want to be free, but capitalism/corporatism doesn't want that to happen.

One solution to this is 'Creative Commons', which offers copyright agreements proposed as being more suited to the digital age than are traditional legal provisions.[28]

There is a growing sense of absurdity about treating immaterial forms of wealth as property or commodities, in the same way that we might treat a sack of potatoes. (If I have a potato and I give it to you, I don't have any potatoes left. On the other hand, if I have an idea and I give it to you, I still have the idea.) The growth of online piracy indicates that it will become increasingly problematic to police this area.

At the moment, it's difficult to envisage what kind of society might develop in practice. A burgeoning 'gift economy' already represents the mindset of people for whom creative cooperation and the public good outweigh personal gain. (Wikipedia is perhaps the most notable example, though there are many others.)

Many people, particularly the most highly gifted and creative, are just not that interested in acquiring a lot of wealth, at least for its own sake. When they do, some of them spend the rest of their lives giving it away, having discovered that there is more lasting satisfaction – not to mention peer esteem and public approval – in helping to make the world a better place than in a lifestyle devoted to yachts, luxury hotels and parties for a select few.

If information is the basis of the new economy, and it becomes increasingly difficult to treat it as a commodity, that may, indeed, call in question the future of capitalism itself.

We could conceive of a future society without copyright laws or similar legal restrictions, where the 'gift economy' flourished and people created work for the sake of it. In such a society, people would work for the creative 'buzz' and peer esteem involved, rather than for the material rewards.

In our own society, of course, the 'gift economy' already flourishes to some extent, particularly among creative people working in the digital sphere. A society where such an economy predominated would be a completely different society from that which exists at present. It would be weirdly ironic if we ended up with the kind of society to which social-ists have traditionally aspired, without having to go through the stage of socialism at all.

Digital technology may open up the possibility of such a society, but it will not of itself bring it about. It is, of course, equally conceivable that we could end up with a nightmare world of total visibility and regimen-tation, with the abolition of privacy that digital technology threatens to bring about, where there is no escape from the all-seeing eye of the corporate state. Such a state would not need camps or barbed wire to contain the population: the whole of society would be a concentration camp.

The crucial question is what we do with the technology: whether we employ it in the service of oppression on the one hand, or of enhanced freedom on the other.

Children are the one section of our society whose lives are free from money, at least for a short time. They inhabit, if they are fortunate, a blissful 'pre-capitalist' world where their needs are supplied and they are free to play and dream as they wish. Of course, such a world is short-lived and artificial, and depends to a great extent on the financial wellbeing of their parents, or guardians. Nevertheless, it does give a glimpse of what a future society might look like, when the pressures of wealth acquisition are alleviated, if not removed entirely.

Of course, the serpent soon enters this Edenic juvenile state, in the form of paid chores, pocket money, and the constant need for mobile-phone credit. Nevertheless, for a short time many children enjoy a wonderful world of freedom where they experience reality primarily in aesthetic terms, in terms of awe and of play – free to a large extent from the constant tug of the 'performance' and 'reality' principles, or the endless need to pursue money for present comfort or future security.

Indeed, this freedom is soon blighted for most children by a regimented school system, and the realisation that, in our society, you have to knuckle down in the present to get what you want in the future. (Whether that future ever materialises is another matter.) The performance principle and the reality principle win out in the end, usually stifling creative freedom before it has a chance to develop.[29]

Nevertheless, remembrances of those childhood days when the sun always seemed to shine survive for many of us – and may indeed help to illuminate one possible future for us all, adults included.

It would, however, be overly sanguine to imagine that a society free of the impositions of capitalism or the state will come about any time soon. This is despite the pressures and tensions to which both will become (increasingly) subject, combined with the tendency, in some quarters at least, to the development of a 'post-materialist' and 'post-productivist' mindset.

The recipe for investor success is, supposedly, to be fearful when others are greedy, and greedy when others are fearful. The number of people who are motivated primarily by fear and greed is not going to diminish at any time soon. Private ownership and control of the means of production, distribution and exchange will not magically vanish, nor will the mindset that the system so assiduously propagates – even among those who benefit least from it, if they benefit at all.

Nevertheless, we can at least hope that the severe tensions and stresses that our society is going through may give way, if only in the long term, to a utopia that – since our present system is not an option – may be the only alternative to dystopia itself.

UBI may, then, be just one step on the long, hard road to an alternative future. No one can say for how long UBI will last, once instituted. Will we even have money in a hundred years? Already, there is serious discussion of a 'cashless' society.[30] (Such a society, where physical cash has been abolished and all transactions are made through the banking system, obviously threatens to give much more power and control to the banks and the state than they have at present, to the detriment of the ordinary citizen.[31])

If we do retain money in the future, the question arises whether it should be under the control of banks, the state, or some alternative structure independent of both.

Electronic developments promise to ease border controls. (This is particularly relevant given the possibility of a 'hard' border on the island of Ireland post-Brexit, with the political dislocation that it potentially threatens). At the same time as the external borders of the EU come under unprecedented pressure – as the indirect result of disruptive military adventurism by the West in North Africa[32] and in the Middle East – nationalists of various hues want to put up the barriers again.

The future role of the state is as uncertain as is the future of capitalism itself. Will we get a breakdown of borders in the interests of international solidarity, or (under the pressure of new forms of nationalism, ethnic exclusivity and protectionism) a reinstatement of the nation states that many had thought had been superseded?

In an Irish context, the nightmare is that of a 'hard border' across the island of Ireland once again, with all the renewed divisiveness which would probably ensue – not to mention greatly increased bureaucracy for businesspeople and ordinary citizens alike. Brexit as a whole seems to promise the triumph of bureaucracy, restriction, small-minded thinking and cultural limitation – surely a major step backwards for a modern state like Britain to take.

At the time of writing, a resurgence of European nationalism seems likely, in parallel with similar phenomena in the UK and the US. The dangers of a Europe of competing nation states don't need to be emphasised – they are familiar enough from recent history, not just in terms of the Second World War but from the more recent wars in the Balkans as well.

Ideally, there should be a lively public discussion about issues such as federation versus confederation in a European context.

Similarly, there should surely be public discussions of issues such as what, exactly, is going to happen when (not if) recreational drugs are legalised and the corporations move in to control their supply and their advertising; of how we can avoid the slide towards a form of global surveillance tyranny; of the need to look at alternatives (such as sortition for example)[33] to political systems that may be outmoded; of the priority of looking for a third (ecological) choice, perhaps based on bioregions, instead of the old dichotomy of globalisation/nationalism – and so on.

Instead, we have populations fixated on 'celebs', soap operas and spectator sports of various kinds. Some of this is a result of deliberate deflection on the part of the media and the culture industry; some of it is just the way the system operates; and some of it is down to mental laziness on the part of many people – for which they are, to some extent at least, accountable in a moral sense. (In other words, it's not all the fault of the 'system'.)

It can only be hoped that UBI – by facilitating a society where freedom becomes more of a thinkable alternative, together with the growth of free association and debate – will help to awaken us from the dreams of mass culture and consumerism, before it's too late. The crisis of contemporary capitalism may become the opportunity for utopia in the long term – or at least the avoidance of dystopia, which may ultimately be the same thing. But we cannot sit back and wait for this to come about. We need to help make it happen.

At this point it's time to sum up.

The money currently wasted on obstructive bureaucracy, destructive military adventurism, bank bailouts and corporate welfare is really our money. It is we who deserve it, not the politicians, bureaucrats, militarists, financiers and CEOs who have caused so many of our problems. This is one major argument for UBI.

The justification for UBI also includes the fact that jobs are unequally distributed, just as wealth is. Much vital work, including the care of children, is currently unremunerated. The resources of nature originally belonged to no one (or to everyone, depending on how you look at it).

Wealth-creating technology is, to a great extent, part of the common cultural inheritance of humanity, so that everyone deserves a share, not just a small section of the population, or those who were fortunate enough to obtain a well-paying job.

There is also the issue of compensation for the injustice of present-day exploitation and colonialism, as well as for past events such as slavery, land clearances, enclosure and expropriation that continue to affect us in the present, in ways that are impossible to quantify.

All of the above are good reasons for the institution of UBI from the point of view of morality and social justice, and they may well feed in to political pressure for UBI in years to come.

But there is also a more compelling reason for UBI, from the point of view of the capitalist system itself. That reason may be equally, or more, persuasive in a political sense than are the many moral arguments that have been put forward from the point of view of freedom, justice, solidarity and related values. It is simply the fact that if you make goods, and there is no one to buy your goods, you will go out of business. If that happens across the board, the market ceases to exist.

What the result of that would look like is impossible to say. It would probably result in financial collapse and anarchy, followed by a tyranny of extreme Left or Right (or of some weird combination of the two, which is also thinkable). Given modern weapon technology and the surveillance techniques at the disposal of the modern state, such a situation could be one of unimaginable horror.

Such a development is in nobody's interest, except for a small number of demagogues at either political extreme. (Though it is not even in their interests in an ultimate sense, since the pursuit of power over others is a destructive, and self-destructive, illusion.)

For the reasons set out above, UBI is not only highly desirable but also, probably, inevitable. It's up to those of us who believe in liberty, equality and fraternity (or, putting it another way, in freedom, justice and solidarity) to make UBI come about in a way that benefits society as a whole, rather than merely a small section of society.

In a society with UBI, the citizen will have a choice between being a lazy couch potato on the one hand, or a vibrant, creative individual on the other. What we make of the opportunities that an economic basis provides is up to us. But at least, with UBI, we will have the freedom to make that kind of choice.

NOTES

Introduction

1   See, for example, John Downing, 'Fianna Fail to Promise Every Citizen €188 per Week', *Independent.ie*, 28 December 2015, http://www.independent.ie/ irish-news/politics/fianna-fil-to-promise-every-citizen-188-every-week-34317330. html. In a UK context see Jeremy Warner, 'Paying All UK Citizens £155 a Week May Be an Idea Whose Time has Come', *Telegraph*, 8 December 2015, http:// www.telegraph.co.uk/finance/economics/12037623/Paying-all-UK-citizens-155-a-week-may-be-an-idea-whose-time-has-come.html; Jonny West, 'SCOTLAND: Scottish National Party Conference Calls for Universal Basic Income', *BIEN: Basic Income Earth Network*, 29 March 2016, http://basicincome.org/news/2016/03/ scotland-conference-members-call-for-universal-income/; Heather Stewart and Jessica Elgot, 'Jeremy Corbyn to Investigate Idea of Universal Basic Income', *Guardian*, 14 September 2016, https://www.theguardian.com/politics/2016/ sep/14/jeremy-corbyn-to-launch-review-into-universal-basic-income.

2   To some extent, this focus on 'silos' or independent lines of enquiry is inevitable. There is, for example, a case for looking at the implications of sociology for physics, in the sense that the search for scientific truth (or its application) may be affected by issues of money, status, 'groupthink' and the like. There is less of a case for the application of, for example, the Everett (or 'many worlds') interpretation of quantum mechanics to sociology. A physicist who subscribed to the notion of multiple dimensions (or indeed to its competitor, the Copenhagen Interpretation) might be regarded as orthodox. A sociologist who

emphasised the relevance of either interpretation for his/her discipline, would be regarded as unorthodox, to say the least.

3   This is (supposedly) the case in the UK and UK-influenced countries. In the US it is said to be the opposite: you learn less and less about more and more until eventually you end up knowing nothing about everything. A (related) cynical observation is that the great thing about a PhD – if you get that far – is that the job you wouldn't get with it would be a lot better than the one you wouldn't have got if you didn't have it. Cynicism apart, it does seem as if the traditional supervisor-student PhD 'model' in the humanities in the UK is coming under increased pressure from the US model, where you have panels of supervisors and mandatory coursework as part of the project (no doubt, in most cases, an improvement on the older, one-to-one model).

4   George Orwell, *Politics and the English Language* (London: Penguin Books, 2013).

5   I have a problem with the term 'neoliberalism' since it comes across as rather anodyne, connoting – incorrectly – both novelty and freedom. However, I occasionally use it, in the absence of a workable alternative.

6   Thanks to Josh Cole for drawing my attention to this concept.

7   'Capitalism' is a complex term and difficult to define, or even to specify with any historical exactitude. Streeck defines it as a modern or 'progressive' system that aims at limitless prosperity, whose reproduction is a spin-off of the search for individual maximisation of profit. In capitalism, the labour process joins private capital with labour power that has been turned into an object to be bought and sold. Capitalism promises to turn private vices into public benefits – a promise that it can no longer keep. Wolfgang Streeck, 'How Will Capitalism End?' *New Left Review 2*, no.87 (May/June 2014), pp.35–64.

8   A contemporary variant of historical materialism might be termed political determinism. To take the example of Western foreign policy vis-à-vis the Middle East, the overestimation of the explanatory power of politics, and the underestimation of 'ideological' factors such as religion, have had catastrophic consequences, when people simply refuse to behave in ways that their 'liberators' expect.

9   The most influential critique of Marx was Karl Popper, *The Open Society and Its Enemies* (London: Routledge, 1966).

10   Anyone who wants to situate him/herself on the Left-Right spectrum might ask the question whether, if he/she were a political representative at the time of the French Revolution, they would be sitting to the right or to the left of the President in the French National Assembly. The vast majority of people nowadays would, presumably, choose the latter.

11   See for example, Edmund Burke, *Reflections on the Revolution in France, and on the Proceedings in Certain Societies in London Relative to that Event*, ed. and introd. Conor Cruise O'Brien (Harmondsworth: Penguin, 1969). See also Friedrich A. von Hayek, *The Road to Serfdom* (London: Routledge, 2001).

12   The figures sometimes disguise the reality. A US employee who formerly worked

at a highly paid job in a factory and now works stacking shelves in a supermarket is still counted among the 'employed', though his/her situation is radically different from before.

13 'Nobody 'Stealing' Your Jobs, You Spend Too Much on Wars, Alibaba founder tells US', *RT*, January 2017, https://www.rt.com/business/374289-alibaba-us-jobs-military/#.WIG87KQq9IY.facebook.

14 The fact that a form of UBI exists, and flourishes, in Alaska may be a riposte to the notion that it is necessarily a Leftist idea. Alaska, whatever else it may be, is not a hotbed of socialism. APFC: Alaska Permanent Fund Corporation, http://www.apfc.org/home/Content/aboutFund/aboutPermFund.cfm.

1: Universal Basic Income

1 Tim Bradshaw, 'Driverless Cars: When Robots Rule the World', *Financial Times*, 4 May 2016, https://next.ft.com/content/0f8e6b60-0bdf-11e6-b0f1-61f222853ff3. See also John Howe, 'Prototype Boulevard', *New Left Review*, Second Series, no.82 (July/August 2013), pp.85–96.

2 Matt Egan, 'Robots Threaten These 8 Jobs', *Financial Times*, 14 May 2015, money.cnn.com/2015/05/13/news/economy/robots-threaten-jobs-unemployment/?iid=EL.

3 Sarah O'Connor, 'How to Robot-proof Your Children's Careers', *Financial Times*, 16 April 2016, https://next.ft.com/content/0c7906d6-be89-11e5-9fdb-87b8d15baec2. For a comprehensive survey of how technology could undermine the labour market, see Martin Ford, *Rise of the Robots: Technology and the Threat of Mass Unemployment* (UK: Oneworld, 2015), and Jerry Kaplan, *Humans Need Not Apply: A Guide to Wealth and Work in the Age of Artificial Intelligence* (Yale University Press, 2015).

4 Or, even more chillingly, the enslavement of humans by machines as foreseen in the film *The Matrix*.

5 See David Levy, *Love and Sex with Robots: The Evolution of Human-Robot Relationships* (New York: Harper, 2007).

6 Ford, *The Rise of the Robots*, pp.26, 27.

7 Ibid., p.52.

8 Ibid., p.79.

9 Ibid., p.83.

10 Ibid., p.117.

11 Ibid., pp.118–119.

12 Ibid., pp.133–149.

13 Ibid., pp.151–168.

14 Ibid., p.170.

15 Ibid., pp.256–274.

16 'Bank of England's Andy Haldane Warns Smart Machines Could Take 15 Million

UK jobs and 80 Million in the US', *Robotenomics: Tracking the Evolution of Robots*, https://robotenomics.com/2015/11/12/bank-of-englands-andy-haldane-warns-smart-machines-could-take-15-million-uk-jobs-and-80-million-in-the-us/.

17   'Bring on the robots but reboot our societies too', *FT Weekend*, 7–8 May 2016, p.10.

18   The account of UBI in this chapter (as referenced where relevant) draws on the website of Basic Income Ireland, http://www.basicincomeireland.com, to which the author contributed with others over a number of years. Daniel Raventós defines UBI as an income paid to every member of society, regardless of their desire for paid work, their financial circumstances, or their domestic arrangements. Daniel Raventós, *Basic Income: The Material Conditions of Freedom*, trans. Julie Wark (London: Pluto, 2007), p.8.

19   Philippe Van Parijs, probably the most notable present-day advocate of UBI, argues that, in principle, UBI can be set at less (as well as more) than whatever level is regarded as enough to fulfil an individual's basic necessities. Philippe Van Parijs, 'Competing Justifications of Basic Income', in Philippe van Parijs, *Arguing for Basic Income: Ethical Foundations for a Radical Reform* (London/New York: Verso, 1992), p.4.

20   An Roinn Coimirce Sóisialaí, Department of Social Protection, Intreo, http://www.welfare.ie/en/Pages/273_Child-Benefit.aspx.

21   What 'everyone' means is a key issue. Should UBI be confined to citizens, or residents, or people who are tax-resident, or have been for a number of years? There might then be legal issues to work out (for example with regard to EU law). Can you receive UBI if you are a recent immigrant, or in prison, or a citizen living abroad? (Perhaps on a Greek island, as one author points out in a critique of the UBI idea – see Brian Barry, 'Equality Yes, Basic Income No', in Philippe Van Parijs, *Arguing for Basic Income*, p.132.) As in so many things, the devil is in the detail. It should be pointed out, though, that many of these issues also arise in the context of current social welfare payments. (An apparently persuasive argument against paying UBI to all residents is that it would attract large numbers of immigrants who would be happy for the state to pay them to sit around watching TV, playing video games and/or smoking dope. This issue is dealt with later.)

22   Eric Morath, 'Jobs Return to Peak, but Quality Lags', *Wall Street Journal*, 9 June 2014, http://www.wsj.com/articles/u-s-adds-217-000-jobs-unemployment-rate-steady-at-6-3-1402058042.

23   See Guy Standing, *The Precariat: The New Dangerous Class* (London: Bloomsbury, 2011).

24   See Naomi Klein, *This Changes Everything: Capitalism vs the Climate* (UK: Penguin/Random House, 2015).

25   See Standing, *The Precariat*, p.250. The propagation of workfare arguably involves more of an issue around authoritarianism than a Left/Right split, though most of those who promote the idea of workfare are probably on the Right. A

note here about definitions: by 'Left' I mean a political position that supports high taxes and high state expenditure. By 'Right' I mean the opposite. (This is, of course, to follow the terms of contemporary popular discourse rather than the complexities of academic debate.) For an attempt – with some limitations – to go beyond the traditional 'Left/Right' dichotomy as an explanatory method, see https://www.politicalcompass.org/analysis2. The argument here is that, in order to understand how society and politics work, we need to think in terms of the distinction between authoritarianism and libertarianism, in addition to that between Left and Right. The traditional, one-dimensional Left-Right axis is, consequently, expanded into two dimensions. One could imagine its further expansion into three dimensions if the (Green-influenced) 'growth-degrowth' dichotomy were introduced. (Though at that point the model becomes rather unwieldy; and it could become even more so, since any further dichotomies – for example nationalism versus supra-nationalism, in the context of debates around the EU for instance – would expand it into hyperspace.)

26   See Anna Coote, 'Help to Work? Britain's Jobless Are Being Forced Into Workfare, More Like', *Guardian*, 28 April 2014, http://www.theguardian.com/commentisfree/2014/apr/28/help-to-work-britains-jobless-forced-workfare-unemployed.

27   Christopher S. Rugaber and Josh Boak, 'Wealth Gap: A Guide To What It Is, Why It Matters', *Excite News*, 27 January 2011, http://apnews.excite.com/article/20140127/DABJ40P00.html. See also Thomas Piketty, *Capital in the Twenty-First Century*, trans. Arthur Goldhammer (Cambridge, MA: Harvard University Press, 2014). Ford points out (*The Rise of the Robots*, p.192) that in 2012, the top 5 per cent of US households reckoned by income engaged in 38 per cent of consumer spending, as compared to 27 per cent in 1992. At the same time, the share of spending by the bottom 80 per cent fell from around 47 per cent to 39 per cent: see Nelson D. Schwartz, 'The Middle Class is Steadily Eroding: Just Ask the Business World', *New York Times*, 2 February 2014, https://www.nytimes.com/2014/02/03/business/the-middle-class-is-steadily-eroding-just-ask-the-business-world.html?_r=0.

28   Angela Monahan, 'US Wealth Inequality: Top 0.1% Worth as Much as the Bottom 90%', https://www.theguardian.com/business/2014/nov/13/us-wealth-inequality-top-01-worth-as-much-as-the-bottom-90. See also Victor Tan Chen, 'All Hollowed Out: The Lonely Poverty of America's White Working Class', 16 January 2016, http://www.theatlantic.com/business/archive/2016/01/white-working-class-poverty/424341/.

29   Standing, *The Precariat*, p.6.

30   Ibid., p.10. Standing (p.15) also distinguishes the notion of the 'precariat' from the Marxian concept of the '*lumpenproletariat*'. (The latter literally means the 'ragged' or – supposedly – unrespectable section of the proletariat.)

31   Ibid., p.20. Standing identifies the historical precursors of the precariat as the *banausoi* of ancient Greece, required to do productive social labour and

socially restricted. With the *metics* (alien craftsmen), and slaves, they did all the necessary work. Citizens did not do necessary work but indulged in *schole* (leisure) and *praxis* (home-based work).

32   Ibid., p.33.

33   Ibid., p.60.

34   Barry O'Rourke, 'No Country for Young Teachers: The Two-Tier Pay Problem', *The Irish Times*, 1 March 2016, http://www.irishtimes.com/news/education/no-country-for-young-teachers-the-two-tier-pay-problem-1.2548352.

35   Standing, *The Precariat*, pp.6, 63, 72, 98, 112-113, 242.

36   Ibid., pp.115–135.

37   Kate Holmquist and Sorcha Pollak, 'All Work and No Pay: Why Ireland's Interns Are Tired of Working for Free', 19 April 2014, *The Irish Times*, http://www.irishtimes.com/life-and-style/people/all-work-and-no-pay-why-ireland-s-interns-are-tired-of-working-for-free-1.1766646. On the issue of precarity (in a German context), see, for instance, Wanda Vrasti, 'Working in Prenzlau', *New Left Review*, Second Series, no.101 (September – October 2016), pp.49–61. For a critique of the concept of precarity from a Left perspective, see Francesco Di Bernardo, 'The Impossibility of Precarity', *Radical Philosophy*, no.198 (July-August 2016), pp.7–14.

38   See Erich Fromm, *To Have or To Be?* As Fromm points out (p.32) some languages don't actually have a word for 'having' or 'to have'. (As it happens, Irish is one of them: perhaps one of the arguments for the continuing usefulness of the Irish language is that it offers an alternative linguistic perspective to that of neoliberalism, or indeed to that of corporatism.)

39   P.D. Anthony, *The Ideology of Work* (London: Tavistock, 1977), p.264.

40   A. Fox, *A Sociology of Work in Industry* (London: Collier Macmillan, 1971), p.68, quoted in Anthony, *The Ideology of Work*, p.264. For a brief critique of GDP as a measuring device, see Bregman, *Utopia for Realists*, pp.162–170.

41   Hannah Arendt, *The Human Condition*, second edition, (Chicago and London: The University of Chicago Press), p.133.

42   For some light on the issue see Anthony, *The Ideology of Work*, and Peter Fleming, *The Mythology of Work: How Capitalism Persists Despite Itself* (London: Pluto, 2015).

43   The key reference for this discussion is the *1844 Manuscripts* of Karl Marx. See Karl Marx, *Economic and Philosophical Manuscripts (1844), in Early Writings*, trans. Rodney Livingstone and Gregor Benton (Harmondsworth/London: Penguin/New Left Review, 1975), pp.279–400 (in particular the section on 'Estranged Labour', pp.322–334). The terminology Marx uses is varied and difficult. For those who read German, the original can be consulted online at Karl Marx, 'Entfremdete Arbeit', Erstes Manuskript, *Oekonomisch-philosophische Manuskripte aus dem Jahre 1844*, *The Marxists Archive*, https://www.marxists.org/deutsch/archiv/marx-engels/1844/oek-phil/1-4_frem.htm. The young Marx (he was in his mid-twenties) describes the situation of alienation/estrangement of labour, characterised by the division of labour and the split between the owners of property on the one hand, and workers without property on the

other. The worker is alienated from the product of labour and from the external world; from the act of production; from nature; and from the individual's species being; and each individual is alienated from the others. The worker's life activity becomes a mere means for the worker's existence. (I have tried to avoid sexist pronouns in the foregoing account but it's a minefield. The translation cited uses masculine pronouns 'he', 'his', and so on as Marx does not dwell on specific forms of alienation that may be experienced by female workers. It might have changed the argument to a considerable extent had he done so.) As a consequence of the situation described by Marx, personal fulfilment is replaced by acquisition and the sense of having (pp.352, 361). Money becomes a 'pimp' that mediates between the individual and others (p.375). A number of questions arise from his analysis. If I am physically deprived of the product of my labour, does that mean that my activity is thereby psychologically unfulfilling? Conversely, even if I'm producing directly for myself or for the community, might I not at the same time feel a sense of non-fulfilment for other reasons (for example existential angst, or an unhappy love affair)? Is it possible to have a society where 'necessary' work is at the same time fulfilling? Or should we not organise society to keep necessary work to a minimum, and thus expand the sphere of freedom? And how might that be done without installing a self-perpetuating bureaucracy? Who would clean the drains, or do other kinds of unpleasant work, without political or economic coercion? (That is to leave aside the possibility that in future all such work – or virtually all of it – could be done by machines.) Presumably – in whatever kind of society it is envisaged would replace the present one – such necessary work as remained for humans to do would have to be made attractive enough in an economic sense. The key question is whether, from Marx's perspective, the basic requirement is the 'disalienation' or 'redemption' of necessary labour, to turn it into some kind of fulfilling activity; or whether such labour is always to be regarded as a necessary evil, to be rationalised in the interest of freedom and what we call 'leisure'. Marx is not very clear on this, though in his later writings he seems to come down on the side of the latter position. In the third volume of *Capital* he points out that the true 'realm of freedom' begins where the realm of necessity ends, though the former can develop only on the basis of the latter: Karl Marx, *Capital: A Critique of Political Economy* Vol.3, Frederick Engels (ed.) (London: Lawrence and Wishart, 1959), p.820. Earlier than that, though, Marx and Engels pointed out that in the current system an individual cannot escape from a narrow area of activity, while in a communist system 'society regulates the general activity' allowing an individual to hunt, fish, rear cattle or engage in criticism, without ever confining themselves to one activity: Karl Marx and Frederick Engels, 'The German Ideology', in *On Historical Materialism: A Collection*, comp. T. Borodulina (Moscow: Progress; 1972), p.33. Questions that might arise here regarding the benevolence (or otherwise) of the regulatory power of society are ignored (not to mention the interests of the animals involved). Leaving those matters aside, it does appear that Marx and Engels assume some kind of future leisure-maximising society on the basis of the rational organisation of necessary work. However, the primary purpose is not to discover what Marx (and/or Engels) 'really' meant (assuming that it's possible to find the answer or that such a pursuit would be a meaningful one) but how their insights (whatever the internal tensions may be) are of use in our contemporary situation. See also, for example, Arendt, *The Human Condition*, pp.87, 118, 128, 130. For an interesting sideline on the issue see Anthony, 'Anarchists and Syndicalists', in *The Ideology of Work*, pp.96–112. Lenin tried to develop a material basis for communism through the introduction of 'Taylorism' (involving, no doubt paradoxically from a Marxist point of view, the extreme intensification of alienation). In our own day, it seems that China is trying to do something similar by outdoing the capitalists at their own game. Whether a command economy can combine successfully with capitalist enterprise remains to be seen – it is certainly an ongoing socioeconomic experiment with high stakes for both China and the world as a whole. (In regard to the notion of 'disalienation' or fulfilling work, there are parallels in the notion of 'flow' in the work of Mihály Csíkszentmihályi, and 'autonomy' in the writings of André Gorz.)

44 See Daniel Raventós, 'The Poor Cannot be Free', in *Basic Income*, pp.107–109.

45 Nicola Fifield, 'Household Chores to be Given Economic Value', *Telegraph*, 16 November 2014, http://www.telegraph.co.uk/news/uknews/11234123/Household-chores-to-be-given-economic-value.html.

46 David Graeber, 'On the Phenomenon of Bullshit Jobs', 17 August 2013, STRIKE! http://www.strikemag.org/bullshit-jobs.

47 This is a result of a number of factors: the pressures of bureaucratisation and time-wasting 'accountability', commodification, overwhelming pressure of student numbers, the distractions of digital technology and a widespread attention deficit that it causes among people of school-leaving age, inappropriate course choices by students (and consequent disengagement) as a result of financial pressure to get well-paying jobs that may be unsuited to their abilities, the replacement of collegiality by a provider–customer relationship, and financial cutbacks. (On the 'commodification' of education and associated issues see Standing, pp.115–126.) For a US perspective on this area see Jennifer Washburne, *University Inc: The Corporate Corruption of American Higher Education* (New York: Basic Books, 2005). (See also the chapter 'Division and Demoralisation' in Anthony, *The Ideology of Work*, pp.146–166.)

48 There is an argument in favour of 'employment' as a goal in itself, i.e. that the worker finds a sense of community among workmates that he/she would not otherwise enjoy. There is some persuasiveness in this, though it perhaps says something about the deficiencies of our atomised home and social lives, that we would prefer paid unfreedom to the freedom to live as we please. The valuation of 'employment' does, however, conflict with the notion of retirement as something desirable. If paid work (whether office or factory work or whatever) is so great, why would anyone ever want to retire? This seems

to be an ideological fudge of industrial society: we are supposed to want to spend our time doing something we have to be paid for in order to do it, yet we are also supposed to be glad to retire at the end of our term of (voluntary or involuntary) servitude. The ideological complexities of the work ethic achieve their ultimate apotheosis in the ghastly irony of the sign at the entrance to Nazi concentration camps: '*Arbeit Macht Frei*' – perhaps the defining slogan of the twentieth century. (Work, presented as freedom, is actually bondage.) Despite its ostensible endorsement of work as an end in itself, fascism based its own rejection of the work ethic (in favour of the values of domination and militarism) on human slavery (see Anthony, p.187).

49 Consequently, there can be a surprising overlap between positive neoliberal attitudes to immigration (which increases the labour pool in the host country) on the one hand, and Leftist approval of immigration on the other – albeit the latter generally arises from humane and internationalist rather than profit-maximising attitudes. The consequences of the failure of the Left to address the problems of the indigenous working class (often blamed on immigration, whether legitimately so or otherwise) may be seen all around us, from Trump in the US to Brexit in the UK, and in the rise of the far-Right in Europe.

50 Lynn Stuart Parramore, 'Why a Medieval Peasant Got More Vacation Time Than You', http://blogs.reuters.com/great-debate/2013/08/29/why-a-medieval-peasant-got-more-vacation-time-than-you/.

51 Anthony Giddens, 'Introduction' to Max Weber, *The Protestant Ethic and the Spirit of Capitalism,* trans. Talcott Parsons, (London: Routledge, 2001), pp.x–xiii. Weber's analysis, though extremely influential, has been the subject of criticism: for example that he misinterpreted Protestantism (and Catholicism); that his empirical studies were flawed; that he drew too sharp a contrast between modern capitalism and preceding forms; that his notion of the relation between Puritanism and capitalism was deficient, and so on (Giddens, pp.xxi–xxiv).

52 Weber, *The Protestant Ethic and the Spirit of Capitalism*, p.67.

53 Ibid., p.69.

54 Ibid., p.104.

55 Ibid., p.116.

56 This is true not just of Protestant countries but of many Catholic countries or regions as well, not to mention countries in East Asia which have been latecomers to capitalism.

57 The term 'fetishism' which Marx applies to commodities could also, in another sense, be applied to work itself. Guy Standing (p.282) calls for an end to the fetishism of jobs. The term 'fetishism' has a rich and diverse history in the writings of (e.g.) Marx and Freud. (See, for example, 'The Fetishism of Commodities and the Secret Thereof' in Volume 1 of Marx's *Capital*, pp.76–87.) 'Fetishism' has the sense of attaching an undeserved importance to something. Ironically, the fetishism or idolatry of work could be seen as being in breach of the first of the Ten Commandments, which forbids idolatry. Intriguingly, though paradoxically, Anthony (p.45) traces the socialist as well as the capitalist ideology

of work to the Protestant ethic. The work ethic probably also has gender implications, in that 'masculine' work in the formal economy has traditionally been valued more highly than 'feminine' work in the home. The fact that, without a socialised workforce (able to talk, tie its shoelaces and use the toilet), the economy would fall apart, is quietly ignored.

58　See Erich Fromm, *Fear of Freedom* (London: Routledge, 2001).

59　Weber, in *The Protestant Ethic and the Spirit of Capitalism* (p.124), notes that in the United States the secularised search for wealth can actually give it the character of a sport.

60　Of course, even activities traditionally described as 'labour' may on occasion be enjoyable: a person working in an office all day may enjoy chopping wood for the fire on a weekend, but in that case something that would otherwise be regarded as labour is transformed into work, or even leisure. Standing (p.201) notes the traditional distinction made by the ancient Greeks between labour, work, play and leisure.

61　Arendt, *The Human Condition*, p.48. Arendt points out (p.80) that, for example, the French language distinguishes between *travailler* and *ouvrer*, and German between *arbeiten* and *werken*. Only the equivalents for 'labour' have resonances of pain and difficulty. She notes (p.126) that the ideals of the human being as the maker of the world have been given up for the goal of abundance. For Arendt (p.127) the artist is the only worker we have in a society of labour. However, elsewhere she points to the phenomenon of workers who prefer certain forms of labour because they are mechanical and allow them some mental freedom. The early Christians similarly justified manual labour, in that it was seen as allowing mental space for contemplation (p.146). Arendt, in a passage which seems to go against the main theme of her argument, writes that 'the blessing of labor' in close association with nature lies in the fact that satisfaction follows effort, consumption follows production (p.106–107): labour can actually be a good thing. One might even, from one perspective, say the same about alienated labour itself, in that the very boredom and repetitiveness of the activity can leave the mind free for daydreaming. See R. Fraser (ed.), *Work* (Harmondsworth: Penguin, 1968), quoted in Anthony, *The Ideology of Work*, p.275.

62　Arendt, *The Human Condition*, p.83.

63　Anthony, *The Ideology of Work*, pp.16–17. Anthony references Aristotle, *Politics* (London: Dent, 1912), 1328b. Anthony (p.17) notes that, for Aristotle, work obstructs the citizen by wasting his time and inhibiting his personal development (the gendered pronoun is inevitable here – citizens in ancient Greece were male and women were largely invisible). Referring to A.W. Zimmern, *The Greek Commonwealth* (London: Oxford University Press, 1915), p.270, Anthony (p.19) notes though that the Greeks did not despise work but subordinated it to the pursuit of such values as beauty and happiness: work for the Greeks was not an end in itself.

64 On this see Oscar Wilde, *The Soul of Man Under Socialism*, https://www. marxists.org/reference/archive/wilde-oscar/soul-man/.

65 Whether this would need some form of socialism to bring it about, or whether it could happen under capitalism (or some variant of capitalism), is an important question. The difficulties are familiar enough. The problem with (state) socialism is that it needs bureaucrats and functionaries to administer it, and such individuals are notoriously averse to freedom (at least for others). The problem with capitalism, as it currently exists at any rate, is that it needs a certain amount of unemployment to maintain the demand for employment and help keep wages down: too few potential workers means pressure to raise wages.

66 Arendt, *The Human Condition*, p.5.

67 See Bregman, *Utopia for Realists*, pp.38–41.

68 The ideal is sometimes held to be the integration of play with work: the example of the artist may be cited in this regard. My own experience of the activities of artist friends is that they take their work much more seriously than that, though it's admittedly difficult to detach their activity from the society of economic rationality and profit-maximisation in which they operate: it can be hard to discern the 'utopian' possibility through the fog of everyday actuality. And some progressive multinationals incorporate the play principle in their workers' environment. Whether non-alienated work could or should incorporate the play principle is a matter of debate. Perhaps we need to understand that both work and leisure (to the latter of which our concept of play is largely relegated) are fragmented and distorted in our society, so that the understanding of what a society would look like where the division had been transcended is difficult to achieve. On the issue of play and the aesthetic dimension see, e.g., Herbert Marcuse, *Eros and Civilisation: A Philosophical Inquiry into Freud* (Boston: Beacon, 1976); Herbert Marcuse, *The Aesthetic Dimension: Toward a Critique of Marxist Aesthetics*, translated and revised by Herbert Marcuse and Erica Sherover (London: Macmillan: 1979) and Friedrich Schiller, *On the Aesthetic Education of Man*. translated by Reginald Snell (New York: Dover, 2004).

69 Max Horkheimer and Theodor Adorno, 'The Culture Industry', in *Dialectic of Enlightenment: Philosophical Fragments*, Gunzelin Schmid Noerr (ed.), Edmond Jephcott (trans.) (Stanford, CA: Stanford University Press, 2002), pp.94–136.

70 This is not to deny the advantages of digital technology in terms of, for example, enhanced connectivity and access to information. Though, on the downside of the Internet, see e.g. Nicholas Carr, *The Shallows: What the Internet is Doing to our Brains* (New York: Norton, 2011).

71 Standing, p.108.

72 Raventós, *Basic Income*, pp.21–22, 37.

73 Carol Pateman, 'Democratizing Citizenship: Some Advantages of a Basic Income', in B. Ackerman, A., Alstott and P. Van Parijs (eds), *Redesigning Distribution* (London/New York: Verso. 2006) p.115, quoted in Raventós, *Basic Income*, p.70.

74   Raventós, *Basic Income*, pp.70–71.
75   Eric Olin Wright, 'Unconditional Basic Income', interview by C.S. Soong, *Against the Grain*, 94.1 KPFA, radio podcast, April 5, 2016, https://kpfa.org/player/?audio=227954. Writings of Eric Olin Wright may be accessed from his website at https://www.ssc.wisc.edu/~wright/.
76   The phrase used by Marx (and others) 'From each according to his abilities, to each according to his needs' sums up the aspiration of a post-capitalist society as envisaged from a nineteenth-century perspective. The phrase raises the question of how necessary work could be extracted from workers without economic or some other form of coercion, which would inevitably involve a diminution of freedom. (Even in capitalist society, people are normally free not to work if they wish, though without independent means they might starve as a result.) In regard to need fulfilment, UBI satisfies that requirement without a socialist system of organisation. Insofar as it is sufficient for a frugal existence, UBI supplies everyone's needs through a universal financial provision – with the exception of people facing physical or mental challenges, who would have to be provided for separately.
77   See Andrew Clark, Yannis Georgellis and Peter Stanley, 'Scarring: The Psychological Impact of Past Unemployment', January 1999, http://ftp.kent.ac.uk/pub/ejr/RePEc/ukc/ukcedp/9903.pdf.
78   So, for example, UBI means that it is potentially easier for an employer to dismiss an employee who is performing unsatisfactorily: the increased security that UBI involves means that employment-protection laws would be less needed. It also means, however, that it's easier for an employee to leave their job if it doesn't suit them, since they have their UBI on which to fall back. Freedom is increased for both employer and employee – a win-win situation. UBI also deals with the problem of 'unintended consequences' (what the Germans call '*Verschlimmbesserung*'), whereby something that is intended to make a situation better actually makes it worse. An example is a law to ensure the permanence and pensionability of part-time workers, which has the (unintended) effect of encouraging employers to get rid of such workers, or to attempt to limit their contracts so that they don't qualify under the law in question. UBI reduces the pressure for such (often self-defeating) legislation. (Current social welfare unemployment provisions, which help to keep people unemployed through poverty traps, are another negative example.)
79   Peter Schiff, 'Minimum Wage, Maximum Stupidity', YouTube video, 24:50, *The Peter Schiff Show podcast*, 27 April 2015, https://www.youtube.com/watch?v=9LYOnQ9E2yg.
80   This is linked to the question of whether UBI favours economic growth. In one way it does, by removing obstacles in the way of a worker finding employment, and consequently contributes to economic growth. In another it does not, since it gives the worker the option to choose leisure over employment, and consequently may militate against economic growth, at least as traditionally

measured. See Van Parijs, *Competing Justifications for Basic Income*, p.28.

81   UBI also has a somewhat paradoxical effect in regard to the Green aspiration of a low-growth (or no-growth, or de-growth) economy. Because it lessens the pressure to obtain employment, it might be seen as diminishing the impetus to growth. On the other hand, insofar as it facilitates people who want to work (but can't under the current system) it might be seen as contributing to the growth imperative. However, if we reinterpret 'growth' to mean growth in things that are desirable (or at least not harmful), this changes the perspective. See Richard Norman, 'Equality, Needs and Basic Income', in Philippe Van Parijs (ed.), *Arguing for Basic Income* (Verso, 1992), p.150. See also, for example, Richard Douthwaite, *The Growth Illusion* (Dublin: Lilliput, 1992). On current issues around the measurement of GDP or Gross Domestic Product, see 'The Modern Economy: How to Measure Prosperity', and 'Measuring Economies: The Trouble with GDP', *The Economist*, 30 April – 6 May 2016, pp.7, 21–24. See also William D. Nordhaus, 'Why Growth Will Fall', review of *American Growth: The US Standard of Living Since the Civil War*, by Robert J. Gordon, *The New York Review of Books* (18 August –28 September 2016), pp.64–68; and 'The Trouble with GDP', *The Economist*, 13 April 2016, pp.21–24. On some issues around growth and global warming, see John Burnside, 'Turning off the Planet's Air Con: What Melting Sea Ice Means for the Future of the Earth', review of *A Farewell to Ice* by Peter Wadhams, *New Statesman* (30 September – 6 October 2016), pp.54–55.

82   There is an obvious question as to whether UBI would encourage or discourage class politics (in the traditional sense). The answer is, probably, that it would do both. By making things easier for workers and the unemployed, it potentially lessens some of their indignation and thereby has the effect of reinforcing capitalism. On the other hand, by giving them more leisure and security, it increases their ability to organise (for example in favour of higher wages, better social services, cooperative and alternative forms of economic activity, greater redistribution of wealth, the socialisation of key industries, an end to bank bailouts, or indeed the abolition, transformation or transcendence of capitalism itself) and therefore could be advocated from a Left perspective. This issue illustrates the fact that UBI tends to go beyond the traditional 'Left/ Right' split. Instead, it invokes the dichotomy between freedom and authority (libertarian/authoritarian) in favour of freedom. From an anarchist point of view, UBI has the paradoxical effect of relying on the state for its implementation, yet reducing the power of the state over individuals' lives. Anarchists of a reformist inclination might then support UBI – as indeed might neoliberal proponents of the 'minimal' state, a position elaborated in Robert Nozick's *Anarchy, State, and Utopia* (New York: Basic Books, 1977). On the other hand, hardline anarchists might oppose UBI insofar as it seems to entrench the state at least in one of its aspects – its redistributive role – though it reduces its influence in others. It is conceivable that dyed-in-the-wool anarchists and communists alike could have a serious issue with UBI, insofar as it might take the wind of indignation out of

the sails of opponents of the state and of the capitalist system – though on the other hand, as stated above, it increases their ability to organise against those institutions, if they wish to do so. (From a Left-wing perspective, UBI could indeed form a very useful 'strike fund' for workers in dispute with management. See Raventós, *Basic Income*, p.74.)

83 Whether the economies of the West (the paradigm being the US economy) can accurately be described as capitalist any more is a moot point. With corporations increasingly enmeshed in the state, cooperating with the state and even dictating its operations through international trade agreements (though such agreements may be problematised by the Trump phenomenon) perhaps 'corporatism' would be a more accurate term.

84 Basic Income Ireland, http://www.basicincomeireland.com/if-you-are-employed. html. Examples of bureaucracy, often due to a bewildering and impenetrable legal maze, abound. See Saoirse Brady, 'Want to Appeal a Social Welfare Decision? Be Warned: It's a Bureaucratic Maze', 30 October 2012, *TheJournal. ie*, http://www.thejournal.ie/readme/appeal-social-welfare-decision-flac-650760-Oct2012/.

85 Basic Income Ireland, http://www.basicincomeireland.com/if-you-are-employed. html.

86 Basic Income Ireland, http://www.basicincomeireland.com/if-you-are-self-employed-or-trying-to-start-a-business.html.

87 Standing points out (p.137) that when the US introduced its state pension scheme in 1935, the retirement age was 65 and average life expectancy was 62. Life expectancy is now 78. Furthermore, in this context, the mind-blowing 'science fictional' possibilities opening up for radical, and perhaps even indefinite, extension of the human lifespan have also been noted: see Steve Johnson, '"Curing Death" Will Create a Vast Pensions Crisis', *FTFM, Financial Times*, 30 May 2016, p.8.

88 Raventós, *Basic Income*, pp.111–112.

89 Arendt, *The Human Condition*, p.40.

90 Raventós, *Basic Income*, pp.112–115.

91 Ibid., pp.119–120.

92 Ibid., p.125.

93 Ibid., pp.128–130.

94 Arguments against public health systems as 'inefficient' often collapse (even in their own terms) when you look at the details. For example, private health insurance can be, in practice, many orders of magnitude more time wasting and bureaucratic for the consumer than its public counterpart. Contrary to frequent capitalist objections, it is a merit of the bureaucratic state that it sometimes has the ability to keep the bureaucracy to itself (as, for example, with state health systems). The downside is when it imposes bureaucracy on the citizens, forcing us to become amateur (and unpaid) accountants.

95 In a US context, Ralph Nader argues for a tactical alliance of progressives and

conservatives/libertarians (on key shared issues such as opposition to bank bailouts, foreign policy interventionism, and the 'war on drugs') in his somewhat optimistically entitled book *Unstoppable: The Emerging Left-Right Alliance to Dismantle the Corporate State* (New York: Nation Books, 2014).

96   Basic Income Ireland, http://www.basicincomeireland.com/if-you-are-young. html.

97   Jillian Berman, *MarketWatch*, 'America's Growing Student-Loan-Debt-Crisis', 19 January 2016, http://www.marketwatch.com/story/americas-growing-student-loan-debt-crisis-2016-01-15.

98   'How much does it cost to study in the UK?' *Top Universities: Worldwide University Rankings, Guides and Events*, Thursday 2 April 2015, http://www.topuniversities.com/student-info/student-finance/how-much-does-it-cost-study-uk.

99   Basic Income Ireland, http://www.basicincomeireland.com/if-you-are-young. html.

100 Basic Income Ireland, http://www.basicincomeireland.com/if-you-care-for -others.html.

101 Though if global warming continues at its present pace, one could imagine the future prospect of underwater tours of Venice.

102 There are some enlightened exceptions, such as the tax exemption for artists that currently exists in Ireland. See *Revenue: Irish Tax and Customs*, http://www.revenue.ie/en/tax/it/reliefs/artists-exemption.html.

103 Basic Income Ireland http://www.basicincomeireland.com/if-you-do-artistic-or-creative-work.html.

104 Paul Mason, *Postcapitalism: A Guide to Our Future* (UK: Allen Lane/Penguin, 2015).

105 Marx (*Capital*, vol.3, p.820), in opposition to the tendencies of many of his 'workerist' followers, believed that the shortening of the working day was the fundamental requirement for the establishment of the realm of freedom, where the development of human energy as a goal in itself could begin. On the (historical) socialist romanticisation of work and its bizarre apotheosis in Stakhanovism, see Anthony, pp.197–198.

106 On the issue of surveillance, the key text is Michel Foucault, *Discipline and Punish: The Birth of the Prison*, trans. Alan Sheridan (Harmondsworth: Penguin, 1979). On the general issue of the dominance of visuality and its critique, see Martin Jay, *Downcast Eyes: The Denigration of Visuality in Twentieth Century French Thought* (Berkeley: University of California Press, 1993).

107 Edgar Manjarin and Maciej Szlinder argue that UBI would improve the bargaining position of workers: 'A Marxist Argumentative Scheme on Basic Income and Wage Share in an Anti-capitalist Agenda', *Basic Income Studies*, 11, no.1 (June 2016), pp.49–59, https://www.degruyter.com/view/j/bis.2016.11.issue-1/bis-2016-0010/bis-2016-0010.xml?format=INT.

2: A Brief History of Basic Income Proposals

1　See, for example, Michael Hardt and Antonio Negri, *Empire* (Cambridge, Mass: Harvard University Press, 2000), p.403; 'Noam Chomsky on Basic Income', YouTube video, 1:55, Kölner Initiative Grundeinkommen e. V., posted by M. Molli, 2 May 2015, https://www.youtube.com/watch?v=Wyjazv90nYs (Chomsky's support as outlined here is somewhat nuanced, but on balance he favours the idea); Naomi Klein, *This Changes Everything: Capitalism Versus the Climate* (UK: Penguin/Random House, 2015), p.26, 461; 'Interview with Yannis Varoufakis', *The Economist*, 31 May 2016, http://www.economist.com/ESDvaroufakis; Paul Mason, *PostCapitalism: A Guide to Our Future* (UK: Penguin/Random House, 2015), pp.284–286; Slavoj Žižek, *Living in the End Times* (London: Verso/New Left Books, 2011), pp.233–143. In a German context and from a different political perspective, the author Thilo Sarrazin also discusses the UBI concept in his controversial book *Deutschland Schafft sich ab: Wie Wir Unser Land aufs Spiel Setzen* (Germany: DVA, 2010), pp.140–147.

2　Žižek, *Living in the End Times*, p. 233.

3　See, for example, Ford, *The Rise of the Robots.*

4　See, for example, Jeremy Warner, 'Paying All UK Citizens £155 a Week may be an Idea Whose Time has Come', 8 December 2015, *Telegraph*, http://www.telegraph.co.uk/finance/economics/12037623/Paying-all-UK-citizens-155-a-week-may-be-an-idea-whose-time-has-come.html; Jon Stone, 'Scrap Benefits System and Bring in Universal "Citizens Wage" Basic Income for Everyone, Think-tank Recommends', 17 December 2015, *Independent*, http://www.independent.co.uk/news/uk/politics/replace-the-benefits-system-with-a-universal-basic-income-paid-to-all-citizens-think-tank-recommends-a6777101.html; Gleb Tsipursky, 'Free Money is not so Funny Anymore: Confessions of a (Former) Skeptic of Basic Income', 21 August 2016, *Salon*, http://www.salon.com/2016/08/21/free-money-is-not-so-funny-anymore-confessions-of-a-former-skeptic-of-basic-income/; Nathan Schneider, 'Why the Tech Elite Is Getting Behind Universal Basic Income', 6 January 2015, *Vice,* https://www.vice.com/en_us/article/something-for-everyone-0000546-v22n1. For a critical perspective of the notion of UBI, see David H. Freedman, 'Basic Income: A Sellout of the American Dream', 13 June 2016, *MIT Technology Review*, https://www.technologyreview.com/s/601499/basic-income-a-sellout-of-the-american-dream/.

5　Steven Shafarman, 'A Brief History of Basic Income Ideas', Unconditional Basic Income Europe, http://basicincome-europe.org/ubie/brief-history-basic-income-ideas/, This site also mentions figures such as Juliet Rhys, Philip Wogaman, Leonard M. Greene, Jeffrey Smith and Gary Flo (the Geonomy Society), Robley E. George, Alfred F. Andersen, Allan Sheahen, Theresa Funiciello, Robert Schutz, Bruce Ackerman and Anne Alstott, and Stevan Shafarman.

6　The discussion here and in the following pages draws to a considerable extent on BIEN: Basic Income Earth Network, History of Basic Income, http://www.basicincome.org/basic-income/history/. The web version, edited and abridged by Simon Birnbaum and Karl Widerquist, is based on Chapter 1 of Yannick Vanderborght and Philippe Van Parijs, *L'Allocation Universelle* (Paris: La Découverte, 2005). (I have also made reference to the latter in this chapter.) For a comprehensive bibliography on UBI (on which I have relied to a great extent in the following material) see The US Basic Income Guarantee Network, BIG Bibliography, http://www.usbig.net/bibliography.php.

7   BIEN, *History of Basic Income*, Part 2, 'Basic Endowment: The Republicans Condorcet ... and Paine.'

8   Thomas Paine, 'Agrarian Justice'. *Rights of Man, Common Sense and Other Political Writings*, Mark Philp (ed.) (Oxford: Oxford University Press, 1995), pp.611, 612–613, quoted in BIEN, *History of Basic Income*, Part 2, 'Basic Endowment: The Republicans Condorcet ... and Paine'. See also Thomas Paine, 'Agrarian Justice', Digital edition 1999 by www.grundskyld.dk, http://piketty.pse.ens.fr/files/Paine1795.pdf. There is a critical elaboration of Paine's ideas in a pamphlet by the English radical Thomas Spence (1750–1814): Thomas Spence [1797], 'The Rights of Infants', in J. Cunliffe and G. Erreygers (eds), *The Origins of Universal Grants* (Basingstoke: Palgrave Macmillan, 2004), pp.81–91. See Vandegborght and Van Parijs, *L'Allocation Universelle*, 13.

9   'Jesus consecrated through his words the right, when one is hungry, to take one's necessities where they are to be found, and that right imposes on the social body the duty to assure to people a minimum of support: since civilization strips from them the first natural right, that of hunting, fishing, gathering, pasture, it must give them a compensation.' Charles Fourier, *La Fausse Industrie* [1867] (Paris: Anthropos, 1967), pp.491–492, quoted in BIEN, *History of Basic Income*, Part 3, 'Basic Income: The Utopian Socialists Charlier ... and Mill' (my translation). The reference is presumably to the passage (e.g. Mark 2: 23–28) where Jesus defends the actions of his followers in plucking the ears of corn from the cornfields, by pointing to a comparable historical action of the Old Testament figure David, and of those with him. However, it has to be admitted that if that is the case the point is a little tenuous: Jesus' main argument here seems to have been to defend, *contra* Jewish orthodoxy, the right to work on the Sabbath in the case of necessity, as distinct from urging the limitations of property rights (the latter is probably there, but if so it is subsidiary to the main point).

10   Philippe Van Parijs, 'Competing Justifications for Basic Income', in Philippe Van Parijs, *Arguing for Basic Income*, 9. See William Cobbett, *The Poor Man's Friend* (New York: Augustus M. Kelley, 1977); Samuel Read, *An Inquiry into the Natural Grounds of Rights to Vendible Property or Wealth* (Edinburgh, 1829); George Poulett Scrope, *Principles of Political Economy* (London: Longman, 1833); Robert Nozick, *Anarchy, State and Utopia* (New York: Basic Books, 1977).

11   Vanderborght and Van Parijs, *L'Allocation Universelle*, p. 12. See Hugo Grotius,

The Rights of War and Peace, Richard Tuck (ed. and introd.), from the edition by Jean Barbeyrac (Indianapolis: Liberty Fund, 2005), 3 vols, 6 July 2016, http://oll. libertyfund.org/titles/1877, and François Huet, *Le Règne Social du Christianisme* (Paris: Firmin Didot/Brussels: Decq, 1853).

12   BIEN, *History of Basic Income,* Part 3, 'Basic Income: The Utopian Socialists Charlier ... and Mill'. The references are to Joseph Charlier, *Solution du Problème Social ou Constitution Humanitaire* (Brussels: Chez Tous les Librairies du Royaume, 1848), and *La Question Sociale Résolue, Précédée du Testament Philosophique d'un Penseur* (Bruxelles: Weissenbruch, 1894). See also John Cunliffe and Guido Erreygers, 'The Enigmatic Legacy of Charles Fourier: Joseph Charlier and Basic Income', *History of Political Economy,* 33, no.3 (2001), pp.459–484. (The BIEN site notes the appeal to the equal ownership of natural resources reappearing in the later work of Herbert Spencer, Henry George, Léon Walras, and Hillel Steiner.)

13   Cited in BIEN, *History of Basic Income,* Part 3, 'Basic Income: The Utopian Socialists Charlier ... and Mill', J.S. Mill, *Principles of Political Economy* [2nd ed., 1849], (New York: Augustus Kelley, 1987), pp.212–214.

14   BIEN, *History of Basic Income in the 20th Century.*

15   BIEN, *History of Basic Income,* Part 4, 'Modest but Real: Alaska's Dividends.' This cites Michael Goldsmith, 'Universal Basic Income and the Future of Citizenship', paper presented at BIEN's sixth Congress, Vienna, 12–14 September 1996. On the Alaska Permanent Fund, see https://pfd.alaska.gov.

16   Quoted in BIEN, *History of Basic Income,* Part 1, 'From Militancy to Respectability: England Between the Wars', from Bertrand Russell, *Roads to Freedom: Socialism, Anarchism and Syndicalism* (London: Unwin Books, 1918), pp.80–81, 127.

17   BIEN, *History of Basic Income,* Part 1, 'From Militancy to Respectability: England between the Wars.' On aspects of the first public emergence of the UBI proposal (including Milner, Douglas, Meade and Cole), the BIEN site cites Walter Van Trier, 'Basisinkomen', in *De Sociale Zekerheid Verzekerd? Referaten van het 22st Vlaams Wetenschappelijk Economisch Congres,* Marc Despontin and Marc Jegers (ed.) (Brussels: VUB Press, 1995), pp.587–618. On Social Credit see, for example, C.H. Douglas, *Economic Democracy* (Epsom: Bloomfield Books, 1974), and C.H. Douglas, *Social Credit* (London: Eyre and Spottiswoode, 1933). For a vigorous (and well-written) political defence of Douglas and his ideas, see Eric de Maré, *A Matter of Life or Debt* (Australia: Veritas, 1986). For a more recent response, see Brent Ranalli, review of *Social Credit Economics,* by M. Oliver Haydorn, *Basic Income Studies* 10, no.2 (December 2015), pp.281–283, https:// www.degruyter.com/view/j/bis.2015.10.issue-2/bis-2015-0022/bis-2015-0022. xml?format=INT. For Milner's ideas see Dennis Milner, *Higher Production by a Bonus on National Output: A Proposal for a Minimum Income for All Varying with National Productivity* (London: George Allen & Unwin, 1920).

18   BIEN, *History of Basic Income,* Part 1, 'From Militancy to Respectability:

England between the Wars.' See James Meade, *Agathotopia: The Economics of Partnership* (Aberdeen: Aberdeen University Press, 1989).

19   BIEN, *History of Basic Income*, Part 1, 'From Militancy to Respectability: England between the Wars'.

20   Ford, *The Rise of the Robots*, pp.30–31. See also Brian Steensland, *The Failed Welfare Revolution: America's Struggle over Guaranteed Income Policy* (Princeton: Princeton University Press, 2011).

21   BIEN, *History of Basic Income*, Part 2, 'Short-lived Effervescence: The United States in the 1960s'. See Milton Friedman, *Capitalism and Freedom* (Chicago: University of Chicago Press, 1982), pp.191–194. On Friedman and negative income tax, see also the illuminating conversation between the Brazilian Left-wing economist and politician Eduardo Matarazzo Suplicy and Friedman in 'The Suplicy-Friedman Exchange', BIEN: The Basic Income Earth Network, *Newsflash* No.3 (May 2000), http://www.basicincome.org/bien.pdf/NewsFlash3.pdf. As pointed out in the introduction to the latter, the phrase 'negative income tax' originates with the French economist Augustine Cournot and was later used by the British economist Abba Lerner in his *Economics of Control* (New York, Macmillan, 1944). Lerner is described as 'the Milton Friedman of the left' in the entry 'Abba Ptachya Lerner (1905–1982)', in *The Concise Encyclopedia of Economics, Library of Economics and Liberty*, http://www.econlib.org/library/ Enc/bios/Lerner.htm. (The entry notes that Lerner was an 'unusual kind of socialist' who opposed the power of government.) Interestingly, Friedman in the interview does not draw a distinction between negative income tax and UBI, arguing that the latter is just another way of introducing the former. He makes the point that: 'A basic income of a thousand units with a 20 per cent rate on earned income is equivalent to a negative income tax with an exemption of five thousand units and a 20 per cent rate below and above five thousand units.' (There are also some illuminating remarks here about the Alaska Permanent Fund, from Friedman's perspective.) See also Joshua Preiss, 'Milton Friedman on Freedom and the Negative Income Tax', *Basic Income Studies* vol.11, issue 2 (December 2015), pp.169–191, https://www.degruyter.com/view/j/bis.2015.10. issue-2/bis-2015-0008/bis-2015-0008.xml?format=INT; Pertti Honkanen, 'Basic Income and Negative Income Tax: a Comparison with a Simulation Model', *Basic Income Studies*l, vol.9, issue 2 (December 2014), pp.119–135, https:// www.degruyter.com/view/j/bis.2014.9.issue-1-2/bis-2014-0009/bis-2014-0009. xml?format=INT. On comparable libertarian lines, for an argument for UBI based on a Hayek-influenced perspective – the maximisation of freedom within and outside the employment structure – see Matt Zwolinski, 'Why Did Hayek Support a Basic Income?' 23 December 2013, http://www.libertarianism.org/ columns/why-did-hayek-support-basic-income. However, while Hayek certainly did support the principle of a social support for the citizenry, I am not aware that he spelt out the issues (e.g. involving unconditionality, means testing and

so on) in any detail, and the extent to which his ideas differ from commonplace social democratic concepts remains open to debate. Hayek defined a 'minimum income for everyone' as a kind of floor affording protection from risks and adverse conditions: one does not have to fall below it even when self-provision is impossible. See Friedrich von Hayek, *Law, Legislation and Liberty*, Vol.3: *The Political Order of a Free People* (Chicago: University of Chicago Press, 1979), pp.54–55, quoted in Ford, *The Rise of the Robots*, pp.256–7. See also Friedrich von Hayek, *The Road to Serfdom* (London: Routledge, 2001).

22   BIEN, *History of Basic Income*, Part 2, 'Short-lived Effervescence: the United States in the 1960s'. See also 'The Suplicy-Tobin Exchange' in BIEN: The Basic Income European Network, Newsflash No.11, September 2001, http://www. basicincome.org/bien/pdf/NewsFlash11.pdf, an interview between Eduardo Matarazzo Suplicy and James Tobin.

23   BIEN, History of Basic Income, History of Basic Income in the Twentieth Century, Part 2, 'Short-lived Effervescence: the United States in the 1960s'.

24   Rutger Bregman, 'Nixon's Basic Income Plan: Why Richard Nixon Once Advocated for Basic Income – and then Turned Against It', *Jacobin: Reason in Revolt*, https://www.jacobinmag.com/2016/05/richard-nixon-ubi-basic-income-welfare/. See also Bregman, *Utopia for Realists*, pp.117–131.

25   Michel Foucault, *The Birth of Biopolitics: Lectures at the Collège de France 1978–1979*, Michel Senellart (ed.), Graham Burchell (trans) (New York: Palgrave Macmillan, 2008), pp.203–207. The book contains some useful footnotes with references for those interested in the history of UBI. For example, for a (very) technical contemporary French-language discussion of negative income tax, see Lionel Stoléru, 'Coût et Efficacité de l'Impôt Négatif', *Revue Économique*, Vol.25, no.5 (1974), pp.745–761, http://www.persee.fr/collection/reco.

26   James S. Albus, *People's Capitalism: The Economics of the Robot Revolution* (Maryland: New World Books, 1976); Stuart M. Speiser, *The USOP Handbook: A Guide to Designing Universal Share Ownership Plans for the United States and Great Britain* (New York: The Council on International and Public Affairs, 1986); Stuart M. Speiser, *Equitable Capitalism: Promoting Economic Opportunity Through Broader Capital Ownership* (New York: Apex Press, 1991).

27   BIEN, *History of Basic Income*, Part 3, 'New Departure: North-Western Europe in the 1980s', See N.I. Meyer, H. Petersen and V. Sorensen [1978], *Revolt from the Center* (London: Marion Boyars, 1981), and J.P. Kuiper, *Arbeid en Inkomen: Twee Plichten en Twee Rechten*, Sociaal Maandblad Arbeid 9, (1976), pp.503–512.

28   BIEN, *History of Basic Income*, Part 3, 'New Departure: North-Western Europe in the 1980s.' See T. Schmid (ed.), *Befreiung von Falscher Arbeit: Thesen zum Garantierten Mindesteinkommen* (Berlin: Wagenbach, 1984).

29   BIEN, *History of Basic Income*, Part 3, 'New Departure: North-Western Europe in the 1980s.' See for example André Gorz, trans. Malcolm Imrie, *Paths to Paradise: On the Liberation from Work* (London: Pluto, 1985).

30   Raymond Crotty, *Ireland in Crisis: A Study in Capitalist Colonial Undevelopment*

(Ireland: Brandon, 1986), p.128.

31 BIEN, *History of Basic Income*, Part 3, 'New Departure: North Western Europe in the 1980s'.

32 Raventós, *Basic Income*, pp.16–17.

33 See The US Basic Income Guarantee Net, http://www.usbig.net/whatisbig.php.

34 Basic Income Studies, http://www.degruyter.com/view/j/bis. This is probably the most relevant site for academics wishing to pursue further research, with reference to contemporary thought on various aspects of UBI. It is particularly useful for research on UBI in different geographical contexts. Abstracts of articles available may be consulted at this site.

35 See for example Seán Ward, 'A Basic Income System for Ireland', in Brigid Reynolds and Seán Healy (eds), *Towards an Adequate Income for All* (Dublin: CORI, 1994), pp.74–137. The website of Social Justice Ireland may be found at http://www.socialjustice.ie.

36 Basic Income Ireland, http://www.basicincomeireland.com.

37 Karl Widerquist, Yannick Vanderborght, José A. Naguera, and Jurgen De Wispelaare, 'Introduction: The Idea of an Unconditional Income for Everyone', in Karl Widerquist, Yannick Vanderborght, José A. Naguera, and Jurgen De Wispelaare (eds), *Basic Income: An Anthology of Contemporary Research* (UK: Wiley Blackwell, 2013), p.xx. This volume is the definitive collection of writings on UBI in book form, and is a valuable research resource for anyone seriously pursuing the area. Further references to this source will be abbreviated in these notes to *BIACR*. The reader is also referred to the journal *Basic Income Studies*, https://www.degruyter.com/view/j/bis, the foremost academic forum for discussion of issues around UBI.

38 The latter is politically ambiguous: the argument (expressed by the individual citizen through the ballot box) that the money would be better off in the citizen's pocket rather than being spent on war or unnecessary bureaucracy is one thing. The argument that I would rather the state give the money to me directly rather than spend it on health or education is quite another. From a Leftist perspective, this issue might be addressed by (e.g.) abolishing private healthcare, private health insurance and private education (at least at first and second level). It would consequently be in everyone's interest to have a good public system of health and education, and the population would then (presumably, but not inevitably) be willing to pay for it through the tax system at the expense of the level of UBI. There is admittedly a risk that UBI would exert pressure to cut back on positive as well as negative forms of state expenditure, though one could argue that such a risk is greatly outweighed by the manifold advantages of UBI to the citizenry as a whole. (See Michael Moore's film *Where to Invade Next?* on the issue of state versus private education, in a Finnish context.)

39 Whether, or to what extent, the most important dichotomy continues to be that of Left versus Right – rooted as the polarity is in the political tensions

of the time of the French Revolution – is a moot point. One could cite other important dichotomies: growth/degrowth (onto which might be mapped the dichotomy between ecological and economic perspectives); freedom versus authoritarianism; nationalism versus supranationalism; or even a putative alliance of conservatives and progressives, on the one hand, against the neo-feudalism of the contemporary corporate state on the other.

3: Freedom, Justice and Solidarity: The Philosophical Basis of UBI

1   David Graeber, *Debt: The First 5000 Years* (New York: Melville House, 2012), pp.94–102.
2   Style requirements can complicate this issue, but it can normally be taken that the theoretical literature referred to in this book refers to 'communism' in the ethically commendable sense, rather than in the sinister sense that the term 'Communism' has acquired.
3   I'm aware of the limitations of this in terms of discussions around animal rights. If we open up the concept of 'fraternity' to include the animal kingdom as well, it adds a whole new dimension to the discussion. See, in particular, Jacques Derrida, 'The Animal that Therefore I Am', *Critical Inquiry*, vol.28, no.2 (winter, 2002), pp.394–395.
4   See John Baker, *Arguing for Equality* (London: Verso, 1987), for a discussion of the concept. Baker (pp.3–5) argues for equality in terms of basic needs, equal respect, equality in terms of economics and politics, and sexual, racial, ethnic and religious equality. The discussion in this chapter draws on some of the arguments in Baker's book.
5   Keith Ansell-Pearson, introduction to *On the Genealogy of Morality*, by Friedrich Nietzsche, Keith Ansell-Pearson (ed.), Carol Diethe (trans.) (Cambridge: Cambridge University Press, 1994), pp.ix–xxiii.
6   Of course, if you believe in karma and reincarnation, or some form of conscious prenatal existence, you could argue that we did choose those circumstances in some way. But even if that were true, it probably shouldn't be the business of the state, since it's better for the state to stay out of affairs involving the supernatural.
7   Kitty Holland, 'Record Number of Dublin Families Became Homeless in January', *The Irish Times*, 26 February 2016, http://www.irishtimes.com/news/social-affairs/record-number-of-dublin-families-became-homeless-in-january-1.2544182.
8   The distinction has sometimes been made between 'natural' and social aristocracy. Natural aristocracy involves things such as good health, attractive looks, strength, creative talent, intelligence and so on. A poor, though highly attractive, individual may be the focus of all eyes as soon as he/she enters a room – whereas their billionaire counterpart may be effectively invisible, at least

to those ignorant of their wealth. (Though while wealth can be an effective social facilitator, a rich person never really knows what the motivations of their friends, or would-be friends, actually are.) Social aristocracy does not necessarily equate to the aristocracy of nature. Indeed, members of the social aristocracy may actually be disadvantaged through reproducing the acquisitive and anti-social traits of their ancestors (either through inheritance or environmental influence, or both). This is in addition to whatever negative genetic factors may have developed as a result of too close attention to maintaining the family bloodline. On the other hand, there is undoubtedly a certain interface between natural and social aristocracy: rich people have, on the whole, a greater choice in terms of pairing-off with attractive people of whatever social class, vis-à-vis those who are not rich. Thus, the distinction between natural and social aristocracy may be blurred to some extent. What a class society does, though, is to throw in material wealth as a factor where it would not otherwise exist in terms of choice of sexual partners, consequently skewing otherwise 'natural' reproductive tendencies within the society.

9 On the face of it, the issue might arise if a person practised no religion at all. However, in Northern Ireland, religious differences are so deeply ingrained that an atheist may be asked (semi-seriously) whether he/she is a Protestant atheist or a Catholic one. (Even today, such jocular remarks tend to be confined to people of a certain educational background – they are by no means risk-free.)

10 The best-known recent analysis of this situation is Thomas Piketty, *Capital in the Twenty-First Century*, trans. Arthur Goldhammer (Cambridge, MA: Harvard University Press, 2014). For an entertaining counterview to that of Piketty, see Peter Schiff, 'Piketty's Envy Problem', 29 May 2014, http://www.europac.com/commentaries/pikettys_envy_problem. See also *Basic Income Studies*, vol.10, no.1 (June 2015), https://www.degruyter.com/view/j/bis.2015.10.issue-1/issue-files/bis.2015.10.issue-1.xml, which has several articles discussing Piketty's *Capital in the Twenty-First Century*, in the context of discussions around UBI. For an Irish perspective on the inequality issue, see Carl O'Brien, 'Ireland at Risk of Reaching US Levels of Inequality, Says Study', *The Irish Times*, 16 February 2015, http://www.irishtimes.com/news/social-affairs/ireland-at-risk-of-reaching-us-levels-of-income-inequality-says-study-1.2105125.

11 Amanda Holpuch, 'Forty Millionaires Ask New York to Raise Taxes on Wealthy in '1% Plan for Fairness'', *The Guardian*, 21 March 2016, https://www.theguardian.com/us-news/2016/mar/21/40-millionaires-ask-new-york-raise-taxes-wealthy-1-percent-plan-fairness.

12 James Surowiecki, in *The Wisdom of Crowds: Why the Many Are Smarter than the Few* (London: Abacus, 2004), pp.112–116, describes a psychological experiment suggesting that, in the context of a game described, people would rather have nothing than let others get away with too much. This seems to illustrate a political point that is not often recognised. The argument about the need to redistribute wealth in the society is not simply that it would make poor people

richer, but that it would also defuse the social resentment that threatens to undermine our whole society. (And that is irrespective of whether or not such resentment is justified – in other words, it's a political point, not a moral one.)

13 See Baker, *Arguing for Equality*, p.52.

14 Bregman, *Utopia for Realists*, pp. 173–191.

15 I realise that it's easy for someone living in a relatively underpopulated country such as Ireland to be dismissive of British (or more specifically English) concerns regarding immigration. The pressure of population numbers is much greater in England than in Ireland. (This is altogether apart from cultural or ethnic issues that have been raised in regard to immigration, and which may indeed function as something of a substitute for a discussion of the issue of population numbers themselves, regardless of the ethnic or cultural make-up of the population.)

16 Damian Carrington, 'Fossil Fuels Subsidised by $10M a Minute, says IMF', *Guardian*, 18 May 2015, https://www.theguardian.com/environment/2015/may/18/fossil-fuel-companies-getting-10m-a-minute-in-subsidies-says-imf.

17 We could speculate that, if it were possible to distribute that money directly to everyone, it could give in the region of $716 per year to every man, woman and child on the planet (less administrative costs of course, and assuming a world population of 7.4 billion). For a family of five, that would be in the region of $3,600 per year. It would help to abolish world poverty, raise productivity and employment by increasing demand for goods and services, and curb population growth by facilitating education and reducing the pressure on poor families to have children as a form of pension fund.

18 Of course, something we naturally desire is not necessarily good – some people may naturally desire to punch someone in the face if they get annoyed, and we generally agree that such behaviour should be discouraged.

19 Even the Nazis, with horrible irony, wrote '*Arbeit Macht Frei*' or 'Work Makes [You] Free' over the gates of their concentration camps, in a cynical gesture to the universal desire for freedom.

20 Baker, *Arguing for Equality*, p.74.

21 ibid., p.107.

22 Hans A. Baer, 'Toward Democratic Eco-socialism as the Next World System', http://thenextsystem.org/wp-content/uploads/2016/04/HansBaer.pdf.

23 The issue of gun control is more complex than the visceral responses of both Right and Left on this issue might suggest. A coherent argument can be made that an armed population provides a potential defence against external invasion on the one hand, and internal oppression on the other. There is an argument, perhaps equally strong, that it leads to mayhem on the streets. (Perhaps the issue is not so much that of gun-possession, as the general level of civilisation in the society in question.)

24 According to one estimate, 1 per cent of the population of the US are psychopaths. Given a population of around 325 million, that equates to over three million. See William Harris, 'Psychopaths are not Neurally Equipped to have Concern for Others', *UChicagoNews*, 24 April 2013, https://news.uchicago.

edu/article/2013/04/24/psychopaths-are-not-neurally-equipped-have-concern-others.

25   Erich Fromm, 'The Psychological Aspects of the Guaranteed Income', in *BIACR* (1966), p.9. The issues around the biblical philosophy of work will be discussed later.

26   Philippe Van Parijs, *Real Freedom for All* (Oxford: Clarendon Press, 1995), pp.1, 5, 59, 19. Van Parijs (p.22) dismisses the distinction between 'freedom from' and 'freedom to' as illusory. Although he does not pursue the issue in this direction, a further consequence of 'real freedom for all' would, it appears, involve something like the argument of John Stuart Mill that it is not the business of the state to police the private behaviour of consenting adults. The latter position, which I advocate, would imply freedom not just to spend your day surfing if you so wish, but also to indulge in activities (including, e.g., recreational drug taking) which do not directly harm others. (Of course, no activity takes place in a vacuum, so the question of what 'direct harm' actually means is not a simple one.) The other side of the coin is the ability to enjoy freedom from coercion, for example in the form of mass medication (e.g. fluoridation of the water supply). It could be argued that the prohibition of recreational drugs on the one hand, and mass medication on the other, while apparently opposite phenomena, both derive from the same mindset: that of the 'nanny state' that knows what is best for its citizens. However, we should be aware that the failure, for so long, to take drug decriminalisation (or legalisation) seriously has left the door wide often for the corporate domination of the market for recreational drugs, and the potential for their further spread throughout society through advertising, product placement and so on. This issue needs to be addressed urgently, if indeed it is not already too late. There is no contradiction between maximising individual freedom and limiting corporate freedom. A corporation is not a person, no matter what legal fictions may assume. See Ralph Nader and Carl J. Mayer, Opinion, 'Corporations are Not Persons', *The New York Times*, 9 April 1988, http://www.nytimes.com/1988/04/09/opinion/corporations-are-not-persons.html.

27   Philippe Van Parijs, 'Why Surfers Should Be Fed: The Crazy-Lazy Challenge', *BIACR*, p.17.

28   Van Parijs, *Real Freedom for All*, p.22.

29   Ibid., p.33.

30   Ibid., p.90.

31   Ibid., p.109.

32   Ibid., p.123.

33   Van Parijs, 'Why Surfers Should Be Fed', *BIACR* p.21. See also p.18.

34   Philippe Van Parijs, 'A Basic Income for All', in Philippe Van Parijs et al, *What's Wrong With A Free Lunch?*, Joshua Cohen and Joel Rogers (eds) (Boston: Beacon Press, 2001), pp.25–26.

35   Van Parijs, *Real Freedom for All*, p.97.

36   Ibid., p.135. The reader who wishes to follow up Van Parijs's incisive though

complex arguments (for example with regard to the labour theory of value) is referred to Chapter 5 of *Real Freedom for All*, 'Exploitation versus Real Freedom'.

37 Ibid., pp.232-233.

38 Van Parijs, 'Competing Justifications of Basic Income', in Philippe van Parijs (ed.), *Arguing for Basic Income: Ethical Foundations for a Radical Reform* (London: Verso, 1992), pp.7, 17. See also Robert van der Veen and Philippe Van Parijs, 'A Capitalist Road to Communism', in *BIACR*, pp.52–54, and Robert van der Veen and Philippe Van Parijs, 'A Capitalist Road to Communism', *Theory and Society* 15, no.5 (1986), pp.635–655. For a recent discussion of this in a US context, see Aaron Major, 'Affording Utopia: The Economic Viability of 'A Capitalist Road to Communism'', *Basic Income Studies* 11, no.2 (December 2016), pp.75–95, https://www.degruyter.com/view/j/bis.2016.11.issue-2/bis-2015-0023/bis-2015-0023.xml?format=INT.

39 Raventós, *Basic Income*, pp.31-32. See also Hillel Steiner, 'Three Just Taxes', in Philippe Van Parijs (ed.), *Arguing for Basic Income: Ethical Foundations for a Radical Reform* (London: Verso, 1992), pp.81-92.

40 John Baker, 'An Egalitarian Case for Basic Income', in Van Parijs (ed.), *Arguing for Basic Income*, pp.122, 124.

41 Bill Jordan, 'Basic Income and the Common Good', in Van Parijs (ed.), *Arguing for Basic Income*, p.165.

42 Ibid., p.171.

43 Ibid., p.173.

44 Jordan, 'Associations and Basic Income', in *BIACR*, pp.72–77.

45 Raventós, *Basic Income*, p.64.

46 Ibid., p.66.

47 Ibid., pp.70–74.

48 Ibid., p.104.

49 Charles Murray, 'Guaranteed Income as a Replacement for the Welfare State', in *BIACR*, p.51.

50 Michael Howard, 'Why Marxists and Socialists Should Favour Basic Income', *BIACR*, pp.55–61.

51 Michael McLeay, Amar Radia and Ryland Thomas, 'Money Creation in the Modern Economy', *Quarterly Bulletin* Q1 (2014), http://www.bankofengland.co.uk/publications/Documents/quarterlybulletin/2014/qb14q102.pdf.

52 There is also, of course, the school system that educates the workers to whatever extent is necessary for them to function in the workforce, the police and army that protect the business from robbery or foreign invasion, the roads on which its vehicles run, and so on. The necessity for these institutions and facilities is an argument for taxation to support them, but the point here is that it's not just labour that deserves remuneration and support, but also the means by which that labour is facilitated.

4: Political Issues: The Implications of UBI for Feminism and the Environment

1 Carolyn Merchant, *The Death of Nature: Women, Ecology and the Scientific Revolution* (London: Wildwood House, 1982). See also, for example, Val Plumwood, *Environmental Culture: The Ecological Crisis of Reason* (London, Routledge, 2002). For a more recent contribution tying in issues of feminism, ecology and Marxism, see Kate Soper, 'Capitalocene', review of *Capitalism in the Web of Life: Ecology and the Accumulation of Capital*, by Jason Moore, *Radical Philosophy*, vol.197 (May/June 2016), pp.49–52.

2 We should not ignore the influence of mass culture with its many gender stereotypes, which militate against women's participation in the workforce.

3 See Tim Jackson, *Prosperity Without Growth: Economics for a Finite Planet* (London, Sterling, VA: Earthscan, 2009); Juan Cole, 'The Last Time Summer Was This Hot, Human Beings Hadn't Yet Left Africa ...', Truthdig, 25 September 2016, http://www.truthdig.com/report/item/the_last_time_summer_was_this_hot_human_beings_hadnt_left_africa_20160925; Horatio Clare, 'Climate Change Writ Large', review of *A Farewell to Ice* by Peter Wadhams, *Guardian* (August 21, 2016) https://www.theguardian.com/books/2016/aug/21/farewell-to-ice-peter-wadhams-review-climate-change; Jan Otto Andersson, 'Degrowth with Basic Income: The Radical Combination' (essay written for the fourteenth BIEN Conference, Munich, September 2012), http://basicincome.org/bien/pdf/munich2012/andersson.pdf.

4 Ann Withorn, 'Is One Man's Ceiling Another Woman's Floor?' in *BIACR*, p.145.

5 Tony Fitzpatrick, 'A Basic Income for Feminists?' in BAICR, pp.163–165.

6 Withorn, 'Is One Man's Ceiling Another Woman's Floor?' in *BAICR*, p.146.

7 Anne Alstott, 'Good for Women', in *BIACR*, p.187. Alstott apparently favours 'stakeholding' (a one-off, unconditional grant to young citizens) over a regular basic income: see Bruce Ackerman and Anne Alstott, *The Stakeholder Society* (New Haven: Yale University Press, 1999), pp.210–216. (It is surely questionable whether it would be wise to give a large sum of money to someone at an early stage of life. In some cases they might make prudent use of it, in others not.)

8 Ingrid Robeyns, 'A Gender Analysis of Basic Income', in *BIACR*, p.160. This article is a valuable empirical and statistical resource on the issue.

9 Withorn, 'Is One Man's Ceiling Another Woman's Floor?' in *BIACR*, p.147.

10 Ann S. Orloff, 'Why Basic Income does not Promote Gender Equality', in *BIACR*, pp.149–150.

11 Ibid., p.150.

12 Ibid., p.151.

13 S. Kesenne, 'Basic Income and Female Labour Supply: An Empirical Analysis', *Cahiers Economiques de Bruxelles*, 125 (1990), pp.81–92; J. Nelissen and S. Polk, 'Basisinkomen: effecten op de arbeidsparticipatie en de inkomensverdeling',

Tijdschrift voor Politieke Economie, vol.18, no.4 (1990), pp.64–82.

14 Ingrid Robeyns, 'A Gender Analysis of Basic Income', in *BIACR*, p.154.

15 Ibid., p.158.

16 Ibid., pp.159.

17 Ibid., pp.156, 159, 160.

18 Tony Fitzpatrick, 'A Basic Income for Feminists?' in *BIACR*, pp.165–167.

19 Ibid., p.167.

20 Carole Pateman, 'Free-riding and the Household', in *BIACR*, p.175.

21 Ibid., p.176.

22 Jewish Women's Archive: Women of Valor, 'Emma Goldman – Women's Rights – Women's Suffrage', http://jwa.org/womenofvalor/goldman/womens-rights/womens-suffrage. See Emma Goldman, 'Woman Suffrage', in *Red Emma Speaks: An Emma Goldman Reader*, Alix Kates Shulman (ed.) (Atlantic Highlands, NJ: Humanities Press International, 1996), pp.192–3, and 195.

23 For a recent discussion of UBI and feminism from the point of view of 'time use', see Corina Rodríguez Enríquez, 'Basic Income and Time Use Democratization', *Basic Income Studies*, vol.11, no.1 (June 2016): 39-48, https://www.degruyter.com/view/j/bis.2016.11.issue-1/bis-2016-0012/bis-2016-0012.xml?format=INT.

24 José A. Noguera and Karl Widerquist, 'Basic Income as a Post-productivist Policy', in *BIACR*, p.260.

25 Claus Offe, 'A Non-productivist Design for Social Policies', in *BIACR*, p.278, 281–282.

26 Tony Fitzpatrick, 'Ecologism and Basic Income', in *BIACR*, p.264.

27 Ibid., p.266.

28 Ibid., pp.266–267. See also Andrew Dobson, *Green Political Thought: An Introduction* (London: Routledge, 1995).

29 Fitzpatrick, 'Ecologism and Basic Income', *BIACR*, p.266.

30 See Ed Cumming, 'Can Hipsters Save the World?', *Guardian*, 8 March 2015, https://www.theguardian.com/uk-news/2015/mar/08/can-hipsters-save-the-world.

31 Fitzpatrick, 'Ecologism and Basic Income', *BIACR*, p.267. Fitzpatrick notes that he is echoing here ideas of James Robertson, André Gorz and Claus Offe.

32 Ibid., pp.266–267. See J. O. Andersson, 'Fundamental Values for a Third Left', *New Left Review*, no.216 (March/April 1996), pp.66–78; and J.O. Andersson. 'Why a Citizen's Income Should be Combined with a Citizen's Wage' (Paper, Sixth International Congress of the Basic Income European Network, Vienna International Centre, Vienna, 12–14 September 1996).

33 Philippe Van Parijs, 'A Green Case for Basic Income?' in *BIACR*, pp.269–273.

34 André Gorz, 'Beyond the Wage-based Society', in *BIACR*, pp.297–298.

35 Ibid., p.304.

36 F. Guattari, 'Vers une "Ecosophie"', *Transversales Science/Culture*, vol.2 (March/April 1990), pp.2-3, cited in André Gorz 'Beyond the Wage-based Society', in *BIACR*, p.306. Gorz notes that the term was introduced in F. Guattari, 'The Three Ecologies', *New Formations*, vol.8 (Summer 1989), pp.131–147, and elaborated in F.

Guattari, Chaosmose (Paris: Galilée, 1992).

37 Gorz 'Beyond the Wage-based Society', in *BIACR*, pp.304–205.

38 Thanks to Joan Healy for insightful comments on this chapter, and assistance with it.

5: Answering Some Objections

1 Supporters of UBI tend to think of rights rather than duties: UBI increases my right to stay at home (or to work in the formal economy) and – to some extent – reduces my duty to do either. However, those for whom duty plays an important role in how they think people should behave may, indeed, argue that this is not necessarily a good thing, and that people should be expected to fulfil some duty to society. (To take one issue, UBI may be compatible with some form of national service – not necessarily military in nature – but arguments around that issue are separate from those around the issue of UBI. You could have UBI with or without national service, and national service with or without UBI. The one is not dependent on the other.)

2 See, for example, Degrowth Conference 2016, http://budapest.degrowth.org.

3 II Thes 3: 10. (References to the Bible are normally to the King James Version.)

4 To what extent Marxist socialism is a form of secularised Christianity is outside the scope of this book, but there are some interesting resemblances, including the implicit morality of equality, not to mention the puritanical elements of state socialism in practice (the latter are attacked, for example, in George Orwell's *Nineteen Eighty-Four*). More specifically, Van Parijs (*Real Freedom for All*, p.157) points out a reference by Marx to a text of Martin Luther in the discussion of surplus value in *Capital*, in Karl Marx, *Das Kapital*, vol.1 (Berlin: Dietz, 1962): 'whoever takes more or better than he gives, this is usury, and is not service, but wrong done to his neighbour, as in the case of theft and plunder.' The reference may also be found in Karl Marx, *Capital: A Critique of Political Economy*, vol.1, trans. Samuel Moore and Edward Aveling, Frederick Engels (ed.) (London: Lawrence and Wishart, 1977), p.187. The reference given by Marx is Martin Luther, 'An die Pfarrherrn wider den Wucher zu Predigen' (Wittenberg: 1540).

5 Gen. 3: 16–19.

6 Matt. 6: 28; Luke 1: 40; Matt. 20: 1–16. See also John Ruskin, 'Unto This Last', Essays from the Cornhill Magazine, http://www.efm.bris.ac.uk/het/ruskin/ruskin.

7 Matt. 25: 14–30.

8 Prov. 6: 6–11; Eccl. 1: 1–11.

9 Acts 2: 44–45.

10 I am using these terms as shorthand. Western society has, arguably – for good or ill – its political and philosophical foundations in ancient Greece, its legal foundations in ancient Rome, and its moral/spiritual basis in ancient Israel.

11 The stories of the manna from heaven (Ex. 16: 11–15) and of the distribution of the loaves and fishes (Matt. 14:14–21) could be cited as counter-examples. However, they do not involve any socioeconomic method of wealth distribution. Even if the account of the multiplying of the loaves and fishes is interpreted, not as divine intervention, but as the result of people being inspired to share with others the food that they had already brought with them, such a sharing would have involved voluntary charity rather than any formal political apparatus. Indeed, Jesus specifically refuses the role of a 'judge or a divider' (Luke 12: 13–14) when asked to intervene in a family dispute, and goes on to urge trust in divine provision (Luke 12: 15–35).

12 Matt. 7: 12.

13 The realm of sadomasochistic role-playing offers an obvious exception. Even then, however, the individual is just playing a game – they can escape from bondage whenever they choose (leaving aside possible unfortunate developments that may transpire in any particular case involving this practice).

14 That is, if negative income tax is seen as a form of UBI, which it arguably is.

15 That in turn, however, might lead to increased inflation, though as we – supposedly – have zero or very low inflation at the moment, that might not necessarily be a bad thing.

16 Raventós, *Basic Income*, p.181.

17 The discussion is made somewhat problematic by the shifting and unclear nature of the definition of work, particularly given issues that have been raised in the relevant literature, such as: the distinction between alienated and non-alienated work; between work and labour; between paid work in the formal economy and unpaid work in the informal economy; between freedom and necessity; between autonomous and heteronymous activity, and so on. We could though have a stab at clarifying the issues, perhaps as follows, and using the term 'activity' rather than 'work' ('A' stands for 'activity'). A1: alienated activity in the formal economy (the traditional negative picture of the alienated factory worker); A2: non-alienated activity in the formal economy: a person who enjoys his/her paid job (rightly or wrongly); A3: alienated activity in the informal economy (for example, the bored homemaker); A4: non-alienated activity in the informal economy (the fulfilled homemaker); A5: non-alienated activity in the sphere of leisure or political participation; A6 lazy, non-productive activity, such as watching TV all day while drinking beer. The proposed scheme is complicated not just by the unfortunate fact that 'A' stands for both 'activity' and 'alienation', but also by the further issue that alienation has (at least) two dimensions, an objective and a subjective one. I could be subjectively non-alienated while engaging in an objectively alienated activity (for example if I practised meditation while engaging in repetitive factory work) and presumably viceversa as well (for example an artist suffering a creative block). However this might be, one could argue that UBI helps to minimise A1 and A3, facilitates A2, A4 and A5, and (perhaps unfortunately, though inevitably) permits A6.

18   Warren E. Buffett, 'Stop Coddling the Super-Rich', *The New York Times*, 14
      August 2011. http://www.nytimes.com/2011/08/15/opinion/stop-coddling-
      the-super-rich.html?_r=0.
19   This is assuming that we are still thinking of a society where types of work are
      divided into full-time and part-time – but we should, arguably, be trying to think
      beyond that.
20   The reasons why this should be are sometimes less than clear-cut. We can
      understand why a medical specialist is paid more than a paramedic. It's less
      clear, though, why a high-ranking banker or financier, who may have contributed
      considerably to our recent financial woes, should be rewarded handsomely for
      his/her efforts – while a nurse, teacher or firefighter may struggle to survive,
      under the ravages of austerity. Presumably, the continuance of such a situation
      depends on the (tacit or active) consent of the population. (Even if people are
      brainwashed by the mass media – as seems largely to be the case – they do,
      arguably, have a certain moral responsibility for allowing that to happen, perhaps
      through intellectual laziness.)
21   The basic reason for poverty is (obviously) that poor people don't have enough
      money. This can (again obviously) be remedied most effectively by giving them
      money, either through private charity or formal redistribution. See Matthew
      Yglesias, 'The Best and Simplest Way to Fight Global Poverty', *Slate,* 29 May 2013,
      http://www.slate.com/articles/business/moneybox/2013/05/unconditional_
      cash_transfers_giving_money_to_the_poor_may_be_the_best_tool.html.
22   Raventós, p. 181–182.
23   Rutger Bregman, *Utopia for Realists: The Case for a Universal Basic Income,
      Open Borders, and a 15-Hour Workweek*, trans. Elizabeth Manton (Netherlands:
      The Correspondent, 2016), p.183. The figure is from Lant Pritchett, 'The Cliff at
      the Border', https://www.hks.harvard.edu/fs/lpritch/Labor%20Mobility%20
      -%20docs/cliff%20at%20the%20borders_submitted.pdf.
24   Ibid., p. 187. See Heidi Schiefholz, 'Immigration and Wages: Methodological
      Advances Confirm Modest Gains for Native Workers', Economic Policy Unit,
      Briefing Paper #255, 4 February 2010, http://www.epi.org/publication/bp255/.
25   Bregman, p.183.
26   Ibid., p.184. See '62 People Own the Same as Half the World, Reveals Oxfam
      Davos Report', 18 January 2016, https://www.oxfam.org/en/pressroom/
      pressreleases/2016-01-18/62-people-own-same-half-world-reveals-oxfam-
      davos-report.
27   For a recent discussion of the immigration issue in regard to UBI, see Alex Boso
      and Mihaela Vancea, 'Basic Income for Immigrants? The Pull Effect of Social
      Benefits on Migration', *Basic Income Studies*, vol.7, no.1 (December 2012), https://
      www.degruyter.com/view/j/bis.2012.7.issue-1/1932-0183.1234/1932-0183.1234.xml.
28   From a political point of view, it seems important to separate the promise
      that UBI holds out of increased freedom from bureaucracy, from the promise
      of the increased justice that a society with a fairer system of distribution

proffers. Otherwise the arguments may become confused. While the goals of freedom and justice are closely connected, it is possible that (depending on the sums involved) a society with UBI could increase freedom (for example by releasing people from poverty traps) without any noticeable effect on fairness of distribution. On the other hand, we could have a much fairer society in economic terms than we currently have, without UBI, through fairer redistribution than exists at present. In other words, to some extent the Left-Right debate, and the debate around the desirability of UBI, are separate discussions. If we do want to emphasise human freedom, perhaps we need, as well as instituting UBI, to break down the 'work/leisure' distinction so that necessary work is simultaneously rationalised, minimised and (as much as possible) shared out. In such a situation the performance of necessary work would be made as fulfilling as possible. At the same time, it would be made as easy as possible for everyone to engage in fulfilling activity, outside of the formal economy. It is true, of course, that not everyone will subscribe to such high-minded goals as creativity, self-development and the like. In a society with UBI, there will no doubt be a certain number of people who wish to spend their time skateboarding, playing video games or surfing. (Though it should be noted – for those to whom such things matter – that such activities may, on occasion, themselves be developed in a professional direction.)

6: Implementation: Making UBI Happen

1   There is a separate issue concerning the effect of UBI on society, for example whether it would lead to a diminution in GDP, due to fewer people working.

2   See Linda J. Bilmes, 'The Financial Legacy of Iraq and Afghanistan: How Wartime Spending Decisions will Constrain Future National Security Budgets', Faculty Research Working Paper Series (March 2013), https://research.hks.harvard.edu/publications/getFile.aspx?Id=923, cited in Bregman, *Utopia for Realists*, p.68. According to that estimate, the wars in Afghanistan and Iraq cost somewhere in the region of $5 trillion. We might take this line of enquiry a bit further, by noting that the population of the US is around 325 million people. If the $5 trillion (or thereabouts) could have been divided equally among the US population, it would have given more than $15,000 to everyone in the US, or more than $75,000 for a family of five. Apart from avoiding the mayhem and instability that have beset the world since the beginning of this ill-advised military adventurism post-9/11, such a direct redistribution would have gone a long way towards solving the problem of poverty in the US.

3   Of course, depending on the sums involved, raising the level of UBI could become a radical means of adjusting distribution in favour of the less well-off in society, but that is a separate issue from the issue of UBI itself. (From a purely

theoretical perspective, it is of relevance to the argument for UBI only when it makes the latter more thinkable, or politically feasible.)

4   On the transition to UBI see Bill Jordan, 'Efficiency and Participation: The Basic Income Approach', in *BIACR*, p.233. Jordan refers to H. Parker, *Instead of the Dole: An Enquiry into Integration of the Tax and Benefit Systems* (London: Routledge, 1989); see also Liberal Democrats, *Common Benefit: Liberal Democrat Policies for the Reform of the Tax and Benefit Systems*, Federal Green Paper no.11 (London, 1990); Netherlands Scientific Council for Government Policy, *Safeguarding Social Security* (The Hague: WRR, 1985).

5   See, for example, Jurgen De Wispelaare and Lindsay Stirton, 'Practical Bottlenecks in the Implementation of a Universal Basic Income', *BIACR*, pp.360–368.

6   To take an example (the figures are used only for illustration): if the cut-off rate is 20,000 (euro/dollars/pounds) and the income tax rate is 50 per cent, then if you earn 30,000 you pay 5,000 in income tax (i.e. 30,000 less 20,000, multiplied by 50 per cent). On the other hand, if you earn 10,000 you receive 5,000 from the state (i.e. 50 per cent of the difference between what you earn and the level – 20,000 – at which you would no longer qualify for a payment). The crucial element is that a person earning nothing at all – for example an unemployed person or a full-time homemaker – would also qualify for the subsidy, and in this case his/her income would be 10,000, i.e. 50 per cent of 20,000. On negative income tax see Milton Friedman, 'Negative Income Tax: The Original Idea', *BIACR*, pp.398–401. Friedman sees a downside (which others might see as an upside) in that the system might be transformed to favour the recipients rather than the taxpayers. Friedman sees no solution to this, except a (perhaps somewhat touching) reliance on the restraint of the population. Here, perhaps, is a possible Leftist riposte to the supposedly Right-wing implications of a negative income tax: once instituted, there would be a natural dynamic for it to develop in favour of the less well off. On negative income tax see also James Tobin, 'The Case for an Income Guarantee', *BIACR*, pp.195–199. For a detailed analysis of experiments in negative income tax, see Karl Widerquist, 'What (If Anything) Can We Learn from the Negative Income Tax Experiments?' in *BIACR*, pp.216–229. On costing negative income tax, see Fred Block and Jeff Manza, 'The Case for a Progressive Negative Income Tax', BIACR, pp.402–416.

7   Bruce Ackerman and Anne Alstott, 'Stakeholding versus Basic Income', *BIACR*, pp.417–428. Unlike in proposals for UBI, there are some elements of conditionality in the proposal: in order to receive principal rather than interest, the individual would be required to complete high school. Criminality could lead to a postponement of payment of the stake. (Selective use of forfeiture could be used as a sanction, in place of lengthy prison terms.) The authors note (in 2004) that the stake of $80,000 could give a lifetime annuity of $400 per month, so the stake could be converted into a basic income if the recipient wanted that. (However, it should be pointed out that $400 equates to a 6 per cent return: such a figure

would, presumably, be problematic at current low rates.) A stakeholder's grant is proposed on the basis that young people may have a need for high expenditure, for example on education. (An obvious problem, though, is that its existence might simply push college fees higher.) The authors point out the intriguing issue that a young person in potential receipt of a basic income for life could, either legally or illegally, capitalise it in any case. The authors also mention the issues of insulation from creditors' claims, as well as the implications for other forms of state payments. (Such questions, of course, arise for UBI as well.) One could point out the (obvious) objection that the young stakeholder might simply blow his/her stakeholding on drink or drugs – but this would arise also in the context of UBI (not to mention present forms of social security, or indeed wages or salary).

8   Stuart White, 'Reciprocity-sensitive Forms of Basic Income', in *BIACR*, p.432.

9   Claus Offe and Johan de Deken, 'Sabbatical Grants', in *BIACR*, pp.447–452.

10   See Anthony B. Atkinson, 'Participation Income', in *BIACR*, pp.435–438; Jurgen de Wispelaere and Lindsay Stirton, 'The Trilemma of Participation Income', in *BIACR*, pp.439–446.

11   See European Commission, Taxation and Customs Union, 'Taxation of the Financial Sector', http://ec.europa.eu/taxation_customs/taxation/other_taxes/financial_sector/index_en.htm.

12   See my article, 'Social Justice Without Socialism: The Advantages of Participatory Capitalism', in Stuart M. Speiser (ed.), *Equitable Capitalism: Promoting Economic Opportunity Through Broader Capital Ownership* (New York: Apex Press, 1991), pp.114–123; Guy Standing, 'A Coming-of-Age Grant versus a Community Capital Grant', *BIACR*, pp.464–470; Seán Healy and Brigid Reynolds, 'Basic Income: Radical Utopia or Practical Solution?' in Brigid Reynolds and Seán Healy (eds), *Basic Income: Radical Utopia or Practical Solution?* (Dublin: Social Justice Ireland, 2016), pp.23–24. This collection will be referred to hereafter as *BIRUPS*.

13   'Quantitative Easing for People: A Rescue Plan for the Eurozone', http://www.qe4people.eu; John Cassidy, 'Printing Money: A Radical Solution to the Current Economic Malaise', *The New Yorker*, 15 November 2013, http://www.newyorker.com/magazine/2015/11/23/printing-money-books-john-cassidy. See Tom Streithorst, 'How Basic Income Solves Capitalism's Fundamental Problem', *Evonomics: The Next Evolution of Economics*, https://evonomics.com/how-universal-basic-income-solves/. On 'helicopter money' as direct provision for the population in order to address the problem of demand, see Adair Turner, *Between Debt and the Devil: Money, Credit and Fixing Global Finance* (Princeton and Oxford: Princeton University Press, 2016), pp.218–222. See also W. Buiter, 'The Simple Analytics of Helicopter Money: Why It Works – Always', *Economics: The Open-Access, Open-Assessment E-Journal* 8: 1-5, http://dx.doi.org/10.5018/economics-ejournal.ja.2014-28.

14   See 'Steve Baker MP at the Historic Debate in UK Parliament on Money Creation', YouTube video, 27:00, posted by Positive Money, 21 November 2014,

https://www.youtube.com/watch?v=bXOkmD8Eozshttps://www.youtube.
com/watch?v=bXOkmD8Eozs; Michael McLeay, Amar Radia and Ryland
Thomas, 'Money Creation in the Modern Economy', *Quarterly Bulletin* 2014 Q1,
pp.14–27, http://www.bankofengland.co.uk/publications/Documents/quarterly-
bulletin/2014/qb14q102.pdf. A video explanation of the last-mentioned may be
found at 'Money Creation in the Modern Economy: Quarterly Bulletin Article',
YouTube video, 5.07, posted by Bank of England, 12 March 2014, https://www.
youtube.com/watch?v=CvRAqR2pAgw.

15   Luis Sanzo and Rafael Pinilla, 'A Household Basic Income', in *BIACR*, pp.461–463.

16   See José A. Noguera, 'Basic Income and Contributory Pensions', in *BIACR*,
pp.346–350.

17   A counter-argument from a theological perspective, as noted previously, may be
found in Matt. 20: 1–16.

18   See Thomas W. Pogge, 'A Global Resources Dividend', in *BIACR*, pp.375–391.
Pogge (382) estimates that a 1 per cent global resource dividend from affluent
nations would raise about $300 billion per year, yielding $250 per year for each
individual whose income is below the international poverty line. This would give
over three times their yearly income on average. Pogge estimates (note 2, figures
for 2000) that the average annual income per head of the global poor of $326 is
equivalent to about $82 at market exchange rates.

19   See Philippe Van Parijs and Yannick Vanderborght, 'From Euro-Stipendium
to Euro-Dividend', *BIACR*, pp.392-397. The authors (p.395, see also note 3)
propose a Euro-dividend for all EU citizens, differentiated to reflect the cost of
living in different countries, with the threshold increased until it covers every
citizen. This could be paid for through a common energy tax, reflecting the
environmental cost of energy-use.

20   Claus Offe, 'Pathways from Here', in *BIACR*, p.563, discusses the difficulties of
implementing a country-specific form of UBI within the EU. (For information about
DiEM25, an international organisation that seeks to preserve the EU while steering
it in a progressive direction, see DiEM25, https://diem25.org.)

21   While one may favour the EU in principle – and I do – it has its downsides. The
euro is a particular case in point: a monetary change that was imposed without
the prior political consolidation that would have facilitated its success. This in
turn made it impossible for individual states that adopted the euro to adjust
their currencies in response to economic pressures, such as the crisis of 2008
and following years. The lack of a federal system in Europe means that intra-EU
transfers cannot be made from one country to another, so that the south
languishes while the north (more or less) prospers. In the past, the EU has been
blamed for exerting undue economic pressure on countries such as Greece,
Ireland and Italy. (More recently, it has been blamed for undue interference
in Ireland's tax affairs.) On the other hand, supporters of liberty should surely
defend the freedom of movement that the dismantling of national borders
(at least within the Union) facilitates. In the specific case of Ireland, the EU has

massively helped to dispel an insular cultural mindset – the kind of mindset that the far-Right currently seems intent on bringing back to the countries of mainland Europe, mirroring the growth of authoritarian nationalism in the US – and, to a lesser extent, in the UK. Globalisation is the main bogy of reactionaries in Europe and the US (a curious deformation of the situation of 15 or 20 years ago, when globalisation was the demon identified by the Left).

22 Of course, the difference between Alaska and most European countries is that Alaska wants to encourage immigration, while most European countries want to discourage it. (Germany, which is looking at a declining indigenous population, may be an exception, at least in some quarters there.) There are also questions to be asked about the role of UBI in Alaska in maintaining the popularity of the resource extraction by which it is financed – another issue for the 'Green' dimension of UBI.

23 For up-to date information on actual and projected pilot schemes in countries such as Finland, Canada, Uganda, Switzerland, Kenya, Brazil, The Netherlands, France, Italy, Namibia and India, see BIEN: Basic Income Earth Network, http://basicincome.org/topic/pilot-experiments/. For a discussion of the UBI experiment in Finland, see Pertti Honkanen and Ville-Veikko Pulkka, 'Tackling Poverty and Social Exclusion with Unconditional Money: Notes on the Finnish Basic Income Experiment', in *BIRUPS*, pp.57–67. See also 'From Idea to Experiment: Report on Universal Basic Income Experiment in Finland', Kela Working Papers 106, Kela/FPA, https://helda.helsinki.fi/handle/10138/167728. For an incisive (and critical) analysis of the Finnish experiment, see Matt Bruenig, Antti Jauhiainen, Joona-Hermanni Mäkinen, 'The UBI Bait and Switch: Finland's UBI Experiment Serves as a Cautionary Tale for Basic Income Proponents on the Left', *Jacobin*, https://www.jacobinmag.com/2017/01/ubi-finland-centre-party-unemployment-jobs/. On the current situation in the Netherlands, see Sjir Hoeijmakers, 'Municipal Basic-income Related Experiments in the Netherlands', in *BIRUPS*, pp.69–73. For further relevant information see Global Basic Income Foundation, http://www.globalincome.org/English/BI-worldwide.html. See also 'Basic Income – International Experience', *American Herald Tribune*, http://ahtribune.com/economy/942-basic-income-part-ii-html. Bregman, *Utopia for Realists* (pp.61–67) provides a useful and informative recent survey of such experiments in a North American context.

24 Philippe Van Parijs, 'Basic Income in the South', *BIACR* 522–526. For discussions of costing in the UK, see Green Party of England and Wales: Basic Income: A Detailed Proposal: April 2015, https://policy.greenparty.org.uk/assets/files/Policy%20files/Basic%20Income%20Consultation%20Paper.pdf; Citizens Income Trust: http://citizensincome.org. In a US context see The US Basic Income Guarantee Network: What is the Basic Income Guarantee? http://www.usbig.net/whatisbig.php. For recent discussions of UBI in a US context, see James A. Yunker, 'The Basic Income Guarantee: A General Equilibrium Evaluation', *Basic Income Studies* 8, no.2 (July 2914): pp.203–233, https://www.degruyter.com/

view/j/bis.2013.8.issue-2/bis-2013-0014/bis-2013-0014.xml?format=INT, and Steven
O. Richardson, 'Entitlement Reform: from Tangled Web to Safety Net', *Basic
Income Studies*, vol.8, no.1 (August 2013), pp.105–137, https://www.degruyter.
com/view/j/bis.2013.8.issue-1/bis-2013-0001/bis-2013-0001.xml?format=INT.

25 Bregman, *Utopia for Realists*, pp.57–58. See GiveDirectly, https://www.
givedirectly.org. Bregman (pp.56–60, and footnotes) provides an informative
survey on the literature covering free transfers of money to poor people.

26 Malcolm Torry, 'Citizen's Basic Income: is it Feasible?' in *BIRUPS*, pp.31–47. For
details of calculations, see Malcolm Torry, 'An Evaluation of a Strictly Revenue
Neutral Citizen's Basic Income Scheme', Institute for Social and Economic
Research Working Paper EM17/14, *Colchester: Institute for Social and Economic
Research,* University of Essex, June 2016, https://www.iser.essex.ac.uk/research/
publications/working-papers/euromod/em5-16. For a proposal with detailed
costings in the UK context see Malcolm Torry (2016) *The Feasibility of Citizen's
Income* (London: Palgrave Macmillan). For further discussions of costing in the
UK, see Green Party of England and Wales: Basic Income: A Detailed Proposal:
April 2015, https://policy.greenparty.org.uk/assets/files/Policy%20files/Basic%20
Income%20Consultation%20Paper.pdf; see also Citizens Income Trust: http://
citizensincome.org. For a costed proposal to combine UBI with a 'National
Living Wage' in a UK context see Anthony Painter, 'Citizenship and Basic
Income', in *BIRUPS*, pp.49–53. See also Anthony Painter and Chris Thoung,
'Creative Citizen, Creative State: The Principled and Pragmatic Case for a
Universal Basic Income', RSA: RSA Reports, 3 December 2015, https://medium.
com/rsa-reports/creative-citizen-creative-state-a3cef3f25775#.exekhqakt.
For a critical view of the possibilities of UBI in a UK context, see Howard
Reed and Stewart Lansley, 'Universal Basic Income: An Idea Whose Time has
Come?' https://www.compassonline.org.uk/wp-content/uploads/2016/05/
UniversalBasicIncomeByCompass-Spreads.pdf.

27 Charles M.A. Clark, 'Cost Estimates for a Basic Income in the United States',
in *BIACR*, pp.255–257. Clark's proposal is in a 2002 context. For a more recent
contribution (from a libertarian perspective) see Michael D. Tanner, letter
to the editor, 26 August 2014, Cato Unbound, https://www.cato-unbound.
org/2014/08/26/basic-income-guarantee-simplicity-what-cost. See also, for
example, Gary Flomenhoft, 'Applying the Alaska Model in a Resource-poor
State: The Example of Vermont', http://usbig.net/pdf/Flomenhoft—
AlaskaModelInVermont.pdf.

28 For a discussion of issues around post-colonialism, globalisation and identity in
an Irish context, see my article 'Hibernian Evanescence: Globalisation, Identity
and the Virtual Shamrock', in *Postcolonial Text* 3, no.3 (2007), http://postcolonial.
org/index.php/pct/article/viewArticle/713. (Things have, admittedly, changed
radically in a socio-economic-political sense in Ireland, in the ten years since the
article was written.)

29 Seán Ward, *BIRUPS*, p.79. See Brendan Dowling, *Integrated Approaches to
Personal Income Taxes and Transfers* (Dublin, NESC, 1977); Rosheen Callender,

'Down to Basics', (1989) in *Making Sense* (May/June).

30 For a survey of these, see Ward in *BIRUPS*, pp.77–91. See for example, *First Report of the Committee on Taxation* (1982) Dublin Stationery Office; Patrick Honohan, 'A Radical Reform of Social Welfare and Income Tax Evaluated', *Administration*, vol.35, no.1 (1987); Tim Callan, C. O'Donoghue, C. O'Neill, *Analysis of Basic Income Schemes for Ireland* (Dublin: ESRI, 1994); Seán Ward, 'A Basic Income System for Ireland', in B. Reynolds and S. Healy (eds), *Towards an Adequate Income for All* (Dublin: CORI, 1994); S. Healy and B. Reynolds, 'Arguing for an Adequate Income Guarantee', in B. Reynolds and S. Healy (eds), *Towards an Adequate Income for All* (Dublin: CORI, 1995), pp.29–49; Charles M.A. Clark and J. Healy, *Pathways to a Basic Income* (Dublin CORI, 1997); Department of the Taoiseach, *Basic Income: A Green Paper* (Dublin: Department of the Taoiseach, 2002); Charles M.A. Clark, *The Basic Income Guarantee: Ensuring Progress and Prosperity in the 21st Century* (Dublin: Oak Tree Press, 2002); Social Justice Ireland, *Building a Fairer Tax System: The Working Poor and the Cost of Refundable Tax Credits* (Dublin: Social Justice Ireland, 2010); Micheál Collins, 'Towards a Basic Income' (paper, TASC Conference, Cork, September 2011), NERI: Nevin Economic Research Institute, http://www.nerinstitute.net/research/towards-a-basic-income/; Micheál Collins, 'Estimating the Cost of a Basic Income for Ireland', (paper, BIEN Congress, Munich, September 2012) http://basicincome.org/bien/pdf/munich2012/Collins.pdf; Seán Healy, M. Murphy, and S. Ward, 'Basic Income: Why and How in Difficult Economic Times: Financing a BI in Ireland', (paper presented at the BIEN World Congress, Munich, 2012), http://basicincome.org/bien/pdf/munich2012/healy.pdf. This gives detailed costings (in a 2012 context) for a proposed UBI in Ireland.

31 Michelle Murphy, 'Pathways to a Basic Income System', in *BIRUPS*, pp.93–107.

32 Eamon Murphy and Seán Ward, 'Costing a Basic Income for Ireland', in *BIRUPS*, pp.125–136. Collins. 'Estimating the Cost of a Basic Income for Ireland', p.7, calculates that a basic income at social welfare rates would require a flat tax of 44.44 per cent. (It should be noted that in practice this would be lower, since UBI is not taxed.)

33 See Ronan Lyons, 'A Right to Housing? The Case for a Universal Housing Subsidy', in *BIRUPS*, pp.137–148.

34 Michael Taft, 'Basic Income and Transformative Strategies', in *BIRUPS*, pp.109–123.

35 On the latter see, for example, Positive Money, http://positivemoney.org.

Conclusion: Summing Up and Looking Forward

1 See, in particular, Horkheimer and Adorno, *Dialectic of Enlightenment*.

2 With some notable exceptions, such as Paul Mason's *PostCapitalism*.

3 See, for example, Žižek, *Living in the End Times*; Wolfgang Streeck, 'How will Capitalism End?', *New Left Review*, vol.2, no.87 (May/June 2014), pp.35–64. On the other hand, there are some more optimistic views, for example Göran

Therborn, 'An Age of Progress?' *New Left Review*, vol.2, no.99 (May–June 2016), pp.27–37, and Bregman, *Utopia for Realists*.

4   See John Pilger, 'The Issue is Not Trump, It Is Us', *Counterpunch*, 17 January 2017, http://www.counterpunch.org/2017/01/17/the-issue-is-not-trump-it-is-us/.

5   Joe Twyman, 'Trump, Brexit, Front National, AfD: Branches of the Same Tree', YouGov UK, 16 November 2016, https://yougov.co.uk/news/2016/11/16/trump-brexit-front-national-afd-branches-same-tree/.

6   See Heather Long, 'Why Doesn't 4.9% Unemployment Feel Great?' CNN Money, 6 February 2016, http://money.cnn.com/2016/02/06/news/economy/obama-us-jobs/.

7   Elena Holodny, 'This Chart Highlights One of Europe's Biggest Problems', Business Insider UK: Finance, 9 July 2016, http://uk.businessinsider.com/youth-unemployment-in-europe-2016-7?r=US&IR=T.

8   At the risk of labouring the point, there is of course a Biblical resonance here: Matt. 7: 13–14.

9   See Ted Benton, 'Why Are Sociologists Naturephobes?' in *After Postmodernism: An Introduction to Critical Realism,* José López and Gary Potter (ed.) (New York: Athlone, 2007), pp.133–145.

10   C.P. Snow, *The Two Cultures*, introd. Stefan Collini (Cambridge: Cambridge Univ. Press, 1993). See also Robert Whelan, 'Fifty Years On, C.P. Snow's "Two Cultures" are United in Desperation', *The Telegraph*, 5 May 2009, http://www.telegraph.co.uk/technology/5273453/Fifty-years-on-CP-Snows-Two-Cultures-are-united-in-desperation.html.

11   This article estimates that the total melting of the Greenland ice sheet would raise sea levels by 7 meters, enough to submerge London: 'Sea Level Rise: Ocean Levels are Getting Higher: Can We do Anything About It?' http://ocean.nationalgeographic.com/ocean/critical-issues-sea-level-rise/. Cambridge, where C.P. Snow was based, is actually between 6 and 24 metres above sea level, so parts of it might escape, depending on the severity of the global meltdown. See The Editors of Encyclopaedia Britannica, 'Cambridge: England, United Kingdom', 3 May 2013, https://www.britannica.com/place/Cambridge-England. If the Antarctic ice sheet were to go the same way, the situation would, of course, be much more drastic. This may start to feed in to property prices in the future, if it has not already done so. Real estate in places such as Scotland and Switzerland will be at a premium, not to mention the higher regions of County Wicklow. (On the other hand, in the future you may not be able to give houses away that are at, or near, sea level.)

12   See Christopher Norris, *Against Relativism: Philosophy of Science, Deconstruction, and Critical Theory* (Oxford: Blackwell, 1997).

13   Of course, that term 'should' is an ethical or 'ought' statement, but we cannot pursue those ramifications any further here.

14   To take a couple of examples, something may be true and yet have bad consequences. If I tell you the truth about my opinion of your new hairstyle, it may be the last straw and cause you to jump off a cliff. In a broader sense, assuming that Darwin's theory of evolution is true, it may, in one sense, have been

better if it had never been formulated, since it gave rise to the phenomenon of 'social Darwinism' which had politically negative consequences (feeding into Nazism, Stalinism and the extreme forms of capitalism that we see today). This is not to say that we should avoid the search for truth, but that we should not imagine that finding the truth will always have desirable consequences. On the other hand, a religious belief that may be false may also be the source of much comfort for an individual. A false belief in the existence of monsters may save a child from the dangers of straying too far from home. And so on.

15 I explore this issue in more detail in 'Aesthetics, Virtual Reality and the Environment', in *Rethinking Nature: Authors and Problems, Teoria*, vol.34, no.2 (2014), pp.139–156, https://www.academia.edu/11358005/Aesthetics_Virtual_Reality_and_the_Environment.

16 Bregman, *Utopia for Realists*, p.22.

17 Ibid., p.23.

18 With some notable exceptions, for example the Electronic Frontier Foundation, https://www.eff.org.

19 See Owen Jones, 'It's Socialism for the Rich and Capitalism for the Rest of Us in Britain', *The Guardian*, 29 August 2014, https://www.theguardian.com/books/2014/aug/29/socialism-for-the-rich.

20 'Peter Schiff on $700 Billion Bailout, Bloomberg', YouTube video, 5:52, televised by Bloomberg on September 22, 2008, posted by Rolf Penner, 22 September 2008, https://www.youtube.com/watch?v=PO-JLGbrpXI.

21 Drew Desilver, 'For Most Workers, Real Wages have Barely Budged for Decades', Pew Research Center, Factank: News in the Numbers, 9 October 2014, http://www.pewresearch.org/fact-tank/.

22 Steven Mufson and Brady Dennis, 'Trump Victory Reverses US Energy and Environmental Priorities', *Washington Post*, 9 November 2016, https://www.washingtonpost.com/news/energy-environment/wp/2016/11/09/trump-victory-reverses-u-s-energy-and-environmental-priorities/?utm_term=.ce58ef8723ce.

23 To take a few examples: why is there anything at all, rather than nothing? Why are there laws of nature, rather than complete randomness and chaos? If a chicken has to go halfway across the road, and then half of the rest of the way, and so on, how can it ever get to the other side? Is everything, including this sentence, part of an all-encompassing delusion on your part? Is the phenomenon of *déjà vu* really a glitch in the matrix? Could you really be a brain in a vat in some scientist's laboratory, with a systematic delusion imposed on you about the nature of reality? Does science tell us the truth about reality? Is there such a thing as truth in the first place? If there is no truth, is that a true statement? Can we know anything independently of thought, perception or language? Is there a logic in history, or is life just a mess? What basis, if any, do we have for good behaviour? If I like the Sex Pistols and you prefer Sibelius, which of us is right, and why (if either is)? And so on.

24 This is, of course, often unconscious, as is the (biblically based) predominance

of the values of (e.g.) forgiveness and church/state separation that characterise Western society, however much these values may be sidelined in practice. (See, for example, John 8: 3–11 and Mark 12: 13–17, respectively.) Much of what passes for secular humanism in Western society is, arguably, a secularised form of biblical (or more specifically New Testament) morality. This is by no means to gloss over some crucial problems with the latter, most notably the philosophical 'problem of evil', and the injustice of a deity who will (supposedly) torture His creation eternally (or allow its eternal torture) as punishment for a finite, temporal infraction – perhaps not even on the part of the individual, but on the part of a distant ancestor whose own existence may have been entirely mythical. This concept of divine justice is, arguably, of questionable help in forming the moral foundation of a society. It may, indeed, explain some of the excesses of our civilisation, from the Crusades to the Inquisition to the murderous religious wars of the seventeenth century. To argue that the militant secularism of the twentieth century has been even worse (at least in terms of numbers killed and suffering caused) is perhaps not a very convincing riposte. (In any case it is at least partly due to the availability of a more lethal technology to Hitler than to Torquemada.)

25   See Warwick Fox, 'Deep Ecology: A New Philosophy of Our Time?' *The Ecologist*, vol.14, no.5–6 (1984), pp.194–200.

26   See the prescient, and warning, remarks of President Eisenhower on leaving office, on the issue of the US military-industrial complex: 'Eisenhower Farewell Address (Full): President Dwight Eisenhower's Farewell Address to the Nation: January 17, 1961', YouTube Video, 15:44, 16 January 2011, posted by 'someoddstuff', https://www.youtube.com/watch?v=CWilYW_fBfY.

27   On the downside, though, they also offer the possibility of payments – for example between employers and workers – taking place beyond the range of the revenue authorities, since such transactions may be difficult or impossible to trace. This has the potential to undermine not just the banking system but the state itself, and indeed the society that depends on it for its functioning.

28   See Creative Commons, https://creativecommons.org.

29   Under the pressure of economic austerity, for example in the UK, the cultural development of second-level students is under threat. See Mark Brown, 'Arts and Culture Being "Systematically Removed from UK Educational System"', *Guardian*, 17 February 2015, https://www.theguardian.com/education/2015/feb/17/arts-and-culture-systematically-removed-from-uk-education-system.

30   Hazel Sheffield, 'If Sweden Becomes the World's First Cashless Society, Could the UK be Next?' *Independent*, 25 November 2016, http://www.independent.co.uk/life-style/gadgets-and-tech/if-sweden-becomes-the-world-s-first-cashless-society-could-the-uk-be-next-a7438656.html.

31   See Tony Joseph, 'Understanding Demonetisation: Why There's a War on Cash: (and You Are in the Middle of It)', *Scroll.in*, 28 January 2017, https://scroll.in/article/827887/understanding-demonetisation-why-theres-a-war-on-cash-and-you-are-in-the-middle-of-it.

32   See for example, Luis Durani, 'The Libyan Failure: Obama and Clinton's Forgotten War', *Modern Diplomacy*, 13 May 2016, http://moderndiplomacy.eu/index. php?option=com_k2&view=item&id=1416:the-libyan-failure-obama-and-clinton-s-forgotten-war&Itemid=566.
33   See, for example, Sortition Ireland: Proposing Sortition as a Possible Solution for Ireland, https://sortitionireland.org.

BIBLIOGRAPHY

The most useful recent resource for further research on this topic, in terms of books, is probably *Basic Income: An Anthology of Contemporary Research*, edited by Karl Widerquist, José A. Noguera, Yannick Vanderborght, and Jurgen de Wispelaere (West Sussex: Wiley Blackwell, 2013). (The title is shortened in the endnotes to *BIACR*.) The best journal resource for recent academic papers on the issue is probably *Basic Income Studies*, https://www.degruyter.com/view/j/bis. In terms of websites, one of the most useful in a general context is BIEN: Basic Income Earth Network, http://basicincome. org. In a UK context, see for example UK Citizens Income Trust, http://citizensincome. org. For costing proposals in the UK, see Malcolm Torry, *The Feasibility of Citizen's Income* (London: Palgrave Macmillan, 2016). For discussions of UBI in a US context, see in particular The US Basic Income Guarantee Network, http://www.usbig.net. In an Irish context, the best recent book resource for researchers is Seán Healy and Brigid Reynolds (eds), *Basic Income: Radical Utopia or Practical Solution?* (Dublin: Social Justice Ireland, 2016). (The last-mentioned title is shortened in notes here to *BIRUPS*.) The most useful websites for discussions of the issue in an Irish context are Basic Income Ireland, http:// www.basicincomeireland.com, and Social Justice Ireland: Working to Build a Just Society, https://www.socialjustice.ie. As mentioned already in the Introduction, the Bibliography that follows includes most of the 'hard-copy' material, in terms of books and journal articles, mentioned in the endnotes, with online links where they were available. It also includes some of the online material mentioned in the endnotes, where they seemed to be of particular relevance.

Ackerman, B., A. Alstott and P. Van Parijs (eds), *Redesigning Distribution* (London/ New York: Verso, 2006).

Ackerman, Bruce and Anne Alstott, *The Stakeholder Society* (New Haven: Yale University Press, 1999).

Ackerman, Bruce and Anne Alstott, 'Stakeholding versus Basic Income' in *Basic Income: An Anthology of Contemporary Research*, Karl Widerquist, José A Noguera, Yannick Vanderborght, Jurgen de Wispelaere (eds) (West Sussex: Wiley Blackwell, 2013), pp.417–428.

Albus, James S., *People's Capitalism: The Economics of the Robot Revolution* (Maryland: New World Books, 1976).

Alstott, Anne, 'Good for Women' in *Basic Income: An Anthology of Contemporary Research*, Karl Widerquist, José A Noguera, Yannick Vanderborght and Jurgen de Wispelaere (eds) (West Sussex: Wiley Blackwell, 2013), pp.186–188.

Andersson, J.O., 'Fundamental Values for a Third Left', *New Left Review*, no.216 (March/April 1996), pp.66–78.

Andersson, J.O., 'Why a Citizen's Income Should be Combined with a Citizen's Wage'. Paper presented at the Sixth International Congress of the Basic Income European Network, Vienna International Centre, Vienna, 12–14 September 1996.

Ansell-Pearson, Keith, Introduction to Friedrich Nietzsche's *On the Genealogy of Morality*, Keith Ansell-Pearson (ed.), Carol Diethe (trans.) (Cambridge: Cambridge University Press, 1994), pp.ix–xxiii.

Anthony, P.D., *The Ideology of Work* (London: Tavistock, 1977).

Arendt, Hannah, *The Human Condition*, Introduced by Margaret Canovan (Chicago: University of Chicago Press, 1998).

Aristotle, *Politics* (London: Dent, 1912).

Atkinson, Anthony B., 'Participation Income' in *Basic Income: An Anthology of Contemporary Research*, Karl Widerquist, José A. Noguera, Yannick Vanderborght and Jurgen de Wispelaere (eds) (West Sussex: Wiley Blackwell, 2013), pp.435–438.

Baer, Hans A. 'Toward Democratic Eco-socialism as the Next World System', http:// thenextsystem.org/wp-content/uploads/2016/04/HansBaer.pdf.

Baker, John, *Arguing for Equality* (London: Verso, 1987).

Baker, John, 'An Egalitarian Case for Basic Income' in *Arguing for Basic Income: Ethical Foundations for a Radical Reform*, Philippe Van Parijs (ed.) (London: Verso, 1992), pp.101–127.

Barry, Brian, 'Equality Yes, Basic Income No' in *Arguing for Basic Income: Ethical Foundations for a Radical Reform*, Philippe Van Parijs (ed.) (London: Verso, 1992), pp.128–140.

Basic Income Ireland, http://www.basicincomeireland.com.

Benton, Ted, 'Why Are Sociologists Naturephobes?' in *After Postmodernism: An Introduction to Critical Realism*, José López and Gary Potter (eds) (New York: Athlone, 2001), pp.133–145.

BIEN: Basic Income Earth Network, http://basicincome.org/topic/pilot-experiments/.

Block, Fred and Jeff Manza, 'The Case for a Progressive Negative Income Tax' in

Basic Income: An Anthology of Contemporary Research, Karl Widerquist, José A. Noguera, Yannick Vanderborght and Jurgen de Wispelaere (eds) (West Sussex: Wiley Blackwell, 2013), pp.402–416.

BIEN: Basic Income Earth Network, 'History of Basic Income', http://www. basicincome.org/basic-income/history/.

Boso, Alex and Mihaela Vancea, 'Basic Income for Immigrants? The Pull Effect of Social Benefits on Migration', *Basic Income Studies* vol.7, no.1 (December 2012). https:// www.degruyter.com/view/j/bis.2012.7.issue-1/1932-0183.1234/1932-0183.1234.xml.

Bregman, Rutger, *Utopia for Realists: The Case for a Universal Basic Income, Open Borders, and a 15-Hour Workweek*, Elizabeth Manton (trans.) (Netherlands: The Correspondent, 2016).

Buiter, W., 'The Simple Analytics of Helicopter Money: Why It Works – Always', *Economics: The Open-Access, Open-Assessment E-Journal*, vol.8, pp.1–5. http:// dx.doi.org/10.5018/economics-ejournal.ja.2014-28.

Burke, Edmund, *Reflections on the Revolution in France, and on the Proceedings in Certain Societies in London Relative to that Event*, Conor Cruise O'Brien (ed. and Introduction) (Harmondsworth: Penguin, 1969).

Callan, Tim, C. O'Donoghue and C. O'Neill, *Analysis of Basic Income Schemes for Ireland* (Dublin: ESRI, 1994).

Callender, Rosheen, 'Down to Basics', *Making Sense* (May/June, 1989).

Carr, Nicholas, *The Shallows: What the Internet is Doing to our Brains* (New York: Norton, 2011).

Cassidy, John, 'Printing Money: A Radical Solution to the Current Economic Malaise', *New Yorker*, 15 November 2013. http://www.newyorker.com/magazine/2015/11/23/ printing-money-books-john-cassidy.

Charlier, Joseph, *La Question Sociale Résolue, Précédée du Testament Philosophique d'un Penseur* (Brussels: Weissenbruch, 1894).

Charlier, Joseph, *Solution du Problème Social ou Constitution Humanitaire* (Brussels: Chez Tous les Librairies du Royaume, 1848).

Citizens Income Trust, http://citizensincome.org.

Clark, Charles M.A., *The Basic Income Guarantee: Ensuring Progress and Prosperity in the 21st Century (*Dublin: Oak Tree Press, 2002).

Clark, Charles M.A., 'Cost Estimates for a Basic Income in the United States' in *Basic Income: An Anthology of Contemporary Research*, Karl Widerquist, José A. Noguera, Yannick Vanderborght and Jurgen de Wispelaere (eds) (West Sussex: Wiley Blackwell, 2013), pp.254–257.

Clark, Charles M.A. and J. Healy, *Pathways to a Basic Income* (Dublin: CORI, 1997).

Cobbett, William, *The Poor Man's Friend* (New York: Augustus M. Kelley, 1977).

Collins, Micheál, 'Estimating the Cost of a Basic Income for Ireland'. Paper presented at the BIEN Congress, Munich, September 2012, pp.1–14. http://basicincome.org/bien/pdf/munich2012/Collins.pdf.

Collins, Micheál, 'Towards a Basic Income.' Paper presented at the TASC Conference, Cork, September 2011. NERI: Nevin Economic Research Institute. http://www.

nerinstitute.net/research/towards-a-basic-income/.

Crotty, Raymond, *Ireland in Crisis: A Study in Capitalist Colonial Undevelopment* (Ireland: Brandon, 1986).

Cunliffe, John and Guido Erreygers, 'The Enigmatic Legacy of Charles Fourier: Joseph Charlier and Basic Income', *History of Political Economy*, vol.33, no.3 (2001), pp.459–484.

De Maré, Eric, *A Matter of Life or Debt* (Australia: Veritas, 1986).

De Wispelaare, Jurgen and Lindsay Stirton, 'Practical Bottlenecks in the Implementation of a Universal Basic Income' in *Basic Income: An Anthology of Contemporary Research*, Karl Widerquist, José A. Noguera, Yannick Vanderborght and Jurgen de Wispelaere (eds) (West Sussex: Wiley Blackwell, 2013), pp.360–368.

De Wispelaere, Jurgen and Lindsay Stirton, 'The Trilemma of Participation Income'. In *Basic Income: An Anthology of Contemporary Research*, Karl Widerquist, José A. Noguera, Yannick Vanderborght and Jurgen de Wispelaere (eds) (West Sussex: Wiley Blackwell, 2013), pp.439–446.

Department of the Taoiseach, *Basic Income: A Green Paper* (Dublin: Department of the Taoiseach, 2002).

Derrida, Jacques, 'The Animal that Therefore I Am', *Critical Inquiry* vol.28, no.2 (winter, 2002), pp.394–395.

Di Bernardo, Francesco, 'The Impossibility of Precarity', *Radical Philosophy*, no.198 (July–August 2016), pp.7–14.

Dobson, Andrew, *Green Political Thought: An Introduction* (London: Routledge, 1995).

Douglas, C.H., *Economic Democracy* (Epsom: Bloomfield Books, 1974).

Douglas, C.H., *Social Credit* (London: Eyre and Spottiswoode, 1933).

Douthwaite, Richard. *The Growth Illusion* (Dublin: Lilliput, 1992).

Enriquez, Corina Rodriguez, 'Basic Income and Time Use Democratization', *Basic Income Studies* vol.11, no 1 (June 2016), pp.39–48. https://www.degruyter.com/view/j/bis.2016.11.issue-1/bis-2016-0012/bis-2016-0012.xml?format=INT.

European Commission: Taxation and Customs Union, 'Taxation of the Financial Sector'. http://ec.europa.eu/taxation_customs/taxation/other_taxes/financial_sector/index_en.htm.

First Report of the Committee on Taxation (Dublin: Dublin Stationery Office, 1982).

Fitzpatrick, Tony, 'A Basic Income for Feminists?' in *Basic Income: An Anthology of Contemporary Research*, Karl Widerquist, José A. Noguera, Yannick Vanderborght and Jurgen de Wispelaere (eds), (West Sussex: Wiley Blackwell, 2013), pp.163–172.

Fitzpatrick, Tony, 'Ecologism and Basic Income', In *Basic Income: An Anthology of Contemporary Research*, Karl Widerquist, José A Noguera, Yannick Vanderborght and Jurgen de Wispelaere (eds) (West Sussex: Wiley Blackwell, 2013), pp.263–268.

Fleming, Peter, *The Mythology of Work: How Capitalism Persists Despite Itself* (London: Pluto, 2015).

Florida, James, *The Rise of the Creative Class, and How It's Transforming Work, Leisure, Community and Everyday Life* (London: Basic Books, 2003).

Ford, Martin, *The Rise of the Robots: Technology and the Threat of Mass*

Unemployment (London: Oneworld, 2015).

Foucault, Michel, *The Birth of Biopolitics: Lectures at the Collège de France 1978–1979*, Michel Senellart (ed.), Graham Burchell (trans.) (New York: Palgrave Macmillan, 2008).

Foucault, Michel, *Discipline and Punish: The Birth of the Prison*, Alan Sheridan (trans.) (Harmondsworth: Penguin, 1979).

Fourier, Charles, *La Fausse Industrie* [1867] (Paris: Anthropos, 1967), pp.491–492.

Fox, A., *A Sociology of Work in Industry* (London: Collier Macmillan, 1971).

Fox, Warwick, 'Deep Ecology: A New Philosophy of Our Time?' *The Ecologist*, vol.14, no.5-6 (1984), pp.194–200.

Fraser, R. (ed.), *Work* (Harmondsworth: Penguin, 1968).

Freud, Sigmund, 'Fetishism', J. Strachey (trans.) in *The Complete Psychological Works of Sigmund Freud* Vol.21 (London: Hogarth and the Institute of Psychoanalysis, 1927).

Friedman, Milton, *Capitalism and Freedom* (Chicago: University of Chicago Press, 1982).

Friedman, Milton, 'Negative Income Tax: The Original Idea' in *Basic Income: An Anthology of Contemporary Research*, Karl Widerquist, José A. Noguera, Yannick Vanderborght and Jurgen de Wispelaere (eds) (West Sussex: Wiley Blackwell, 2013), pp.398–401.

Fromm, Erich, *Fear of Freedom* (London: Routledge, 2001).

Fromm, Erich, 'The Psychological Aspects of the Guaranteed Income' in *Basic Income: An Anthology of Contemporary Research* Karl Widerquist, José A Noguera, Yannick Vanderborght and Jurgen de Wispelaere (eds) (West Sussex: Wiley Blackwell, 2013), pp.5–10.

Fromm, Erich, *To Have or To Be?* (London: Jonathan Cape, 1978).

Giddens, Anthony, Introduction to Max Weber's *The Protestant Ethic and the Spirit of Capitalism*, Talcott Parsons (trans.) (London: Routledge, 2001), pp.x–xiii.

Global Basic Income Foundation, http://www.globalincome.org/English/BI-worldwide.html.

Goldman, Emma, 'Woman Suffrage' in *Red Emma Speaks: An Emma Goldman Reader*, Alix Kates Shulman (ed.) (Atlantic Highlands, NJ: Humanities Press International, 1996).

Gorz, André, *Paths to Paradise: On the Liberation from Work*, Malcolm Imrie (trans.) (London: Pluto, 1985).

Graeber, David, *Debt: The First 5000 Years* (New York: Melville House, 2012).

Green Party of England and Wales, *Basic Income: A Detailed Proposal* (April 2015). https://policy.greenparty.org.uk/assets/files/Policy%20files/Basic%20Income%20Consultation%20Paper.pdf.

Grotius, Hugo, *The Rights of War and Peace*, Richard Tuck (ed. and Introduction), from the edition by Jean Barbeyrac (Indianapolis: Liberty Fund, 2005), 3 vols, 6 July 2016. http://oll.libertyfund.org/titles/1877.

Guattari, Félix, *Chaosmose* (Paris: Galilée, 1992).

Guattari, Félix, 'The Three Ecologies', New Formations, vol.8 (Summer 1989), pp.131–147.

Hardt, Michael and Antonio Negri, Empire (Cambridge, Mass: Harvard University Press, 2000).

Hayek, Friedrich A. von, Law, Legislation and Liberty. Vol.3: The Political Order of a Free People (Chicago: University of Chicago Press, 1979)

Hayek, Friedrich A. von, The Road to Serfdom (London: Routledge, 2001).

Healy, Seán and Brigid Reynolds, 'Arguing for an Adequate Income Guarantee' in Towards an Adequate Income for All, Brigid Reynolds and Seán Healy (eds) (Dublin: CORI, 1995), pp.29–49.

Healy, Seán and Brigid Reynolds, 'Basic Income: Radical Utopia or Practical Solution?' in Basic Income: Radical Utopia or Practical Solution?, Seán Healy and Brigid Reynolds (eds) (Dublin: Social Justice Ireland, 2016), pp.1–30.

Healy, Seán, M. Murphy and S. Ward, 'Basic Income: Why and How in Difficult Economic Times: Financing a BI in Ireland.' Paper presented at the BIEN World Congress, Munich 2012. http://basicincome.org/bien/pdf/munich2012/healy.pdf.

Hoeijmakers, Sjir, 'Municipal Basic-income Related Experiments in the Netherlands' in Basic Income: Radical Utopia or Practical Solution?, Seán Healy and Brigid Reynolds (eds) (Dublin: Social Justice Ireland, 2016), pp.69–73.

Honkanen, Pertti, 'Basic Income and Negative Income Tax: A Comparison with a Simulation Model', Basic Income Studies, vol.9, no.2 (December 2014), pp.119–135. https://www.degruyter.com/view/j/bis.2014.9.issue-1-2/bis-2014-0009/bis-2014-0009.xml?format=INT.

Honkanen, Pertti and Ville-Veikko Pulkka, 'Tackling Poverty and Social Exclusion with Unconditional Money: Notes on the Finnish Basic Income Experiment' in Basic Income: Radical Utopia or Practical Solution? Brigid Reynolds and Seán Healy (eds), (Dublin: Social Justice Ireland, 2016), pp.57–73.

Honohan, Patrick, 'A Radical Reform of Social Welfare and Income Tax Evaluated', Administration, vol.35, no.1 (1987), pp.69–87.

Horkheimer, Max and Theodor Adorno, 'The Culture Industry' in Dialectic of Enlightenment: Philosophical Fragments, Gunzelin Schmid Noerr (ed.), Edmond Jephcott (trans.), (Stanford, CA: Stanford University Press, 2002), pp.94–136.

Horkheimer, Max and Theodor Adorno, Dialectic of Enlightenment: Philosophical Fragments, Gunzelin Schmid Noerr (ed.) Edmond Jephcott (trans.) (Stanford, CA: Stanford University Press, 2002).

Howard, Michael, 'Why Marxists and Socialists Should Favour Basic Income' in Basic Income: An Anthology of Contemporary Research, Karl Widerquist, José A Noguera, Yannick Vanderborght and Jurgen de Wispelaere (eds) (West Sussex: Wiley Blackwell, 2013), pp.55–61.

Howe, John, 'Prototype Boulevard', New Left Review, Second Series, no.82 (July/August 2013), pp.85–96.

Huet, François, Le Règne Social du Christianisme (Paris: Firmin Didot/Brussels: Decq, 1853). https://books.google.ie/books?id=46pJAAAAcAAJ&printsec=frontcover&source=gbs_ge_summary_r&cad=0#v=onepage&q&f=false.

Jackson, Tim, Prosperity Without Growth: Economics for a Finite Planet (London,

Sterling, VA: Earthscan, 2009).

Jay, Martin, *Downcast Eyes: The Denigration of Visuality in Twentieth Century French Thought* (Berkeley: University of California Press, 1993).

Jordan, Bill, 'Basic Income and the Common Good' in *Arguing for Basic Income: Ethical Foundations for a Radical Reform*, Philippe Van Parijs (eds) (London: Verso, 1992), pp.155–177.

Jordan, Bill, 'Efficiency and Participation: The Basic Income Approach' in *Basic Income: An Anthology of Contemporary Research*, Karl Widerquist, José A. Noguera, Yannick Vanderborght and Jurgen de Wispelaere (eds) (West Sussex: Wiley Blackwell, 2013), pp.230-234.

Kaplan, Jerry, *Humans Need Not Apply: A Guide to Wealth and Work in the Age of Artificial Intelligence* (New Haven: Yale University Press, 2015).

Kela Working Papers 106, Kela/FPA, 'From Idea to Experiment: Report on Universal Basic Income Experiment in Finland'. https://helda.helsinki.fi/handle/10138/167728.

Kesenne, S., 'Basic Income and Female Labour Supply: An Empirical Analysis' in *Cahiers Economiques de Bruxelles*, no.125 (1990), pp.81–92.

Klein, Naomi, *This Changes Everything: Capitalism Versus the Climate* (UK: Penguin/ Random House, 2015).

Kuiper, J.P., 'Arbeid en Inkomen: Twee Plichten en Twee Rechten', *Sociaal Maandblad Arbeid*, vol.31, no.9 (1976), pp.503–512.

Lerner, Abba, *Economics of Control* (New York: Macmillan, 1944).

Levy, David, *Love and Sex with Robots: The Evolution of Human-Robot Relationships* (New York: Harper, 2007).

Liberal Democrats, *Common Benefit: Liberal Democrat Policies for the Reform of the Tax and Benefit Systems* (London: Federal Green Paper no.11, 1990).

Luther, Martin, 'An die Pfarrhern wider den Wucher zu predigen' (Wittenberg, 1540).

Lyons, Ronan, 'A Right to Housing? The Case for a Universal Housing Subsidy' in *Basic Income: Radical Utopia or Practical Solution?*, Brigid Reynolds and Seán Healy (eds) (Dublin: Social Justice Ireland, 2016), pp.137–148.

Major, Aaron, 'Affording Utopia: The Economic Viability of "A Capitalist Road to Communism"', *Basic Income Studies*, vol.11, no.2 (December 2016), pp.75–95. https://www.degruyter.com/view/j/bis.2016.11.issue-2/bis-2015-0023/bis-2015-0023. xml?format=INT.

Manjarin, Edgar and Maciej Szlinder, 'A Marxist Argumentative Scheme on Basic Income and Wage Share in an Anti-capitalist Agenda', *Basic Income Studies*, vol.11, no.1 (June 2016), pp.49–59. https://www.degruyter.com/view/j/bis.2016.11.issue-1/ bis-2016-0010/bis-2016-0010.xml?format=INT.

Marcuse, Herbert, *The Aesthetic Dimension: Toward a Critique of Marxist Aesthetics* Herbert Marcuse and Erica Sherover (trans. and rev.) (London: Macmillan, 1979).

Marcuse, Herbert, *Eros and Civilization: A Philosophical Inquiry into Freud* (Boston: Beacon, 1974).

Marx, Karl, *Capital: A Critique of Political Economy* Vol.1, Frederick Engels (ed.), Samuel Moore and Edward Aveling (trans.) (London: Lawrence and Wishart, 1977).

Marx, Karl, *Capital: A Critique of Political Economy* Vol.3, Frederick Engels (ed.)

(London: Lawrence and Wishart, 1959).

Marx, Karl, *Das Kapital* Vol.1 (Berlin: Dietz, 1962).

Marx, Karl, 'Economic and Philosophical Manuscripts (1844)' in *Karl Marx: Early Writings*, Lucio Colletti (Introduction) Rodney Livingstone and Gregor Benton (trans.) (Harmondsworth/London: Penguin/New Left Review, 1975), pp.279–400.

Marx, Karl, 'Entfremdete Arbeit'. Erstes Manuskript. *Oekonomisch-philosophische Manuskripte aus dem Jahre 1844*. The Marxists Archive. https://www.marxists.org/deutsch/archiv/marx-engels/1844/oek-phil/1-4_frem.htm.

Marx, Karl and Frederick Engels, 'From the German Ideology', in *On Historical Materialism: A Collection*, compiled by T. Borodulina (Moscow: Progress, 1972), pp.14–76.

Mason, Paul, *Postcapitalism: A Guide to Our Future* (UK: Allen Lane, 2015).

McLeay, Michael, Amar Radia and Ryland Thomas, 'Money Creation in the Modern Economy', *Quarterly Bulletin*, Q1 (2014), pp.14–27. http://www.bankofengland.co.uk/publications/Documents/quarterlybulletin/2014/qb14q102.pdf.

Meade, James, *Agathotopia: The Economics of Partnership* (Aberdeen: Aberdeen University Press, 1989).

Merchant, Carolyn, *The Death of Nature: Women, Ecology and the Scientific Revolution* (London: Wildwood House, 1982).

Meyer, N.I., H. Petersen and V. Sorensen, *Revolt from the Center* (London: Marion Boyars, 1981).

Mill, J.S., *Principles of Political Economy* [2nd ed., 1849]. (New York: Augustus Kelley, 1987).

Milner, Dennis, *Higher Production by a Bonus on National Output: A Proposal for a Minimum Income for All Varying with National Productivity* (London: George Allen & Unwin, 1920).

Murphy, Eamon and Seán Ward, 'Costing a Basic Income for Ireland' in *Basic Income: Radical Utopia or Practical Solution?*, Brigid Reynolds and Seán Healy (eds) (Dublin: Social Justice Ireland, 2016), pp.125–136.

Murphy, Michelle, 'Pathways to a Basic Income System' in *Basic Income: Radical Utopia or Practical Solution?*, Brigid Reynolds and Seán Healy (eds), (Dublin: Social Justice Ireland, 2016), pp.93–107.

Murray, Charles, 'Guaranteed Income as a Replacement for the Welfare State' in *Basic Income: An Anthology of Contemporary Research*, Karl Widerquist, José A Noguera, Yannick Vanderborght and Jurgen de Wispelaere (eds), (West Sussex: Wiley Blackwell, 2013), pp.49–51.

Nader, Ralph, *Unstoppable: The Emerging Left-Right Alliance to Dismantle the Corporate State* (New York: Nation Books, 2014).

Nelissen, J. and S. Polk, 'Basisinkomen: effecten op de arbeidsparticipatie en de inkomensverdeling', *Tijdschrift voor Politieke Economie*, vol.18, no.4 (1990), pp.64–82.

Netherlands Scientific Council for Government Policy, *Safeguarding Social Security* (The Hague: WRR, 1985).

Nietzsche, Friedrich, *On the Genealogy of Morality*, Keith Ansell-Pearson (ed.), Carol Diethe (trans.) (Cambridge: Cambridge University Press, 1994).

Noguera, José A., 'Basic Income and Contributory Pensions' in *Basic Income: An Anthology of Contemporary Research*, Karl Widerquist, José A. Noguera, Yannick Vanderborght and Jurgen de Wispelaere (eds), pp.346–350 (West Sussex: Wiley Blackwell, 2013).

Norris, Christopher, *Against Relativism: Philosophy of Science, Deconstruction, and Critical Theory* (Oxford: Blackwell, 1997).

Nozick, Robert, *Anarchy, State, and Utopia* (New York: Basic Books, 1977).

O'Brien, Paul, 'Aesthetics, Virtual Reality and the Environment', *Rethinking Nature: Authors and Problems, Teoria*, vol.34, no.2 (2014), pp.139–156. https://www.academia.edu/11358005/Aesthetics_Virtual_Reality_and_the_Environment.

O'Brien, Paul, 'Hibernian Evanescence: Globalisation, Identity and the Virtual Shamrock', *Postcolonial Text*, vol.3, no.3 (2007). http://postcolonial.org/index.php/pct/article/viewArticle/713.

O'Brien, Paul, 'Social Justice Without Socialism: The Advantages of Participatory Capitalism' in *Equitable Capitalism: Promoting Economic Opportunity Through Broader Capital Ownership*, Stuart M. Speiser (ed.) (New York: Apex Press, 1991), pp.114–123.

Offe, Claus, 'A Non-productivist Design for Social Policies' in *Basic Income: An Anthology of Contemporary Research*, Karl Widerquist, José A Noguera, Yannick Vanderborght and Jurgen de Wispelaere (eds) (West Sussex: Wiley Blackwell, 2013), pp.275–282.

Offe, Claus, 'Pathways from Here' in *Basic Income: An Anthology of Contemporary Research*, Karl Widerquist, José A. Noguera, Yannick Vanderborght and Jurgen de Wispelaere (eds) (West Sussex: Wiley Blackwell, 2013), pp.560–563.

Offe, Claus and Johan de Deken, 'Sabbatical Grants' in *Basic Income: An Anthology of Contemporary Research*, Karl Widerquist, José A. Noguera, Yannick Vanderborght and Jurgen de Wispelaere (eds), (West Sussex: Wiley Blackwell, 2013) pp.447–452.

Orloff, Ann S., 'Why Basic Income does not Promote Gender Equality' in *Basic Income: An Anthology of Contemporary Research*, Karl Widerquist, José A Noguera, Yannick Vanderborght and Jurgen de Wispelaere (eds) (West Sussex: Wiley Blackwell, 2013), pp.149–152.

Orwell, George, *Nineteen Eighty-Four* (London: Penguin, 2008).

Orwell, George, *Politics and the English Language* (London: Penguin, 2013).

Paine, Thomas, 'Agrarian Justice', Digital edition 1999 by www.grundskyld.dk. http://piketty.pse.ens.fr/files/Paine1795.pdf.

Paine, Thomas, 'Agrarian Justice' in *Rights of Man, Common Sense and Other Political Writings* Mark Philp (ed.) (Oxford: Oxford University Press, 1995), pp.409–433.

Painter, Anthony, 'Citizenship and Basic Income' in *Basic Income: Radical Utopia or Practical Solution?*, Brigid Reynolds and Seán Healy (eds) (Dublin: Social Justice Ireland, 2016), pp.49–53.

Parker, H., *Instead of the Dole: An Enquiry into Integration of the Tax and Benefit*

Systems (London: Routledge, 1989).

Pateman, Carol, 'Democratizing Citizenship: Some Advantages of a Basic Income'. In *Redesigning Distribution*, B. Ackerman, A., Alstott and P. Van Parijs (eds) (London/New York: Verso, 2006).

Pateman, Carole, 'Free-riding and the Household'. In *Basic Income: An Anthology of Contemporary Research*, Karl Widerquist, José A Noguera, Yannick Vanderborght and Jurgen de Wispelaere (eds) (West Sussex: Wiley Blackwell, 2013), pp.173–177.

Piketty, Thomas, *Capital in the Twenty-First Century*, Arthur Goldhammer (trans.) (Cambridge, MA: Harvard University Press, 2014).

Plumwood, Val, *Environmental Culture: The Ecological Crisis of Reason* (London, Routledge, 2002).

Pogge, Thomas W., 'A Global Resources Dividend' in *Basic Income: An Anthology of Contemporary Research*, Karl Widerquist, José A. Noguera, Yannick Vanderborght and Jurgen de Wispelaere (eds) (West Sussex: Wiley Blackwell, 2013), pp.375–391.

Political Compass, The, http://www.politicalcompass.org.

Popper, Karl, *The Open Society and Its Enemies* (London: Routledge, 1966).

Poulett Scrope, George, *Principles of Political Economy* (London: Longman, 1833).

Preiss, Joshua, 'Milton Friedman on Freedom and the Negative Income Tax'. *Basic Income Studies*, vol.11, no.2 (December 2015), pp.169–191. https://www.degruyter.com/view/j/bis.2015.10.issue-2/bis-2015-0008/bis-2015-0008.xml?format=INT.

Pritchett, Lant, 'The Cliff at the Border.' https://www.hks.harvard.edu/fs/lpritch/Labor%20Mobility%20-%20docs/cliff%20at%20the%20borders_submitted.pdf.

Quantitative Easing for People: A Rescue Plan for the Eurozone. http://www.qe4people.eu.

Ranalli, Brent, Review of M. Oliver Haydorn's *Social Credit Economics*, *Basic Income Studies*, vol.10, no.2 (December 2015), pp.281–283. https://www.degruyter.com/view/j/bis.2015.10.issue-2/bis-2015-0022/bis-2015-0022.xml?format=INT.

Raventós, Daniel, *Basic Income: The Material Conditions of Freedom*, Julie Wark (trans.) (London: Pluto, 2007).

Rawls, John, *A Theory of Justice* [Revised Edition] (Cambridge, MA: Harvard University Press/Belknap Press, 1999).

Read, Samuel, *An Inquiry into the Natural Grounds of Rights to Vendible Property or Wealth* (Edinburgh: 1829).

Reed, Howard and Stewart Lansley, 'Universal Basic Income: An Idea Whose Time has Come?' https://www.compassonline.org.uk/wp-content/uploads/2016/05/UniversalBasicIncomeByCompass-Spreads.pdf.

Reich, Wilhelm, *The Mass Psychology of Fascism*, Vincent R. Carfagno (trans.) (Harmondsworth: Penguin, 1983).

Richardson, Steven O., 'Entitlement Reform: From Tangled Web to Safety Net', *Basic Income Studies*, vol.8, no.1 (August 2013), pp.105–137. https://www.degruyter.com/view/j/bis.2013.8.issue-1/bis-2013-0001/bis-2013-0001.xml?format=INT.

Robeyns, Ingrid, 'A Gender Analysis of Basic Income' in *Basic Income: An Anthology of Contemporary Research*, Karl Widerquist, José A Noguera, Yannick Vanderborght and Jurgen de Wispelaere (eds) (West Sussex: Wiley Blackwell, 2013), pp.153–162.

Ruskin, John, 'Unto This Last.' Essays from the Cornhill Magazine, http://www.efm. bris.ac.uk/het/ruskin/ruskin.

Russell, Bertrand, Roads to Freedom: Socialism, Anarchism and Syndicalism (London: Unwin Books, 1918).

Sanzo, Luis and Rafael Pinilla, 'A Household Basic Income'. In Basic Income: An Anthology of Contemporary Research, Karl Widerquist, José A. Noguera, Yannick Vanderborght and Jurgen de Wispelaere (eds) (West Sussex: Wiley Blackwell, 2013), pp.461–463.

Sarrazin, Thilo, Deutschland Schafft sich ab: Wie Wir Unser Land aufs Spiel Setzen (Munich: DVA, 2010).

Schiller, Friedrich, On the Aesthetic Education of Man, Reginald Snell (trans.) (New York: Dover: 2004).

Schmid, T. (ed.), Befreiung von Falscher Arbeit: Thesen zum Garantierten Mindesteinkommen (Berlin: Wagenbach, 1984).

Snow, C.P., The Two Cultures, Stefan Collini (Introduction) (Cambridge: Cambridge University Press, 1993).

Social Justice Ireland. Building a Fairer Tax System: The Working Poor and the Cost of Refundable Tax Credits (Dublin: Social Justice Ireland, 2010).

Soper, Kate, 'Capitalocene', review of Jason Moore's Capitalism in the Web of Life: Ecology and the Accumulation of Capital, Radical Philosophy, vol.197 (May/June 2016), pp.49–52.

Speiser, Stuart M., Equitable Capitalism: Promoting Economic Opportunity Through Broader Capital Ownership (New York: Apex Press, 1991).

Speiser, Stuart M., The USOP Handbook: A Guide to Designing Universal Share Ownership Plans for the United States and Great Britain (New York: The Council on International and Public Affairs, 1986).

Spence, Thomas [1797], 'The Rights of Infants' in The Origins of Universal Grants, J. Cunliffe and G. Erreygers (eds) (Basingstoke: Palgrave Macmillan, 2004), pp.81–91.

Standing, Guy, 'A Coming-of-Age Grant Versus a Community Capital Grant' in Basic Income: An Anthology of Contemporary Research, Karl Widerquist, José A. Noguera, Yannick Vanderborght and Jurgen de Wispelaere (eds) (West Sussex: Wiley Blackwell, 2013), pp.464–470.

Standing, Guy, The Precariat: The New Dangerous Class (London, Bloomsbury, 2014)

Steensland, Brian, The Failed Welfare Revolution: America's Struggle over Guaranteed Income Policy (Princeton: Princeton University Press, 2011).

Steiner, Hillel, 'Three Just Taxes' in Arguing for Basic Income: Ethical Foundations for a Radical Reform, Philippe Van Parijs (ed.) (London: Verso, 1992), pp.81–92.

Stoléru, Lionel, 'Coût et Efficacité de l'Impôt Négatif', Revue Économique, vol.25, no.5 (1974), pp.745–761. http://www.persee.fr/collection/reco.

Streeck, Wolfgang, 'How Will Capitalism End?', New Left Review, Second Series, no.87 (May/June 2014), pp.35–64.

Surowiecki, James, The Wisdom of Crowds: Why the Many Are Smarter than the Few (London: Abacus, 2004).

Taft, Michael, 'Basic Income and Transformative Strategies' in *Basic Income: Radical Utopia or Practical Solution?*, Brigid Reynolds and Seán Healy (eds) |(Dublin: Social Justice Ireland, 2016), pp.109–123.

Therborn, Göran, 'An Age of Progress?' *New Left Review*, Second Series, no.99 (May–June 2016), pp.27–37.

Tobin, James, 'The Case for an Income Guarantee' in *Basic Income: An Anthology of Contemporary Research*, Karl Widerquist, José A. Noguera, Yannick Vanderborght and Jurgen de Wispelaere (eds) (West Sussex: Wiley Blackwell, 2013), pp.195–199.

Torry, Malcolm, 'Citizen's Basic Income: is it Feasible?' in *Basic Income: Radical Utopia or Practical Solution?* Brigid Reynolds and Seán Healy (ed.) (Dublin: Social Justice Ireland, 2016), pp.31–47.

Torry, Malcolm, 'An Evaluation of a Strictly Revenue Neutral Citizen's Basic Income Scheme', Institute for Social and Economic Research Working Paper EM17/14. Colchester: Institute for Social and Economic Research, University of Essex, June 2016. https://www.iser.essex.ac.uk/research/publications/working-papers/euromod/em5-16.

Torry, Malcolm, *The Feasibility of Citizen's Income* (London: Palgrave Macmillan, 2016).

Turner, Adair, *Between Debt and the Devil: Money, Credit and Fixing Global Finance* (Princeton and Oxford: Princeton University Press, 2016).

US Basic Income Guarantee Network: What is the Basic Income Guarantee? http://www.usbig.net/whatisbig.php.

Van der Veen, Robert and Philippe Van Parijs, 'A Capitalist Road to Communism' in *Basic Income: An Anthology of Contemporary Research*, Karl Widerquist, José A. Noguera, Yannick Vanderborght and Jurgen de Wispelaere (eds) (West Sussex: Wiley Blackwell, 2013), pp.52–54.

Van der Veen, Robert and Philippe Van Parijs, 'A Capitalist Road to Communism' *Theory and Society*, vol.15, no.5, pp.635–655.

Van Parijs, Philippe (ed.), *Arguing for Basic Income: Ethical Foundations for a Radical Reform* (London/New York: Verso, 1992).

Van Parijs, Philippe, 'A Basic Income for All' in Philippe Van Parijs, *What's Wrong With A Free Lunch?*, Joshua Cohen and Joel Rogers (eds) (Boston: Beacon Press, 2001), pp.3–26.

Van Parijs, Philippe, 'A Green Case for Basic Income?' in *Basic Income: An Anthology of Contemporary Research*, Karl Widerquist, José A Noguera, Yannick Vanderborght and Jurgen de Wispelaere (eds) (West Sussex: Wiley Blackwell, 2013), pp.269–274.

Van Parijs, Philippe, 'Basic Income in the South' in *Basic Income: An Anthology of Contemporary Research*, Karl Widerquist, José A. Noguera, Yannick Vanderborght, and Jurgen de Wispelaere (eds) (West Sussex: Wiley Blackwell, 2013), pp.522–526.

Van Parijs, Philippe, 'Competing Justifications of Basic Income' in *Arguing for Basic Income: Ethical Foundations for a Radical Reform*, Philippe Van Parijs (ed.), (London: Verso, 1992) pp.3–43.

Van Parijs, Philippe, *Real Freedom for All* (Oxford: Clarendon Press, 1995).

Van Parijs, Philippe, *What's Wrong With A Free Lunch?* Joshua Cohen and Joel Rogers.

(eds) (Boston: Beacon Press, 2001).

Van Parijs, Philippe, 'Why Surfers Should Be Fed: The Crazy-Lazy Challenge' in *Basic Income: An Anthology of Contemporary Research*, Karl Widerquist, José A Noguera, Yannick Vanderborght and Jurgen de Wispelaere (eds) (West Sussex: Wiley Blackwell, 2013), pp.17–22.

Van Parijs, Philippe and Yannick Vanderborght, 'From Euro-Stipendium to Euro-Dividend' in *Basic Income: An Anthology of Contemporary Research*, Karl Widerquist, José A. Noguera, Yannick Vanderborght and Jurgen de Wispelaere (eds), (West Sussex: Wiley Blackwell, 2013), pp.392–397.

Van Trier, Walter, 'Basisinkomen' in *De Sociale Zekerheid Verzekerd? Referaten van het 22st Vlaams Wetenschappelijk Economisch Congres*, Marc Despontin and Marc Jegers (eds) (Brussels: VUB Press, 1995), pp.587–618.

Vanderborght, Yannick and Philippe Van Parijs, *L'Allocation Universelle* (Paris: La Découverte, 2005).

Vrasti, Wanda, 'Working in Prenzlau', *New Left Review*, Second Series, no.101 (September–October 2016), pp.49–61.

Ward, Seán, 'A Basic Income System for Ireland' in *Towards an Adequate Income for All*, Brigid Reynolds and Sean Healy (eds) (Dublin: CORI, 1994), pp.74–137.

Ward, Seán, 'History and Recent Developments on Basic Income in Ireland' in *Basic Income: Radical Utopia or Practical Solution?*, Brigid Reynolds and Seán Healy (eds) (Dublin: Social Justice Ireland, 2016), pp.77–91.

Washburne, Jennifer, *University Inc: The Corporate Corruption of American Higher Education* (New York: Basic Books, 2005).

Weber, Max, *The Protestant Ethic and the Spirit of Capitalism*, Talcott Parsons (trans.), Anthony Giddens (Introduction) (London: Routledge, 2001).

White, Stuart, 'Reciprocity-sensitive Forms of Basic Income' in *Basic Income: An Anthology of Contemporary Research*, Karl Widerquist, José A. Noguera, Yannick Vanderborght and Jurgen de Wispelaere (eds) (West Sussex: Wiley Blackwell, 2013), pp.429–434.

Widerquist, Karl, 'What (If Anything) Can We Learn from the Negative Income Tax Experiments?' in *Basic Income: An Anthology of Contemporary Research*, Karl Widerquist, José A. Noguera, Yannick Vanderborght and Jurgen de Wispelaere (eds) (West Sussex: Wiley Blackwell, 2013), pp.216–229.

Widerquist, Karl, José A. Noguera, Yannick Banderborght and Jurgen De Wispelaare (eds) *Basic Income: An Anthology of Contemporary Research* (UK: Wiley Blackwell, 2013).

Widerquist, Karl, José A. Noguera, Yannick Banderborght and Jurgen De Wispelaare. Introduction ['The Idea of an Unconditional Income for Everyone'] to *Basic Income: An Anthology of Contemporary Research*, Karl Widerquist, José A. Noguera, Yannick Banderborght and Jurgen De Wispelaare (eds) (UK: Wiley Blackwell, 2013), pp.xiii-xxvi.

Wilde, Oscar, *The Soul of Man Under Socialism*, https://www.marxists.org/reference/archive/wilde-oscar/soul-man/.

Withorn, Ann, 'Is One Man's Ceiling Another Woman's Floor?' in *Basic Income: An Anthology of Contemporary Research*, Karl Widerquist, José A Noguera, Yannick

Vanderborght and Jurgen de Wispelaere (West Sussex: Wiley Blackwell, 2013), pp.145–148.

Yunker, James A., 'The Basic Income Guarantee: A General Equilibrium Evaluation'. *Basic Income Studies*, vol.8, no.2 (December 2013): 203–233. https://www. degruyter.com/view/j/bis.2013.8.issue-2/bis-2013-0014/bis-2013-0014. xml?format=INT.

Zimmern, A.W., *The Greek Commonwealth* (London: Oxford University Press, 1915).

Žižek, Slavoj. *Living in the End Times* (London: Verso/New Left Books, 2011).

Zwolinski, Matt, 'Why Did Hayek Support a Basic Income?' 23 December 2013. http:// www.libertarianism.org/columns/why-did-hayek-support-basic-income.